Governing Migration through Paperwork

Lifeworlds: Knowledge, Politics, Histories

General Editor: Narmala Halstead, University of Sussex

Lifeworlds: Knowledges, Politics, Histories aims to capture anthropological explorations of contemporary social life around the globe. The Series Editors welcome manuscripts on pertinent happenings and movements of people in diverse contexts with an emphasis on fine-grained ethnography. An openness to the study of knowledges, politics and histories – to small-scale as much as large-scale contexts – is central to making sense of peoples' habitations. Thus, the series is interested in the tensions between scales of social life; lifeworlds are as much about the intimacy of social relations (including in digital worlds) as wider socio-political institutions including the law and state. The series invites studies that explore connections as much as tensions between the social and the political and how this unfolds in contemporary settings.

Volume 6
Governing Migration through Paperwork
Legitimation Practices, Exclusive Inclusion and Differentation
Edited by Sophie Andreetta and Lisa Marie Borrelli

Volume 5
Boaters of London
Alternative Living on the Water
Benjamin O.L. Bowles

Volume 4
State Intimacies
Sterilization, Care and Reproductive Chronicity in Rural North India
Eva Fiks

Volume 3
Compliance
Cultures and Networks of Accommodation
Edited by Will Rollason and Eric Hirsch

Volume 2
Individually Ourselves
Personhood, Ethics and Everyday Life in School
Sarah Winkler-Reid

Volume 1
A Magpie's Tale
Ethnographic and Historical Perspectives on the Kazakh of Western Mongolia
Anna Odland Portisch

Governing Migration through Paperwork

Legitimation Practices, Exclusive Inclusion and Differentiation

Sophie Andreetta and Lisa Marie Borrelli

berghahn
NEW YORK • OXFORD
www.berghahnbooks.com

First published in 2024 by
Berghahn Books
www.berghahnbooks.com

Library of Congress Cataloging-in-Publication Data

Names: Andreetta, Sophie, editor. | Borrelli, Lisa Marie, 1988- editor.
Title: Governing migration through paperwork : legitimation practices, exclusive inclusion, and differentiation / [edited by] Sophie Andreetta and Lisa M. Borrelli.
Description: New York : Berghahn Books, 2024. | Series: Lifeworlds : knowledges, politics, histories ; Volume 6 | Includes bibliographical references and index.
Identifiers: LCCN 2024013505 (print) | LCCN 2024013506 (ebook) | ISBN 9781805396116 (hardback) | ISBN 9781805396222 (epub) | ISBN 9781805396130 (adobe pdf)
Subjects: LCSH: Emigration and immigration law--Case studies.
Classification: LCC K3275 .G68 2024 (print) | LCC K3275 (ebook) | DDC 342.08/2--dc23/eng/20240511
LC record available at https://lccn.loc.gov/2024013505
LC ebook record available at https://lccn.loc.gov/2024013506

British Library Cataloguing in Publication Data

A catalogue record for this book is available from the British Library

ISBN 978-1-80539-611-6 hardback
ISBN 978-1-80539-622-2 epub
ISBN 978-1-80539-613-0 web pdf

https://doi.org/10.3167/9781805396116

Contents

Introduction

Governing Migration through Paperwork

Exclusive Inclusion, Differentiation and State Legitimacy

Sophie Andreetta and Lisa Marie Borrelli

Sociolegal scholars have been focusing on immigration policies and on how these policies are implemented by street-level bureaucrats or asylum judges in various contexts (Eule et al. 2019; Fassin and Kobelinsky 2012; Johannesson 2018; Kelly 2012; Spire 2008). Their work considers the place of doubt and evidence, the everyday practices of public administrations and the discretion of those directly involved in introducing or deciding on immigration claims, called street-level bureaucrats (Lipsky 2010). Focusing on street-level practices indeed allows for a nuanced analysis of 'the state' and its institutions 'at work' (Bierschenk and Olivier de Sardan 2014), which can otherwise be perceived as 'magic' due to the uncertainty and ambiguity of bureaucratic procedures (Das and Poole 2004; Hoag 2010). Studying governance through administrative practices also provides valuable insights into both legal and policy implementation (Eule et al. 2019; Fassin 2013; Lipsky 2010).

In order to further such anthropological accounts of 'the state', its policies, laws and practices, the materialization of immigration laws and policies has gained scholarly attention. Documentation functions as a form of statecraft (see Navaro-Yashin 2007; Nugent 2010), allowing the state to govern populations and to legitimize a particular moral ethos. Paperwork thus functions as a signature of the state and a constitutive element of bureaucratic authority (Bierschenk and Olivier de Sardan 2014) that normalizes existing social inequalities (Corrigan and Sayer 1985; Gupta 2012). The continuous devaluation of asylum seekers' claims, for example – from their being perceived as refugees, to asylum shoppers, and from economic migrants to 'cunning trickster' and terrorists (c.f. Ataç 2019; Guiraudon 2000; Scheel 2019) – and the growing suspicious examination of migrants' credibility has increased the importance of material artefacts in and beyond immigration proceedings (see Johannesson 2012; see Berg, chapter 6). Generally, scholarship on migration has noted a change from asylum being framed as a right to being increasingly perceived as a privilege, thereby forcing migrants to support their claims with a growing amount of (paper) evidence (Berg and Millbank 2009; Kagan 2002). This shift also holds true for access to more stable forms of residency or, finally, citizenship for migrants with all kinds of legal status. Facing stronger barriers towards reaching citizenship, migrants need to prove their integration and participation, e.g. in the labour market, very thoroughly (see Gargiulo, chapter 3). At the same time, public administrations face heavy paper-based documentation in their everyday practices, as well as a proliferation of new databases, online services and technologies for data collection.

Paperwork – in both physical and digital form – is indeed a crucial part of everyday life within bureaucracies (Hull 2012; Mathur 2016): it translates policy actions into realities, which at times becomes a seemingly Sisyphean task for civil servants. Documents produced and processed by bureaucracies also have serious effects on those who are exposed to them (Bosworth 2016; Tuckett 2015, 2018). There has, however, been only marginal interest in studying how bureaucrats' and migrant individuals' actions are shaped through and mediated by material artefacts, or how documents are charged with meaning (Navaro-Yashin 2007), create and shape realities and bureaucratic outcomes, and at the same time are used in order to both legitimize and contest certain practices (Feldman 2016; Johannesson 2012). The documentary practices of those 'who do the documenting' (Hull 2012: 255), in particular, have hardly been explored. In order to fill in such a gap, this book focuses on the core artefact of bureaucratic work: documents, which come in various manifestations such as certificates, letters, reports, case files, decisions, internal guidelines and judgements. It builds on the idea that migration governance can be better understood through the concrete, everyday work and practices of bureaucrats, which are intertwined with migrants' strategies to navigate state practices (Hollifield 2004). Because of their materiality, as well as semiotic meaning (Pigg, Erikson and Inglis 2018), migration regimes indeed inherit the powerful ability to (de)legitimize the stay of migrants with precarious legal status, hence upholding a strong influence on their lives. The final two chapters in this book explore how paperwork affects the mobility of asylum applicants: Sophie Nakueira shows how refugees' fabricated documents regularly end up hampering their relocation claims in the competition for the 'most vulnerable'; Hanna Berg shows how identity documents and current relocation procedures are mimicking and furthering much older systems of humanitarian governance. Broadening the scope to other categories of migrants, Enrico Gargiulo shows how municipal records and registration practices in Italy, beyond their official monitoring purpose, actively select those registered and create undocumented migrants in practice. In Swedish deportation centres, Lisa Marie Borrelli and Annika Lindberg further illustrate the controlling power of paperwork, even towards bureaucrats themselves. Against this backdrop, Sophie Andreetta demonstrates how welfare workers can sometimes write reports in favour of claimants and use dependency as an argument against deportability in welfare courts. Further thinking about the way public servants engage with the state, Larissa Vetters shows how immigration bureaucrats create shifts in administrative guidelines 'from the bottom up'. Building on the idea that migration policies are shaped, in practice, by laws, shifting policies and by interactions between various actors – including migrants, state agents, and private and nongovernmental actors – the chapters in this book explore the role of paperwork in mediating, shaping, producing or fixing and amending those relationships. In doing so, and as highlighted by Thomas Bierschenk in the concluding postscript, they illustrate the double-edged nature of paper trails as tools for both migrant control and agency, exclusion, and inclusion on various levels of state bureaucracies, as well as within the broader migration regime that takes into account nongovernmental actors and the agency of migrants themselves.

Paperwork Practices, Bureaucracies and Migration Control

In this book, we not only treat documents or artefacts within the migration regime as crucial providers of knowledge practices (Riles 2006) but also explore how these documents produce legitimacy and establish 'truths' upon which bureaucrats as well as migrants act. In addition, the way individuals use material artefacts discloses power relations, often hidden to the public eye and by bureaucratic procedures. Focusing our analytical lens on these artefacts can therefore help illuminate how different levels of agency and the ability to shape or manipulate administrative practices are created through doing paperwork.

Research has shown that the use of 'documents as an opaque medium of interaction' (Allard 2012) can reduce the agency of migrants in a context where the meaning of these documents is not necessarily shared (see

Nakueira's chapter). Actors involved in the migration regime 'attach fundamentally different symbolic attributes to travel documents' (Alpes 2017: 267), and paper production is strongly linked to knowledge on how to fill in these papers (Tuckett 2018). These asymmetrical relations further play out within the everyday interaction between bureaucrats and migrants. Prior academic work (Ibid.) critically examines how migrants with precarious legal status try to navigate and adapt to the requirements of state bureaucracies and shows that while incredibly complicated, official rules may at times be easily circumvented through the creation of paper trails. Paperwork, or paper trails, which are crucial to immigration procedures, indeed allow migrants to create stories in order to secure some legal status yet also cause them to engage in uncertain practices – forging and thus endangering future prospects, or even their own lives and the lives of their families. Similarly, Maybritt Jill Alpes (2017) examines how the process of migrating is contingent upon obtaining and filling out the right papers. There is a certain power lying not only within documents but also in the work with those documents, at times increasing agency on both sides (see Borrelli and Lindberg's chapter). The role that individuals grant to documents and the relevance of 'having the right kind' (or not having any) are both of crucial importance when steering through the migration regime (Berg, this volume). Indeed, refraining from signing documents, the accumulation of documents to provide evidence or the destruction of 'relevant' paperwork (such as in Nakueira's chapter) shows how migrant individuals contest this regime, but also underlines the spaces of highly asymmetrical power (Eule, Loher and Wyss 2018; Eule et al. 2019).

Besides the multiple shifts of agency between bureaucrats and migrant individuals, enhanced or hindered by paperwork, documents remain an essential part of everyday work within bureaucracies. The state materializes and gains power through forms, documents and signatures. Documents can be used as sources of evidence but are also agents and components of dynamic networks (Prior 2008). Texts such as regulations (see Vetters, this volume) have meaning, change along with each actor working on and with them and thus give documents a performative role in organizational action that is materially and practically entangled in policy-making. At the same time, documents embody organizational memory (Weisser 2014; Kosciejew 2017; see also Berg, this volume). States try to render populations legible, they sort and classify residents through documentation – which is also how they come into being (Scott 1998). At the same time, the 'tyranny of paper regimes set up to control movement' (Dhupelia-Mesthrie 2014: 11) is a lived reality in migration enforcement (Bosworth 2016) and for migrant individuals. However, paperwork not only legitimizes the official practices and procedures of the state; it also allows for administrative discretion and policy implementation. Paperwork functions as a regulatory instrument and as part of a 'ritual construction of collective bureaucratic authority and agents', which provides 'opportunities for functionaries to pursue their own interest' (Hull 2003: 287, 310).

The chapters in this book share a similar understanding of paperwork as paper 'at work', which includes the work that paper does – establishing administrative truths, granting or withdrawing rights – as well as the work that people do with/on paper – providing evidence, filling out forms and reports, or interpreting statutory laws through written internal guidelines. We therefore understand paperwork as a set of practices and processes through which power circulates, and identities and boundaries are produced and materialize. Despite this shared understanding, all authors pay close ethnographic attention to the specificity of different documentary genres, to the function and the types of 'paperwork': producing identity or counter documents to asylum applicants' claims (Berg; Nakueira), writing reports (Andreetta), interpreting immigration law in internal guidelines (Vetters), withdrawing residence permits or producing population records (Gargiulo) but also how bureaucrats may advance the legitimacy of their profession and, as such, the 'state' (Lindberg and Borrelli) while at times also contesting seemingly unjust practices of exclusion. As such, we highlight how various migrant categories are influenced by paperwork but also able to produce evidence that allows them to claim rights (or, at least, to try to do so).

Paperwork indeed functions as a mechanism that allows various actors to continuously negotiate but also to set up a codified set of rules, which permits bureaucracies to maintain an air of standardized practice. Documents allow for the ritual construction of a collective project (Hull 2003); in our presented context legitimacy is given to an otherwise fragmented state that both includes and excludes (see Chauvin and Garcés-Mascareñas 2020). And while paperwork stabilizes information and produces social relations (Kosciejew 2017), this form of bureaucracy does not need to automatically oppose individual treatment but allows for both – control and care, domination and protection (see Bierschenk, closing commentary; Hunter 2008). As a process, 'paperwork' thus enables us to explore how individuals 'work' with given knowledge, how information is transformed into material artefacts and eventually transported via those artefacts. Paper trails, which can be defined as 'series of documents providing written evidence of a sequence of events or the activities of a person or organization' (*Oxford Dictionary*), are produced as a consequence. Those trails function as means to materialize someone's existence (Gargiulo), their itinerary, their work and whereabouts (Cabot 2012, Berg, this volume). Asylum seekers need to visualize their history of suffering (Nakueira); foreign national workers need to show their continued employment in order to receive a more regular residence status (Tuckett 2018) and bureaucrats must collect enough evidence to revoke residence permits (Pfirter 2019). In a context where state–migrant interactions are largely mediated by documents, reflecting on the processes through which these documents are produced and used within and outside of immigration desks has become a crucial part of studying such interactions.

Focusing on the place and the role of documents also contains an implicit methodological stance: that of taking the views and practices of our 'natives' seriously and trying to understand the reasons for their seemingly 'absurd' behaviour (Beek and Bierschenk 2020) – as illustrated by welfare workers trying to get their own administration sued (Andreetta, this volume). Most of our contributions, however, focus on what documents achieve and how they circulate or are mobilized in daily state–migrant encounters: the actual process of writing them up is often invisible to the ethnographer (Vetters; Borrelli and Lindberg, this volume) because it happens online through a database (Gargiulo, this volume), behind closed office doors or because the documents that we study were already written once we got to the field (Nakueira, this volume). Much like studying bureaucrats as experts, focusing on documents nevertheless 'opens the way for a more symmetric anthropology where researcher and researched meet on a more equal footing' (Beek and Bierschenk 2020: 12): the ways in which bureaucrats and migrants write reports, rely on paper trails or collect documents resembles in many ways our own paperwork practices.

Governing Migration through Paperwork – between Agency and Control

Based on ethnographic research, the various chapters in this book discuss in what manner paper realities can shape the mobility, agency and decisions of migrant individuals, but also how they influence bureaucratic practices and contribute to the making of immigration law. Contributions explore how paperwork guides and legitimizes bureaucratic practices, while at the same time showing how the documents produced can be contested by various actors within the migration regime. The usefulness of the collected contributions thus lies in understanding not only how documents become our informants in ethnographic research (see Riles 2006) but also how they become objects which bureaucrats and migrants act upon, contest, manipulate and produce. Drawing from Tatjana Thelen and colleagues' (2017) idea of a relational anthropology of the state, we explore interactions between documents and various kinds of actors who try to make sense of an often highly illegible migration regime (Eule et al. 2019) through three interconnected processes: migrants' and street-level bureaucrat's agency and the effects that these agencies produce; the standardization of bureaucratic practices; and how the aforementioned practices relate to various forms of perceptions of and engagements with the state. Individual contributions also focus on different sets of actors in order to understand how they use, produce and engage with paperwork in a variety of national contexts and institutions, showing how the practices of street-level bureaucrats can be understood.

The contributions by Hanna Berg, Sophie Nakueira, Enrico Gargiulo and Lisa Marie Borrelli and Annika Lindberg critically analyse the effects of paperwork for various categories of migrants. The reality of bureaucracy asking for a constant paper trail comes into being and clashes with the unstable everyday lives of migrants, who might not be able to secure such a coherent documentation (Gargiulo). Berg shows how the use of documents as a tool for controlling migrants' mobility is far from new: based on a combination of archival and ethnographic research, she highlights continuities and similarities between old and new systems of refugee documentation. Nakueira critically examines how documents regulate lived realities of refugees in Ugandan camps and studies the processes of negotiation and agency taken on by migrant individuals. Gargiulo shows how population registers, because of their selective nature in practice, end up performing and selecting legitimate residents, based, amongst other things, on avoiding dependency. Borrelli and Lindberg examine processes of deportation enforcement in Sweden and explore the role of paperwork in mediating and legitimating the detainment, deportation and discriminatory treatment of 'unwanted' migrants. Their work therefore illustrates how paperwork becomes a productive tool of control (Gargiulo; Borrelli and Lindberg, this volume), since its obscurity hinders migrants (with a more or less precarious legal status) in contesting paperwork (Nakueira, this volume) while also being forced to create it and perform according to bureaucratic rules.

Sophie Andreetta and Larissa Vetters, on the other hand, both focus on street-level bureaucrats' perspective, discourses and practices, and show how they sometimes struggle with and contest controversial guidelines. They delve into street-level bureaucrats' attempts to codify their own practices and, in doing so, describe 'immigration law in the making' (Vetters) and identify ways in which street-level workers challenge restrictive migration policies through 'writing for the client' (Andreetta). Looking at how welfare bureaucracies deal with social-assistance requests from irregular migrants, Andreetta shows how street-level bureaucrats write both for and against the state (see also Eckert et al. 2014) in their reports, which they hope will be used as grounds for contestation against the administration. Through the production of paperwork, she describes policy implementation as a fragmented, sedimented process, wherein social workers are constantly dealing with competing and changing interpretations of law. Vetters, on the other hand, studies administrative guidelines as an internally produced and used documentary genre with which German immigration officials attempt to standardize their own administrative practices.

Together, the contributions show how paperwork enables, mediates and constrains power, and deconstruct the struggles of all actors involved in their daily attempt to legitimize their claims, without discrediting the difficulty bureaucrats may face in their job. Concluding with a postscript by Thomas Bierschenk, this book addresses wider concerns in the anthropology of bureaucracy, including the Janus-faced bureaucracies which researchers and migrants encounter, displaying the oppressive and dominating regimes of protection and control. This book therefore ultimately shows how studying the documentary practices of the state and of the migrants who engage with it helps unpack the way immigration laws and policies are implemented, interpreted and questioned on a daily basis within various bureaucracies. It shows how civil servants can both produce statehood in restricting migrants' movements and limiting access to legal statutes and benefits, in line with current political agendas in many countries, while at the same time questioning their own practices and regularly using their discretion in order to help migrants. The different contributions, finally, help to highlight organizational and professional differences in the way civil servants deal with migrants, relate to the state and its policies, and define their obligations towards migrants and towards the state. We thus contribute to the study of the state as documentary practice and highlight the role of paperwork as a serious practice of migration control.

Acknowledgements

This research was funded by the Max Planck Institute for Social Anthropology and the Swiss National Science Foundation within the National Center of Competence in Research (nccr) – on the move (51NF40-182897).

Sophie Andreetta works as a FRS-FNRS Research Associate within the University of Liège. Her work focuses on the place, and the many potential roles/strategies of law in policy areas generally perceived as functioning based on informal logics. At the intersection of social–legal studies and the anthropology of the state, her publications use ethnographic methods to delve into (non)citizens' relationships with law and state institutions, and the concrete implementation of public policies. Email: sandreetta@uliege.be

Lisa Marie Borrelli works as an Associate Professor at the University of Applied Science – HES-SO Valais-Wallis, Institute of Social Work, Switzerland. Her research interests circle around the broader concepts of exclusion and banishment, including a focus on how noncitizens' rights are restricted by states in the fields of migration law, welfare policies and public administration. She follows an ethnographic approach and is interested in qualitative methodologies to study the decision-making of (non)state actors, bureaucratic practices, policy discourses and legal case work. Email: lisa.borrelli@hevs.ch

References

Allard, O. (2012), 'Bureaucratic Anxiety: Asymmetrical Interactions and the Role of Documents in the Orinoco Delta, Venezuela', *HAU: Journal of Ethnographic Theory* 2(2): 234–56, https://doi.org//10.14318/hau2.2.013.

Alpes, M.J. (2017), 'Papers That Work: Migration Brokers, State/Market Boundaries, and the Place of Law', *PoLAR: Political and Legal Anthropology Review* 40(2): 262–77, https://doi.org/10.1111/plar.12219.

Ataç, I. (2019), 'Deserving Shelter: Conditional Access to Accommodation for Rejected Asylum Seekers in Austria, the Netherlands, and Sweden', *Journal of Immigrant & Refugee Studies* 17(1): 44–60, https://doi.org//10.1080/15562948.2018.1530401.

Beek, J. and T. Bierschenk (2020), 'Bureaucrats as Para-Ethnologists: The Use of Culture in State Practices'. *Sociologus* 70(1): 1–17. https://doi.org/10.3790/soc.70.1.1.

Berg, L. and J. Millbank (2009), 'Constructing the Personal Narratives of Lesbian, Gay and Bisexual Asylum Claimants', *Journal of Refugee Studies* 22(2): 195–223.

Bierschenk, T. and J-P. Olivier de Sardan (2014), *States at Work: Dynamics of African Bureaucracies*. Leiden: Brill.

Bosworth, M. (2016), 'Paperwork and Administrative Power in Detention', Oxford Law Faculty Blog, 13 June. Retrieved 12 February 2024 from https://www.law.ox.ac.uk/research-subject-groups/centre-criminology/centreborder-criminologies/blog/2016/06/paperwork-and.

Cabot, H. (2012), 'The Governance of Things: Documenting Limbo in the Greek Asylum Procedure', *PoLAR: Political and Legal Anthropology Review* 35(1): 11–29, https://doi.org//10.1111/j.1555-2934.2012.01177.x.

Chauvin, S. and B. Garcés-Mascareñas (2020), 'Contradictions in the Moral Economy of Migrant Irregularity', in S. Spencer and A. Triandafyllidou (eds), *Migrants with Irregular Status in Europe*, Cham: SpringerOpen, pp. 33–49.

Corrigan, P. and D. Sayer (1985), *The Great Arch: English State Formation as Cultural Revolution*. Oxford: Blackwell.

Das, V. and D. Poole (2004), 'State and Its Margins: Comparative Ethnographies', in Veena Das and Deborah Poole (eds), *Anthropology in the Margins of the State*. Oxford: Oxford University Press, pp. 3–34.

Dhupelia-Mesthrie, U. (2014), 'Paper Regimes', *Kronos* 40: 10–22.

Eckert, J., B. Donahoe, C. Strumpell and Z.O. Biner (2014), *Law Against the State. Ethnographic Forays into Law's Transformations*. Cambridge: Cambridge University Press.

Eule, T.G., L.M. Borrelli, A. Lindberg and A. Wyss (2019), *Migrants Before the Law: Contested Migration Control in Europe*. London: Palgrave Macmillan.

Eule, T.G., D. Loher and A. Wyss (2018), 'Contested Control at the Margins of the State', *Journal of Ethnic and Migration Studies* 16(1): 2717–29, https://doi.org//10.1080/1369183X.2017.1401511.

Fassin, D. (2013), *Enforcing Order: An Ethnography of Urban Policing*. Cambridge: Polity.

Fassin, D. and C. Kobelinsky (2012), 'Comment on Juge l'asile. L'institution Comme Agent Moral', *Revue Française de Sociologie* 53(4): 657–88.

Feldman, G. (2016), '"With My Head on the Pillow": Sovereignty, Ethics, and Evil among Undercover Police Investigators', *Comparative Studies in Society and History* 58(2): 491–518.

Guiraudon, V. (2000), 'European Integration and Migration Policy: Vertical Policy-Making as Venue Shopping', *Journal of Common Market Studies* 38(2): 251–71, https://doi.org//10.1111/1468-5965.00219.

Gupta, A. (2012), *Red Tape: Bureaucracy, Structural Violence, and Poverty in India*. Durham, NC: Duke University Press.

Hoag, C.B. (2010), 'The Magic of the Populace: An Ethnography of Illegibility in the South African Immigration Bureaucracy', *PoLAR: Political and Legal Anthropology Review* 33(1): 6–25.

Hollifield, J.F. (2004), 'The Emerging Migration State', *International Migration Review* 38(3): 885–912, https://doi.org/10.1111/j.1747-7379.2004.tb00223.x.

Hull, M.S. (2003), 'The File: Agency, Authority, and Autography in an Islamabad Bureaucracy', *Language & Communication* 23(3–4): 287–314, https://doi.org//10.1016/S0271-5309(03)00019-3.

_______ (2012), *Government of Paper: The Materiality of Bureaucracy in Urban Pakistan*. Berkeley: University of California Press.

Hunter, S. (2008), 'Living Documents: A Feminist Psychosocial Approach to the Relational Politics of Policy Documentation', *Critical Social Policy* 28(4), 506–28.

Johannesson, L. (2012), 'Performing Credibility: Assessments of Asylum Claims in Swedish Migration Courts', *Retfærd Årgang* 35(138): 69–84.

_______ (2018), 'Exploring the "Liberal Paradox" from the Inside: Evidence from the Swedish Migration Courts', *International Migration Review* 52(4): 1162–85, https://doi.org//10.1177/0197918318767928.

Kagan, M. (2002), 'Is Truth in the Eye of the Beholder? Objective Credibility Assessment in Refugee Status Determination', *Georgetown Immigration Law Journal* 17(3): 367–415.

Kelly, T. (2012), 'Sympathy and Suspicion: Torture, Asylum, and Humanity',

Journal of the Royal Anthropological Institute 18(4): 753–68, https://doi.org//10.1111/j.1467-9655.2012.01790.x.

Kosciejew, M. (2017), 'A Material-Documentary Literacy: Documents, Practices, and the Materialization of Information', *The Minnesota Review* 88: 96–111, doi: 10.1215/00265667-3787426.

Lipsky, M. (2010), *Street-Level Bureaucracy: The Dilemmas of the Individual in Public Service*. New York: Russell Sage Foundation.

Mathur, N. (2016), *Paper Tiger: Law, Bureaucracy and the Developmental State in Himalayan India*. Delhi: Cambridge University Press.

Navaro-Yashin, Y. (2007), 'Make-Believe Papers, Legal Forms and the Counterfeit: Affective Interactions between Documents and People in Britain and Cyprus', *Anthropological Theory* 7(1): 79–98, https://doi.org//10.1177/1463499607074294.

Nugent, D. (2010), 'States, Secrecy, Subversives: APRA and Political Fantasy in Mid-20th-Century Peru', *American Ethnologist* 37(4): 681–702, https://doi.org/10.1111/j.1548-1425.2010.01278.x.

Pfirter, L. (2019), 'Constructing "Unteachability" through Menacing Warnings: the Coupling of Welfare Benefits and Migration Control in Switzerland', *Journal of Legal Anthropology* 3 (2): 29–49, doi: 10.3167/jla.2019.030203.

Pigg, S.L., S.L. Erikson and K. Inglis (2018), 'Introduction. Document/ation: Power, Interests, Accountabilities', *Anthropologica* 60(1): 167–89, https://doi.org/10.3138/anth.60.1.t16.

Prior, L. (2008), 'Repositioning Documents in Social Research', *Sociology* 42(5): 821–36, doi: 10.1177/0038038508094564.

Riles, A. (ed.) (2006), *Documents: Artifacts of Modern Knowledge*. Ann Arbor: University of Michigan Press.

Scheel, S. (2019), *Autonomy of Migration? Appropriating Mobility within Biometric Border Regimes*. London: Routledge.

Scott, James C. (1998), *Seeing Like a State: How Certain Schemes to Improve the Human Condition Have Failed*. New Haven, CT: Yale University Press.

Spire, A. (2008), *Accueillir Ou Reconduire: Enquête Sur Les Guichets de l'immigration*. Paris: Raisons d'agir.

Thelen, T., L. Vetters and K. von Benda-Beckmann (2017), *Stategraphy: Toward a Relational Anthropology of the State*. Oxford: Berghahn Books.

Tuckett, A. (2015), 'Strategies of Navigation: Migrants' Everyday Encounters with Italian Immigration Bureaucracy', *Cambridge Journal of Anthropology* 33(1): 113–28, https://doi.org/10.3167/ca.2015.330109.

——— (2018), *Rules, Paper, Status: Migrants and Precarious Bureaucracy in Contemporary Italy*. Stanford, CA: Stanford University Press.

Weisser, F. (2014), 'Practices, Politics, Performativities: Documents in the International Negotiations on Climate Change', *Political Geography* 40: 46–55.

1

Administrative Guidelines as a Source of Immigration Law?

Ethnographic Perspectives on Law at Work and in the Making

Larissa Vetters

Introduction

This chapter suggests that closer ethnographic attention to *practical* standardization and codification as part of the everyday activities of bureaucrats can contribute to a better understanding (and critique) of the complex realities and politics of migration governance.[1]

Central to such an approach is the ethnographic study of administrative guidelines as a unique genre of documents. Studying how various actors, who are embedded in multiplex social relations and textual webs of references, produce, use and circulate legal meanings and act upon such legal meanings requires an ethnographic approach that takes into account the legal content and context of a variety of documents as well as the diverse forms of practical work done with and upon these documents.

The chapter contextualizes the conceptual and methodological discussion on how migration is governed through paperwork into two broader fields: understandings of state and non-state law in debates about legal pluralism, and the more recent interest in street-level bureaucrats' discretionary practices and paperwork in the anthropology of the state. How bureaucratic paperwork becomes key to migration governance then emerges through ethnographic data.

First, I trace the doctrinal ordering of different sources of law in order to highlight the (contested) legal quality of administrative guidelines according to this doctrinal systematization and to sketch the larger system of ideas in which bureaucratic action is embedded. I next map out how the administrative guidelines of the Foreigners' Registration Office of the city state of Berlin (Ausländerbehörde Berlin – ABB)[2] and the visa guidelines of the Federal Foreign Office (Auswärtiges Amt – AA) come into being, how they are being used by various actors and continuously adapted based on practical experience. Then I demonstrate that they become an important 'source of law' in the everyday governance of migration, by focusing on judicial and political processes during which instructions in these guidelines are contested. In these processes, the micropolitics of the making of immigration law through paperwork, in which a plurality of actors partake, becomes most visible. The chapter argues that an understanding of the politics and practices of lawmaking that emerge around administrative guidelines paves the way for a form of critique that differs from current trends in critical ethnographic scholarship on migration.

The Anthropology of Law and the State – Conceptual Resources for Studying Immigration Governance

When the paradigm of legal pluralism brought the state and its law into the purview of anthropologists (F. von Benda-Beckmann 2008: 87), it also led to a lively, if not heated, debate between legal anthropologists and more doctrinally oriented legal scholars (cf. Griffiths 1986, Tamanaha 1993, F. von Benda-Beckmann 2002). Proponents (mostly anthropologists) and opponents (mostly legal scholars) differed on whether the state was to be seen as the ultimate source and enforcer of law, or whether norms not emanating from and sanctioned by the state could be considered law. Legal anthropologists, who argued for an analytical perspective that was open to the possibility of plural normative orders and who ethnographically documented the widespread practice of actors to resort to different normative orders, shared an underlying epistemological orientation towards a non-state-centric conception of law. They found themselves defending such a stance against what John Griffiths called the ideology of 'legal centralism' (Griffiths 1986: 3–4, see, also, F. von Benda-Beckmann 2008: 97–98). Unwittingly though, the terms of this debate had the side effect of shielding the various norm-making processes through which state law comes into being from ethnographic scrutiny and conceptual analysis. Finding themselves in opposition to overly state-centric visions of law, legal anthropologists by and large did not examine the inner workings or the making of official state law in its own right and with the same fine-grained ethnographic attention that they devoted to other normative orders (be they local or transnational in scope).[3] As a somewhat paradoxical effect, abstract conceptualizations of state law as developed within political or legal theory and put forward by doctrinally oriented legal scholars remained the unchallenged dominant legal ideology, particularly in research settings characterized as 'anthropology at home' and certainly for such legal fields as administrative law (including immigration and asylum law). Closer attention to the inner workings of state law only became more frequent with the gradual acceptance of 'legal pluralism' and 'governance' not merely as analytical but also as normative concepts within mainstream legal scholarship (K. von Benda-Beckmann and Turner 2018: 260, 265–66).

While the making and inner workings of state law in such legal fields as public law, and by extension administrative law, have thus remained relatively understudied within the paradigm of legal pluralism, state actors and their interactions with citizens have received ample attention in the expanding subfield of the anthropology of bureaucracy and the state.[4] Here, theoretical and methodological approaches to studying state bureaucracies quickly diversified and scholars soon called for a closer study of the practices of street-level bureaucrats, their thought-work in shaping organizational worldviews (Heyman 1995), their practical norms (Bierschenk and Olivier de Sardan 2014; Olivier de Sardan 2015) and moral subjectivities (Fassin et al. 2015, Eckert 2020, Andreetta et al. 2022), and their embeddedness in social relations as well as the boundary work they perform in upholding the idea of a division between state and society (Thelen, Vetters and K. von Benda-Beckmann 2018). While these studies often focused on the interactions between bureaucrats and citizens, another strand of research within the emerging anthropology of bureaucracy and the state took an interest in the materiality and generative force of documents as well as the internal documentary practices of bureaucrats (Cabot 2012; Hull 2003, 2012b; Göpfert 2013; Mathur 2016). Central to the first line of study is the role of bureaucrats' discretionary decision-making. Authors such as Jean-Pierre Olivier de Sardan (2015) for the African context, Fassin et al. (2015) for the French context, Tobias Eule (2014) for the German context, or Eule and colleagues (2019) in the European context have taken up Michael Lipsky's (1980) conceptualization of street-level bureaucracy and interpreted the use of discretion as a form of administrative policy-making – rather than the mere execution or implementation of policy. Central to the second line of study is an argument – often, but not always, inspired by actor-network theory – about the co-constitutive or productive force of documentary practices and bureaucratic objects when it comes to the implementation of state laws by bureaucrats and judges (Latour 2002; see also Riles 2006: 21). Authors have variously focused on list-making (Dorondel and Popa 2018), the use of identity documents (Cabot 2012), police records and report-writing (Göpfert 2013; Komter 2006) and letters (Mathur 2016), or the production of case files (Hull 2003; Scheffer 2007) and their role in judicial decision-making (Kubal 2019: 78–101; Latour 2002; Oorschot 2014). Increasingly, this second strand has also been extended to studying the role of 'bureaucratic inscription' and the 'transformative potential of documents' in migrants' interactions with state officials and laws (Horton 2020: 3; Abarca and Coutin 2018: 7).

Though these ethnographies of law, state and bureaucracy have significantly expanded our conceptual vocabulary, they share a tendency to locate sociolegal change and transformative agency outside the parameters of codified law. Conceptually, transformative agency tends to be located either in the everyday, informal social practices of bureaucrats (shaped by workplace constraints, worldviews and moral judgements or webs of social relationships) or in the material, affective and aesthetic dimensions of documents that – by binding together actors, events and decisions – become constitutive of bureaucratic rules and subjectivities. Thus, the ways by which street-level and backstage bureaucrats standardize and codify their own practices in relation to existing codified law, and the effects this has on the wider web of 'state law', remain underexamined.

Building on the insights provided by legal pluralism and the anthropology of the state, while also addressing their blind spots, this chapter offers an in-depth exploration of the role of administrative guidelines in the doctrinal system of legal ideas, in the inner workings and in the practical making of immigration law.

Ethnographic Engagements with Law and Immigration Bureaucracies

That administrative guidelines are a documentary genre that warrants closer ethnographic attention became apparent during a research project exploring transformative dynamics in German immigration and – by extension – administrative law. This sociolegal and ethnographic project aimed to study immigration law in action, hypothesizing that transformative dynamics emerged in interactions and negotiations between migrants, bureaucrats, lawyers, legal-aid providers and judges around specific immigration and asylum claims (Vetters, Eggers and Hahn 2017). As such, it largely shared the conviction of Bierschenk and Olivier de Sardan (2019: 246, 249) that ethnographic methods – such as participant observation, interviews in a conversational mode and socializing both in and outside of the workplace – are ideally suited to investigating how informal practices, pragmatic rules and practical norms interact with formal rules in formal organizations such as bureaucracies and courts. During a 3-year period, from 2015 to 2018, a team of three researchers consisting of myself, another anthropologist and a lawyer observed hearings at the administrative court and interacted with judges on a regular basis, accompanied legal-aid providers and lawyers in their counselling, and carried out internships as well as short-term visits in select branches of the administration concerned with issues of migration and integration in the city of Berlin. We also participated in a range of events and meetings where these actors interacted and conducted additional semi-formal interviews and informal conversations. However, the omnipresence of documents in our field meant that obtaining, reading and understanding the documents our interlocutors used, produced or referred to also constituted an integral part of fieldwork. Like in other bureaucratic and legal research settings (Kubal 2019: 78–101, Latour 2002, Lowenkron and Ferreira 2014), where documents become important ethnographic artefacts, 'ethnographing documents' (Lowenkron and Fereira 2014: 81) is as much part of fieldwork as participant observation. In this context, frequent referrals to the administrative guidelines of Berlin's Foreigners' Registration Office attracted our attention. They became a topic of recurrent conversation and opened a window into a larger system of legal meanings held by our interlocutors. To understand this larger system of legal meanings, we complemented our original ethnographic focus on what actors did and how they interacted with an immersion into the world of doctrinal legal reasoning.[5] Legal texts such as constitutions and statutory laws, but also scholarly commentaries and legal opinions or court judgments, which we encountered through acts of reference by our interlocutors (c.f. Latour 2002; Oorschot and Schinkel 2015), formed part of our ethnographic field. Textual artefacts, therefore, require a double ethnographic engagement that builds on methodological traditions in both fields – the anthropological study of street-level bureaucrats and the anthropological study of law. Tracing how these artefacts (which form distinct documentary genres) are practically constructed and used by our interlocutors, generate socialities and subjectivities, and acquire a performativity of their own became as important as understanding the web of legal meanings emanating from such texts and how actors navigated this web of meanings. The following section portrays the larger web of legal meanings, of which administrative guidelines are a part.

State-Law Ideology

Our interlocutors noted that a well-defined hierarchy of sources of law is central to the function of law in a democratic society and that this core notion is held in high regard by German public-law scholars and practitioners of the postwar era. Next to the constitutional text conceived by the *pouvoir constituant*, the highest authority has traditionally been accorded to a nation-state's elected legislative body. In principle, therefore, a democratically elected parliament is seen as the highest lawmaking authority in society and all state action has to be grounded in parliamentary law in order to be legitimate. This parliamentary lawmaking prerogative must be fully realized and represented in the organizational set-up of the state apparatus. According to the equally central principle of the division of powers, the administration then merely implements parliamentary laws but has no legislative power. Only under certain – legally specified and strictly circumscribed – conditions are executive state bodies granted permission to act as a norm-producing authority and to pass sublegal acts such as ordinances (*Verordnungen*), statutes (*Satzungen*) and administrative guidelines (*Verwaltungsvorschriften*). Described by some legal scholars (e.g. Wahl 2003: 571) as a third layer of norms, administrative guidelines are the most widespread executive activity with a regulatory character. In the hierarchy of norms, these are not considered legal sources in the strict sense but are rather seen as internal provisions of a general character issued by a higher administrative authority for subordinate authorities, or by the head of an administrative authority to provide guidance on how to implement relevant laws and carry out tasks. Administrative guidelines appear under a range of different designations such as directive, decree, administrative circular, internal instruction or procedural guidance (*Richtlinien, Erlasse, Rundverfügungen, innerdienstliche Weisung, Verfahrenshinweise*).

Traditionally, administrative guidelines are not to be understood as a legal norm but only as a declaration of intent of the issuing administrative body (Sachs 2018: margin number 111). They are considered to have only an internally binding character, without any *direct* external effects on citizens. The internal character of administrative guidelines also shields them from judicial control, and thus they can be neither the object of nor a standard for judicial control. The breach of an administrative guideline does not qualify an administrative act as unlawful and an administrative guideline cannot be subjected to an abstract judicial-review procedure (Maurer and Waldhoff 2017: 686). According to this doctrinal ideology, administrative guidelines are clearly demarcated from statutory law.

However, in recent decades, a vibrant doctrinal debate has developed on the question of the legal quality, the external effects and the extent of judicial control over administrative guidelines (Baars 2010; Ossenbühl 2007; Sauerland 2005; Saurer 2006; Wahl 2003). Jurisprudence of the higher courts and legal scholarship have together created ever finer differentiations within the category of administrative guidelines, with different approaches accounting for the *indirect* external effects of administrative guidelines and determining their legal quality in relation to statutory administrative law. First, organizational and staff regulations are distinguished from guidelines providing guidance on the application of a concrete law. The latter are further differentiated into 'norm-interpreting guidelines' (*norminterpretierende Verwaltungsvorschriften*), clarifying indeterminate legal concepts in those parts of a norm dealing with legal facts, and 'discretion-steering guidelines' (*ermessenslenkende Verwaltungsvorschriften*), providing guidance on making use of legally mandated discretion in those parts of a norm determining legal consequences. Different degrees of judicial control are then posited for norm-interpreting and for discretion-steering guidelines.

In a second line of argument, an indirect external effect (allowing for judicial control) is deduced by considering the principle of equality before the law (art. 3, par. 1 German Basic Law). Here it is the actual uniform administrative practice (*Behördenpraxis*) which establishes a right to equal treatment, because the administration is bound by its own acts. Though the existence of an administrative guideline is a strong indicator of a uniform administrative practice, legal doctrine is careful to emphasize that it is the actual practice and not the guideline which establishes a right to equal treatment (Maurer and Waldhoff 2017: 689; Sachs 2018: Rn 111). Another line of reasoning having recourse to the general principle of protection of legitimate expectation has somewhat limited traction among courts and scholars in Germany, as it is not seen to emanate directly from a constitutionally enshrined right.[6] Finally, some legal scholars have advocated recognizing a direct external effect of administrative guidelines based on the argument that the administration has an original lawmaking/regulatory competence (Ossenbühl 2007; Wahl 2003; see also Maurer and Waldhoff 2017: 693). This is a clear departure from the traditional doctrinal view.

At the core of these doctrinal arguments is an attempt to patrol the boundaries between statutory law and an executive norm-making activity (traditionally portrayed solely as a form of interpretation and implementation). What is contested is the scope and intensity of the binding force of administrative guidelines as a type of norm that does not emanate from the democratically elected legislature and therefore creates plural sources of normative authority within the state. This debate attests to the difficulties that legal scholars, judges and public bureaucrats face in upholding and adhering to the traditional theory of hierarchy of norms as well as to the principle of separation of powers within public-law doctrine.

A closer look at state-law ideology thus shows that it provides, on the one hand, a set of ideas that offers legitimacy and a space for the actions of bureaucrats that is clearly demarcated from parliamentary lawmaking. On the other hand, this set of ideas is much less stable than assumed and constant doctrinal work[7] is necessary to uphold the coherence and legitimacy of this system of meaning. It is within this universe of doctrinal ideas and tensions that immigration bureaucrats carry out their daily work. As discussed below, they simultaneously refer to classic notions of the separation of powers or the hierarchy of sources of law and actively take part in norm-making activities through the use and production of administrative guidelines as part of their everyday work.

State Law at Work

When we met officials of the Foreigners' Registration Office (Ausländerbehörde Berlin – ABB) acting as legal representatives in immigration hearings at the Administrative Court of Berlin, they frequently complained about the quick pace of legislative change and the increasing number of package amendments. 'I no longer acquire new digest copies of the relevant laws, since they become outdated so quickly', confided Mrs Beier[8] and – pointing to a stack of printouts – continued, 'I consult our administrative guidelines and, if necessary, print out the relevant norm in its latest version.' Ethnographers doing research in immigration bureaucracies are often struck by the complexity of rules governing migration and find that this sense of complexity is shared by their interlocutors, who seem to be equally overwhelmed with having to keep track of regulatory changes at different levels of the hierarchy of legal sources (Eule 2014: 43–54; Eule et al. 2019; Gill and Good 2019: 21–22). While some researchers have pointed to the oral transmission and production of legal knowledge (Eule 2014) or to the formation of local epistemic communities of interpretation (Affolter, Miaz and Poertner 2019), my interlocutors often highlighted the role of written administrative guidelines as a means to counter this complexity. Norms regulating immigration can be found in national German laws, in European directives and in international treaties, which together form a complex, multilevel and often quickly changing legal landscape. Many of these legal sources contain indeterminate legal concepts and provide room for executive discretion. Comparing the field of immigration law with the field of construction law, one judge, who heard cases in both fields, explained to me that the comparatively large number of ordinances and administrative guidelines in immigration law was not surprising given the need to concretize legal concepts in these various norms and to steer the use of executive discretion according to political and social conditions in specific localities.

In the city state of Berlin, the ABB had published such guidelines for the application of several laws in the form of a compendium, the so-called Procedural Instructions of the ABB (*Verfahrenshinweise der Ausländerbehörde Berlin* – VAB), since 2005. My analysis of VAB versions published in the past has shown that the volume of instructions has steadily increased: in 2005, the guidelines consisted of 233 pages; by the autumn of 2018, this had risen to over 800 pages. Updated versions of the VAB were published on the ABB's website. Each new version contained a host of changes to individual stipulations that had accumulated over the preceding weeks or months, and the frequency with which new versions were published also steadily increased over the years. As Mr Klaus, a member of the ABB's litigation team, pointed out, changes in the VAB can be systematized according to whether they result from changes in legislation, are a response to a (higher instance) court decision, are based on instructions of the Senator of the Interior of the city state of Berlin or are the outcome of an internal decision-making process within the ABB.

I turn to field data to demonstrate how this internal decision-making process takes place. Asked how new instructions are incorporated into the VAB or older ones adapted, Mrs Koenig, the head of the legal division of the ABB, first portrayed this as a relatively structured top-down process in which the policy-issues department drafted such changes in anticipation of and in response to changes in legislation or to directives from the Senate of Berlin. However, when our conversation continued, it became apparent that there were other avenues for change as well. She noted that if, for example, a practice specified by instructions in the VAB is challenged in the course of a claim at the administrative court, this will be reported back to the office by the attending Foreigners ABB's representative. As head of the legal division, she might then decide to introduce a proposal for changing this instruction in the regular meetings of heads of sections. In fact, she continued, every employee can suggest improvements, but only the heads of sections could submit such proposals for discussion at their meetings. Such a meeting occurs every four weeks and, considering previous meetings, she confirmed that proposals for changes in the VAB were frequently on the agenda.

With regard to how the VAB were used by front-line officials, Mrs Koch from the legal division commented:

> These guidelines are the bible on which front-line employees base their daily work. They can't look up everything in the constitution, now, can they? Of course, this does not mean that we ask them to disregard the constitution, but it is *our* task to make

> sure that the guidelines are in line with the constitution and existing laws, so that our front-line staff does not have to worry about this.

In practice, therefore, administrative guidelines, such as the VAB, become the law that is applied, and executive actors participate in the construction of this 'law at work' by standardizing their own convictions, practical experience and informal norms and inserting them into the written guidelines in a bottom-up manner.

A similar in-house process of proposing, drafting and implementing changes to the administrative guidelines regulating the issuing of visas (*Visumshandbuch des Auswärtigen Amtes* – VAA) was explained to us during a discussion in 2017 with members of various sections of the AA dealing with migration policy, visa processing and visa litigation. These civil servants confidently spoke of their legal division as a kind of specialized in-house law firm, and emphasized that because of the circumscribed nature of their mandate they were able to acquire an in-depth expertise in all questions pertaining to visa regulations. In a weekly meeting, cases that were proving problematic in the daily practice of German missions abroad were jointly discussed. Often, they said they were confronted with having to deliberate on the meaning of a sub-subclause of an article in the Residence Act, which previously had no relevance simply because such cases did not occur, but now – due to new circumstances such as the war in Syria – such constellations arose on a daily basis. These civil servants felt they simply could not wait until German courts had established a uniform jurisprudence, and they had to provide guidance to the missions abroad that decided on visa applications. They thought it was best done through instructions in the VAA – a compilation that today runs to over 500 pages; is regularly updated; and, since 2016, has been published as an online document.

When discussing their own active role in the transformation of particular immigration norms, these civil servants pointed to an internally much-debated example describing a complex interplay of repeated cycles of administrative interpretations, judicial reviews, administrative reformulations and legislative changes. This example demonstrates how immigration officials simultaneously navigate a multilevel universe of legal meanings that both underlies their work and is challenged in that immigration officials insert their own practical, situated experience and convictions into the interpretation and reformulation of specific immigration norms. In 2004, a European directive (2004/114/EC) regulating the admission of third-country nationals to European Union (EU) member states for the purpose of study had been passed and subsequently transposed to German immigration law. The respective passage in the German Residence Act had been phrased in language that provided immigration officials with a degree of legally guaranteed (*de jure*) discretion for either granting or denying a student visa. In the AA, guidelines were formulated to further specify how to exercise this *de jure* discretion. These instructions built on a shared conviction among front-line officials (forming an organizational worldview based on personal experience as well as hearsay) that student visas were frequently merely a means to enter Germany, not so much with the intention to study as to seek employment or family reunification before applying for a more advantageous residence title from within the country. While proof of successful enrolment at a German university was a prerequisite for a visa application, embassy officials doubted that university administrations were qualified to assess the validity and authenticity of the submitted certificates, suspecting further opportunities for fraud.

To counter this perceived abuse of student visas, the guidelines encouraged officials to make broad use of their *de jure* discretion, critically reviewing and even rejecting applicants who fulfilled all formal requirements. This restrictive practice was challenged in court by one visa applicant who had been repeatedly rejected and the case was eventually referred to the European Court of Justice (ECJ), which, in a preliminary ruling in 2014, rejected the manner in which the stipulations of the European directive had been transposed to the German Residence Act. Subsequently, discretion in determining the legal outcome was formally reduced: if all formal requirements were met, a visa *had* to be granted, whereas before, according to the German wording, authorities *could* grant a visa but were not obliged to do so. Subsequently, the AA changed its legal opinion and revised the VAA. These now provided extensive instructions on how to assess the supporting evidence needed to complete an application in order to evaluate whether applicants sincerely intended to study in Germany. A comprehensive plausibility review was introduced, and embassy officials were counselled to consider a wide range of circumstantial evidence as indicators that applicants might intend to enter Germany for other purposes than university studies. If indicators of intentional abuse could be found, then applicants should be rejected. However, now the rejection was no longer founded on *de jure* discretion but needed to be justified with reference to a *de facto* discretion deriving from the assessment of facts.

We can appreciate the reformulation of this particular part of the visa guidelines as an attempt to move away from a form of *de jure* discretion that was challenged by the ECJ towards a form of *de facto* discretion in the manner in which evidence for meeting the requirements set out in the norm is requested and assessed. This latter form of discretion is still subject to judicial control, but now assessed according to the standards of German administrative law, which provides some leeway. This shift allowed immigration officials to largely uphold their original practice based on the perception that – as one of our interlocutors phrased it – embassy officials saw themselves as 'the last instance of control against inexperienced admission staff at universities and the abuse of student visas'. At the same time, they remained within the margins of interpretation that the doctrinal systematization of different forms of discretion and judicial control within German administrative law offered them. Noting that a new directive for student visas had just replaced the old one at the European level and was now being put into effect through amendments to the German Residence Act, our counterparts in the Federal Foreign Office saw future opportunities for asserting their point of view.

Demonstrating how immigration norms are internally assessed and guidelines made and reformulated by bureaucrats within a larger web of legal ideas, which are at once created by and contained in a variety of cross-referring legal texts originating at different levels (EU directives, national laws, EU and national court decisions, guidelines, administrative decisions), adds to current discussions of the role of street-level discretion in the governance of migration. Beyond the finding that street-level bureaucrats exercise *de facto* discretion in the face of uncertainty, complexity and resource constraints, I consider the formulation of administrative guidelines as an attempt by astute bureaucrats to codify their practical norms and to shield these from external challenges by inserting them into the space that the larger web of public-law doctrine provides for bureaucratic margins of interpretation. What Josiah Heyman (1995) describes as bureaucratic thought-work in relation to worldviews and Julia Eckert (2020) refers to as bureaucratic ethics tied to specific notions of the commonweal is momentarily standardized and codified trough what could perhaps be called 'second-order' doctrinal work – the skilful navigation of public-law doctrine. In this ongoing process of inserting practical norms and convictions into the guidelines and either defending them successfully against external challenges or having to reformulate them, *state law at work becomes state law in the making* – as discussed below. Publicly available, these administrative guidelines attract the attention of external actors and become yet another source of reference. As an object of reference and contestation, they connect migrants and their lawyers, legal-aid providers and interest organizations, as well as bureaucrats and judges, in an ongoing struggle of interpretation and norm-making.

State Law in the Making

Immigration lawyers who want to contest the outcome of administrative decisions based on the visa guidelines or VAB have to do so by filing an appeal in an individual case, claiming that the ABB or the AA incorrectly exercised its discretion in that particular case. In conversations with lawyers, contrary to my initial expectation, the VAB or VAA were not perceived as problematic in terms of limiting the procedural and substantive rights of their clients or restricting the scope of judicial control. On the contrary, relatively frequently, lawyers saw them as a resource that could be strategically mobilized as one element among a variety of documentary practices, which Susan Coutin (2020: 136–40) has described as the "legal craft" of lawyers and legal-aid providers. Lawyers often commented positively on the fact that the ABB published the VAB on its web page,[9] and used them as a standard to which bureaucrats could be held accountable by insisting on the legal principal of equal treatment.

Regarding another agency, the Federal Office for Migration and Refugees (Bundesamt für Migration und Flüchtlinge – BAMF), we witnessed one such challenge in an asylum case at the administrative court of appeal, which involved an assessment of the situation in Syria. The presiding judge, the lawyer and the representative of BAMF became involved in a verbal exchange over a handwritten note in the administrative file of the applicant's daughter, who had lived with her in Syria. While the mother had only been granted subsidiary protection, the daughter had received full asylum status. The daughter's file contained a note saying that – as established by internal guidelines – the region in which she resided in Syria was generally considered unsafe territory (since it was held by oppositional forces and its residents were therefore considered opponents of the regime). In the German wording, the term 'internal guidelines' (*Leitlinien*) was ambiguous, making it unclear whether a formal administrative guideline was meant; upon being questioned by the presiding judge, Mr Baum, the BAMF representative vehemently denied that such an internally binding guideline had existed. He repeatedly said the note in the file did not represent a generalizable and standardized decision-making practice of BAMF. Mrs Kofti, the lawyer, on the other hand, challenged this account, insisting that some form of standardized internal guidelines on how to treat various categories of Syrian asylum applicants must have existed. She saw the fact that BAMF had temporarily issued standardized written decisions without further oral hearings or individual evaluations as further proof that such internal guidelines must have existed, and explicitly likened their legal character to the VAB of Berlin's Foreigners' Registration Office. In this case, the judge did not follow up on Mrs Kofti's line of argument. Had she been successful in convincing the judge that a standardized decision-making practice had existed – and even been laid down in written guidelines – she would have had grounds for requesting equal treatment of mother and daughter. The guidelines would then – as proof of a general practice and by means of a detour through judicial control – have acquired a binding force for BAMF.

In Berlin, lawyers and their migrant clients were acutely aware of the immense practical importance of the VAB for immigration officials' decision-making. While they attempted to strategically use the VAB and other administrative guidelines to their advantage in individual appeals (thereby judicializing their content), they also, together with migrant interest organizations, lobbied for more external oversight and stakeholder participation in the actual process of formulating and updating these administrative guidelines. When, in 2016, a new government was elected for the city state of Berlin and a governing coalition comprising the Green Party, the Left Party and the Social Democrat Party was formed, this coalition was receptive to the proposals of migrants' and lawyers' associations. In the coalition contract, the establishment of an expert committee that would advise on VAB revisions and submit its own suggestions for revisions was agreed. The committee was to be formed by delegates from local migrant associations, the refugee council of Berlin, the so-called Härtefallkommission – a governmental committee for hearing petitions in cases of hardship in immigration law – large welfare organizations, trade unions, employer associations and professional lawyers' associations, but also representatives of the ABB and of other public agencies tasked with carrying out immigration- and integration-related activities. As guiding principle for the committee's work, the coalition partners affirmed their intention to make full use of their scope of discretion in implementing federal law at the city level according to an integration-oriented liberal local policy vision that considered the humanitarian aspects of cases.

It took a year and a half until the committee was fully established, and only at the end of 2019 did it issue its first batch of recommendations, which were then yet to be either accepted or rejected by Berlin's Senator of the Interior. It was thus difficult to assess the impact of the committee's work on the reformulation and revision of the VAB, but its internal dynamics illustrate the complex and contested micropolitics around the implementation and (re)formulation of immigration law at this local level.

On the one hand, the establishment of the committee indicates that an internal and non-transparent process of executive norm-making, to which bureaucrats significantly contribute by standardizing and codifying their own practical norms, is being brought back into a public form of political deliberation. Importantly, this is not the deliberation of elected representatives, who have the legitimate democratic mandate to debate on and pass parliamentary laws, but rather a deliberation among representatives of several interest organizations and stakeholders. Among them are organizations representing the interests of migrants (who largely lack direct political representation), but also representatives of federal and state bureaucracies and other societal interest groups. The consultative participation of this expert committee in the continuous reformulation of the VAB further pluralizes the range of norm-making actors involved in the field of immigration governance at the local level.

On the other hand, even this merely consultative participation was – according to some of my interlocutors among the civil society and migrant associations – met with strong resistance by the ABB, which did not want to relinquish its authority over and authorship of the VAB. Very few of the recommendations put forward by the representatives of refugee and migrant associations were supported by the representative of the ABB.

Viewing the social life of administrative guidelines, such as the VAB or the VAA, through the ethnographic lens has, thus, revealed how this documentary genre connects various social actors. It shows how they were drawn into a process of mutually interdependent activities of norm-interpretation; norm-contestation; and, ultimately, norm-making in the ambiguous and contested space between deciding on individual cases and abstract, general codification. It also shows how individual and collective actors struggle to have their diverging interests incorporated into a pluralized norm-making process. This process is by nature political and shaped by the unequally distributed legal, institutional, material and symbolic resources of those attempting to govern and control migration and those who, as migrants, are being subjected to this governance.

Law, Paperwork and the Critical Study of Migration Governance

This chapter has offered a closer ethnographic look at how German immigration law is produced as a subfield of administrative law. Administrative guidelines that are doctrinally theorized as an ambivalent source of law in need of constant doctrinal maintenance work are, in practice, produced as a complex form of executive norm-making to which street-level bureaucrats and legal advisors of immigration authorities actively contribute in a bottom-up process. They are contested and brought back into a process of political deliberation in which the interests of different social actors – among them (non-naturalized) migrants, who are excluded from the formal legislative process – are renegotiated. Actors variously engage with and contribute to the formulation of administrative guidelines, and become enmeshed in a larger web of legal meaning. This finding reveals a plurality of norm-making actors and norm-making processes at different levels and sites. It defies a conceptualization of state law as a monolithic and hierarchical source of authority and instead resonates with conceptualizations of normativity developed in anthropological research on legal pluralism.

I have also suggested shifting attention from *de facto* discretion or deviation from formal norms (the focus of much of the literature on street-level bureaucrats' discretionary practices) to a broader continuum of interpreting and remaking norms in which bureaucrats partake in their daily decision-making. Studying that continuum has highlighted attempts of immigration bureaucrats to standardize and codify their own practical norms. This calls for new research questions about the effects of street-level bureaucrats' discretionary power, and about state power more generally. As outlined in this volume's introduction (Andreetta and Borrelli), research on street-level bureaucrats' discretion in the field of immigration governance often explores the operating of power exactly through the unreadability and unpredictability of paperwork. What from the perspective of those who are subjected to it is too often experienced – at best – as unreadable and arbitrary (Nakueira, this volume) and – at worst – as structural violence within a discriminatory and racialized 'system' (Lindberg and Borrelli, this volume), can from another perspective be ethnographically unpacked as social practices within a larger system of meaning built on doctrinal notions of public law that are intended to safeguard individual liberty, equality, democratic representation and the legitimacy as well as the accountability of state actions (see also Andreetta, this volume). Understanding how bureaucrats and other social actors, motivated by complex and situated bundles of interests, act in reference to this system of meaning, how they make use of the margins of interpretation it offers and contribute to its practical reformulation, can provide another critical edge to ethnographic research on immigration law and bureaucracies: it complements ethnographic studies, which explore the power nexus between state and migrants as materialized in documents and experienced by migrants (Heyman 2020: 229), with a perspective that focuses on the experiences and documentary practices of state officials. Rather than taking a standpoint external to the legal-professional worldview of bureaucrats, such a critical exploration starts from within the normative universe they inhabit (see also Bierschenk and Olivier de Sardan 2019). Thus, my ethnographic account of administrative guidelines as a documentary genre intimately tied to bureaucratic practice has served to connect with and illustrate how core notions of democracy – such as the rule of law, legitimacy and political representation – that are taken to constitute pillars of our social order and have been enshrined in public law are (re)constructed and can become intertwined with forms of exclusion and inequality in and through the daily practice of immigration law. Along with Heyman (2020: 242), who argues that identity documents for migrants are a vital avenue to penetrate citizenship inequalities and therefore warrant critical anthropological attention, I call for equal critical attention to inner-administrative documentary genres and practices that structure the interpretation, application and transformation of immigration law.

Acknowledgements

I thank my co-researchers Judith Eggers and Lisa Hahn, as well as all our research partners and interlocutors, for their readiness to share their experience and knowledge. For critical discussions and comments, I am indebted to Jonas Bens, Jonathan Bernaerts, Marc Hertogh, Thomas Bierschenk and Bertram Turner as well as my co-panellists or discussants in Onati and Halle, and the anonymous reviewers. Funding details: research for this chapter was funded by the Fritz Thyssen Stiftung (grant number 10.15.2.002RE).

Larissa Vetters is Senior Research Fellow at the Max Planck Institute for Social Anthropology in Halle, Germany. Her research interests lie in the fields of legal anthropology and the anthropology of the state.

Notes

1. I do not follow the frequent distinction made by policy-makers (and researchers) between forced and voluntary migration and between immigration and asylum law, but instead favour a holistic approach to the study of migration governance that builds on a growing literature critically questioning this distinction. See Crawley and Skleparis (2018) and Vetters (2022).
2. In January 2020, the ABB was renamed the Berlin Immigration Office (Landesamt für Einwanderung).
3. While state actors were part of ethnographic analyses from early on (K. von Benda-Beckmann and F. von Benda-Beckmann 1998), the inner workings of state law often only came into view when contested by (marginalized) citizens and in situations where sub- or supranational norms were levied against state norms (e.g. Eckert 2006, Randeria 2007). Recently, Zenker and Hoehne (2018) have fruitfully brought together the legal-pluralism lens with insights from the anthropology of the state in an edited volume discussing the application of customary law within state law by African bureaucrats.
4. For overviews on the anthropology of the state, see Sharma and Gupta (2006); Stepputat and Nuijten (2018); and Thelen, Vetters and K. von Benda-Beckmann (2018). For the ethnographic study of public-service delivery and bureaucracies, see also Bear and Mathur (2015); Bierschenk and Olivier de Sardan (2014, 2019); Hoag (2011); and Hull (2012a).
5. This immersion into doctrinal reasoning was further facilitated by our project's institutional affiliation to the law faculty of one of the two major universities in Berlin. This affiliation not only offered the anthropologists among

us a space of learning and guidance on doctrinal matters but also played an important role in easing our access to (legally trained) interlocutors in various settings in Berlin. In the process, the boundaries between academic 'home' and 'ethnographic field' became blurred.

6. The publication of a guideline, however, establishes a strong legitimate expectation.
7. I take inspiration from Josiah Heyman's (1995) notion of bureaucratic thought-work here, but refashion it in a manner that reflects my specific analytical interest in bureaucrats' self-understanding as 'law implementers' or 'law makers'. This particular interest notwithstanding and as will be shown below, thought-work as doctrinal work cannot be separated from thought-work on substantive worldviews and moral evaluations (see also Heyman 2000; Eckert 2020).
8. All names are pseudonyms.
9. Many other federal and state immigration agencies did not publish their guidelines, since – if published – this would strengthen the argument for their external effect. With the introduction of freedom of information legislation (1999 in Berlin, 2006 on the federal level), citizens could, however, demand publication. The AA began publishing its visa guidelines following the judicial order to comply with requests for information made under the Freedom of Information Act.

References

Abarca G.A. and S.B. Coutin (2018), 'Sovereign Intimacies: The Lives of Documents within US State – Noncitizen Relationships', *American Ethnologist* 45(1): 7–19.

Affolter, L., J. Miaz and E. Poertner (2019), 'Taking the "Just" Decision: Caseworkers and Their Communities of Interpretation in the Swiss Asylum System', in N. Gill and A. Good (eds), *Asylum Determination in Europe. Ethnographic Perspectives*. Cham: Palgrave Macmillan, pp. 263–83.

Andreetta, S., L. Enria, P. Jarroux and S. Verheul (2022), 'States of Feeling. Public Servants' Affective Entanglements in the Making of the State', *Cambridge Journal of Anthropology* 40(2): 1–20.

Baars, A. (2010), *Rechtsfolgen fehlerhafter Verwaltungsvorschriften*. Baden-Baden: Nomos.

Bear, L. and N. Mathur (2015), 'Introduction. Remaking the Public Good: A New Anthropology of Bureaucracy', *Cambridge Journal of Anthropology* 33(1): 2–17.

Benda-Beckmann, F. von (2002), 'Who's Afraid of Legal Pluralism?' *Journal of Legal Pluralism and Unofficial Law* 34(47): 37–82.

——— (2008), 'Riding or Killing the Centaur? Reflections on the Identities of Legal Anthropology', *International Journal of Law in Context* 4(2): 85–110.

Benda-Beckmann, F. von and K. von Benda-Beckmann (1998), 'Where Structures Merge: State and Off-State Involvement in Rural Social Security on Ambon, Indonesia', in S.N. Pannell and F. von Benda-Beckmann (eds), *Old World Places, New World Problems: Exploring Resource Management Issues in Eastern Indonesia*. Canberra: Australian National University, Centre for Resource and Environmental Studies, pp. 143–80.

Benda-Beckmann, K. von and B. Turner (2018), 'Legal Pluralism, Social Theory, and the State', *Journal of Legal Pluralism and Unofficial Law* 50(3): 255–74.

Bierschenk, T. and J.-P. Olivier de Sardan (eds) (2014), '*States at Work. Dynamics of African Bureaucracies*. Leiden: Brill.

Bierschenk, T. and J.-P. Olivier de Sardan (2019), 'How to Study Bureaucracies Ethnographically?' *Critique of Anthropology* 39(2): 243–57.

Cabot, H. (2012), 'The Governance of Things: Documenting Limbo in the Greek Asylum Procedure', *PoLAR: Political and Legal Anthropology Review* 35(1): 11–29.

Crawley, H. and D. Skleparis (2018), 'Refugees, Migrants, Neither, Both: Categorial Fetishism and the Politics of Bounding in Europe's "Migration Crisis"', *Journal of Ethnic and Migration Studies* 44(1): 48–64.

Coutin, S.B. (2020), 'Opportunities and Double Binds. Legal Craft in an Era of Uncertainty', in S.B. Horton and J. Heyman (eds), *Paper Trails: Migrants, Documents, and Legal Insecurity*. Global Insecurities. Durham, NC: Duke University Press, pp. 130–52.

Dorondel, S. and M. Popa (2018), 'Workings of the State: Administrative Lists, European Union Food Aid and the Local Practices of Distribution in Rural Romania', in T. Thelen, L. Vetters and K. von Benda-Beckmann (eds), *Stategraphy. Toward a Relational Anthropology of the State*. New York: Berghahn, pp. 124–40.

Eckert, J. (2006), 'From Subjects to Citizens: Legalism from Below and the Homogenization of the Legal Sphere', *Journal of Legal Pluralism and Unofficial Law* 38(53–54): 45–75.

——— (2020), 'The Office. Ethos and Ethics in Migration Bureaucracies', in J. Eckert (ed.), *The Bureaucratic Production of Difference. Ethos and Ethics in Migration Administrations*. Bielefeld: Transcript, pp. 7–26.

Eule, T. (2014), *Inside Immigration Law: Migration Management and Policy Application in Germany*. Farnham: Ashgate.

Eule, T., L. Borrelli, A. Lindberg and A. Wyss (2019), *Migrants Before the Law. Contested Migration Control in Europe*. Cham: Palgrave Macmillan.

Fassin, D. et al. (2015), *At the Heart of the State. The Moral World of Institutions*. London: Pluto Press.

Gill, N. and A. Good (eds) (2019), *Asylum Determination in Europe. Ethnographic Perspectives*. Cham: Palgrave Macmillan.

Göpfert, M. (2013), 'Bureaucratic Aesthetics: Report Writing in the Nigerian Gendarmerie', *American Ethnologist* 40(2): 324–34.

Griffiths, J. (1986), 'What is Legal Pluralism?' *Journal of Legal Pluralism and Unofficial Law* 24: 1–55.

Heyman, J. (1995), 'Putting Power in the Anthropology of Bureaucracy. The Immigration and Naturalization Service at the Mexico–United States Border', *Current Anthropology* 36(2): 261–87.

——— (2000), 'Respect for Outsiders? Respect for the Law? The Moral Evaluation of High-Scale Issues by US Immigration Officers', *Journal of the Royal Anthropological Institute* 6(4): 635–52.

——— (2020), 'Conclusion. Documents as Power', in S.B. Horton and J. Heyman (eds), *Paper Trails: Migrants, Documents, and Legal Insecurity*. Global Insecurities. Durham, NC: Duke University Press, pp. 229–47.

Hoag, C. (2011), 'Assembling Partial Perspectives: Thoughts on the Anthropology of Bureaucracy', *PoLAR: Political and Legal Anthropology Review* 34(1): 81–94.

Horton, S.B. (2020), 'Introduction. Paper Trails: Migrants, Bureaucratic Inscription, and Legal Recognition', in S.B. Horton and J. Heyman (eds), *Paper Trails: Migrants, Documents, and Legal Insecurity*. Global Insecurities. Durham, NC: Duke University Press, pp. 1–26.

Horton, S.B. and J. Heyman (eds) (2020), *Paper Trails: Migrants, Documents, and Legal Insecurity*. Global Insecurities. Durham, NC: Duke University Press.

Hull, M. (2003), 'The File: Agency, Authority, and Autography in an Islamabad Bureaucracy', *Language & Communication* 23(3–4): 287–314.

——— (2012a), 'Documents and Paper', *Annual Review of Anthropology* 41: 251–67.

——— (2012b), *The Government of Paper. The Materiality of Bureaucracy in Urban Pakistan*. Berkeley: University of California Press.

Komter, M.L. (2006), 'From Talk to Text: The Interactional Construction of a Police Record', *Research on Language and Interaction* 39(3): 201–28.

Kubal, A. (2019), *Immigration and Refugee Law in Russia. Socio-legal Perspectives*. Cambridge: Cambridge University Press.

Latour, B. (2002), *La Fabrique du droit, une ethnolgie du Conseil d'Ètat*. Paris: La Découverte.

Lipsky, M. (1980), *Street-level Bureaucracy. Dilemmas of the Individual in Public Services*. New York: Russell Sage Foundation.

Lowenkron, L. and L. Ferreira (2014), 'Anthropological Perspectives on Documents. Ethnographic Dialogues on the Trail of Police Papers', *Vibrant. Virtual Brazilian Anthropology* 11(2): 76–112.

Mathur, N. (2016), *Paper Tiger. Law, Bureaucracy and the Developmental State in Himalayan India*. Cambridge: Cambridge University Press.

Maurer, H. and C. Waldhoff (2017), *Allgemeines Verwaltungsrecht*, 19th edn. Munich: C.H. Beck.

Olivier de Sardan, J.-P. (2015), 'Practical Norms: Informal Regulations within Public Bureaucracies (in Africa and Beyond)', in T. de Herdt and J.-P. Olivier de Sardan (eds), *Real Governance and Practical Norms in Sub-Saharan Africa. The Game of the Rules*. New York: Routledge, pp. 19–62.

Oorschot, I. van (2014), 'Seeing the Case Clearly: File Work, Material Mediation, and Visualizing Practices in a Dutch Criminal Court', *Symbolic Interaction* 37(4): 439–57.

Oorschot, I. van and W. Schinkel (2015), 'The Legal Case File as a Border Object: On Self-Reference and Other-Reference in Criminal Law', *Journal of Law and Society* 42(4): 499–527.

Ossenbühl, F. (2007), '§ 104. Autonome Rechtsetzung der Verwaltung', in J. Isensee and P. Kirchhof (eds), *Handbuch des Staatsrechts der Bundesrepublik Deutschland* Bd. V. Heidelberg: C.F. Müller, pp. 305–51.

Randeria, S. (2007), 'The State of Globalization: Legal Plurality, Overlapping Sovereignties and Ambiguous Alliances between Civil Society and the Cunning State in India', *Theory, Culture and Society* 24(1): pp. 1–33.

Riles, A. (2006), 'Introduction: In Response', in A. Riles (ed.), *Documents. Artifacts of Modern Knowledge*. Ann Arbor: University of Michigan Press, pp. 1–38.

Sachs, M. (2018), '§ 40 Verwaltungsverfahrensgesetz, Ermessen', in P. Stelkens, H.-H. Bonk and M. Sachs (eds), *Verwaltungsverfahrensgesetz Kommentar*. Munich: C.H. Beck, margin numbers 1–238.

Sauerland, T. (2005), *Die Verwaltungsvorschrift im System der Rechtsquellen*. Berlin: Duncker & Humblot.

Saurer, J. (2006), 'Die neueren Theorien zur Normkategorie der Verwaltungsvorschriften', *Verwaltungsarchiv* 9(7): 249–69.

Scheffer, T. (2007), 'File Work, Legal Care and Professional Habitus – An Ethnographic Reflection on Different Styles of Advocacy', *International Journal of the Legal Profession* 14(1): 57–80.

Sharma, A. and A. Gupta (eds) (2006), *The Anthropology of the State. A Reader*. Malden, MA: Blackwell, pp. 1–44.

Stepputat, F. and M. Nuijten (2018), 'Anthropology and the Enigma of the State', in H. Wystra and B. Thomassen (eds), *Handbook of Political Anthropology*. Cheltenham and Northampton, MA: Edward Elgar Publishing, pp. 127–44.

Tamanaha, B.Z. (1993), 'The Folly of the "Social Scientific" Concept of Legal Pluralism', *Journal of Law & Society* 20(2): 192–217.

Thelen, T., L. Vetters and K. von Benda-Beckmann (eds) (2018), *Stategraphy. Toward a Relational Anthropology of the State*. New York: Berghahn.

Vetters, L. (2022), 'Making Sense of Noncitizens' Rights Claims in Asylum Appeal Hearings: Practices and Sentiments of Procedural Justice Among German Administrative Judges', *Citizenship Studies* 26 (7): 927–43.

Vetters, L., J. Eggers and L. Hahn (2017), *Migration and the Transformation of German Administrative Law: An Interdisciplinary Research Agenda*. MPI for

Social Anthropology Working Papers 188. Halle/Saale: Max Planck Institute for Social Anthropology.

Wahl, R. (2003), 'Verwaltungsvorschriften: Die ungesicherte dritte Kategorie des Rechts', in E. Schmidt-Aßmann et al. (eds), *Festgabe 50 Jahre Bundesverwaltungsgericht*. Cologne: Carl Heymanns, pp. 571–98.

Zenker, O. and M.V. Hoehne (eds) (2018), *The State and the Paradox of Customary Law in Africa*. London: Routledge.

♦

2

Paperwork Performances

Legitimating State Violence in the Swedish Deportation Regime

Annika Lindberg and Lisa Marie Borrelli

Governing Migration through Paperwork

Paperwork is a key feature of statecraft and plays a crucial role organizing and performing power in 'complex and unequal societies' (Heyman 1995, 261). It is essential to state actors' efforts to render populations legible and governable (Scott 1998), while it also serves to render the state readable and accountable to the population (Bierschenk, this volume; Horton 2020). It is also constitutive of difference, a key function of borderwork: the various state technologies put in place to record, categorize, verify and analyse the identity of individuals and which simultaneously delineate the citizenry and produce categories of 'wanted' and 'unwanted' others (Herzfeld 1992; see also Joppke 1998). For people attempting to cross borders, papers produce and legitimize the conditions of vulnerability, discrimination and exclusion *and* inclusion (however precarious or subordinate) in the nation-state (Coutin 2020). Those classified as 'unwanted' are, in turn, exposed to different forms of coercion and social marginalization via illegalization, criminalization, detention, formal abandonment and deportation. Such coercive state practices require legitimation work (Ellermann 2009); in the contemporary European migration regime, this is achieved in part through the strategic linking of migration to transborder crime, insecurity and terrorism (Salter 2006), and in part through the ways these coercive, discriminatory and essentially punitive measures (Bosworth, Parmar and Vázquez 2018) are enforced through mundane administrative practices.

In this chapter, we explore the role of administrative paperwork in enforcing and legitimating coercive migration-control practices, and in constructing and rationalizing bureaucratic power as such (Das 2004). Given states' heavy reliance on paperwork in the coercive control of populations, studies of the concrete ways in which paperwork, as a symbolic and material practice, produces the social world remain relatively few – albeit with notable exceptions (Gupta 2012, 55; Horton and Heyman 2020; Hull 2012). In consequence, the chapter contributes to the limited but growing literature on the role of paperwork in the enforcement of border and migration policies (Cabot 2012; Coutin 2000; Horton and Heyman 2020; Rozakou 2019). Empirically, the chapter focuses on the documentary practices that inform the everyday work of Swedish border police and migration custody officials, whose work entails controlling, incarcerating and deporting people whose presence has been illegalized and classified as 'unwanted'. It thus adds to the scholarly literature exploring documentation practices as a form of statecraft (Corrigan and Sayer 1985; Gupta 2012; Navaro-Yashin 2007; Riles 2006; Stoler 2004) and to deportation studies (Drotbohm and Hasselberg 2015), respectively.

The empirical material is based on qualitative, ethnographically informed fieldwork with street-level bureaucrats (Lipsky 1980) working within border police units and migration-related detention centres in Sweden.[1] The research was undertaken as part of our respective doctoral studies, which traced the enforcement of deportation policies in Sweden (Lindberg 2022) and street-level officials' discretionary practices and moral dilemmas in enforcing control over illegalized migration (Borrelli et al. 2023; Borrelli 2018). Throughout our research, we found paperwork – forged and authenticated – to be central to the operation of state power to differentiate and control people whose presence had been illegalized. It was also used to resist and subvert state power to exclude, detain and deport (Eule et al. 2019; Horton 2020) – for instance, by destroying papers, borrowing those of others or forging identity documents, illegalized people made themselves illegible to the state (see also Horton 2020). Importantly, however, these practices mimic and appropriate 'official' practices of paperwork production, including forgery done by state actors and bureaucratic misrepresentations by state institutions. Our entry into the field was one of student-observers – although we later, upon completion of our fieldwork, came to engage in various platforms and initiatives by grassroots movements and organizations for migrant rights, wherein we shared and discussed our empirical insights. We learned from these engagements that instead of seeking to identify fraudulent or faulting practices by state actors, it was more fruitful to critically study the 'truths' that state-produced documentation helps to produce and their often drastic and violent implications. Bearing this in mind, we collectively analysed our empirical material, and identified four distinct ways in which paperwork is used by street-level officials to produce a sense of order, to forge facts and to legitimate state actions. The first subsection covering the Swedish deportation regime, below, illustrates the productive role of paperwork in shaping the unequal and often asymmetrical relations between the migration-control apparatus and migrants seeking permission to enter or remain. While the uses of documentation generally have a disempowering effect on people classified as unwanted migrants, and are crucial for officials to produce and exchange information about them, in our second subsection we show how paperwork can be tedious and 'unreadable' also for state officials. Yet, uncertain information is nevertheless used as a basis of bureaucratic decision-making. In a third subsection, we show how paperwork is used to obscure the violence inherent to detention and deportation procedures. Our final example demonstrates how documentation justifies discriminatory state practices. Such discrimination acquired a structural dimension through two documentary practices. On one hand, structurally abandoned urban areas designated as 'vulnerable' by the police, with a higher share of minority-racialized residents, lead them to return and repeat controls. On the other hand, border police officials rely on so-called hints that come in through calls from the population, reporting allegedly suspicious behaviour. These hints are noted down, thus formalized, and then evaluated according to their relevance – finally enshrining discrimination. These four examples and related arguments are summarized in a conclusion, where we discuss the importance of paperwork in producing legitimacy for the Swedish deportation regime and for the enactment and normalization of state violence more broadly.

The Centrality of Paperwork to Statecraft

We conceive paperwork quite literally as the work done with and upon material artefacts or documents, which 'are among the primary paraphernalia of modern states [and] are its material culture' (Navaro-Yashin 2007: 84). Practices of writing, producing statistics and reports, are all 'a constitutive function of the state' (Gupta 2012: 144). Paperwork plays a crucial role in state-making, because 'state-like structures make themselves evident to the persons who inhabit their domains in the form of materialities' (Navaro-Yashin 2007: 94). Indeed, documents and formularies are among the most common forms in which the state materializes in the everyday life of (non)citizens (Horton and Heyman 2020). Documents, such as identify cards or passports, are 'concrete distillations of the law in time and space' (Horton 2020: 5), while the law itself is changing and 'living'. Hence, paper trails simultaneously produce and justify the (unequal) distribution of rights and resources (e.g. as some documents are associated with certain resources, see Heyman 2009), and enable bureaucracies to 'establish . . . a seemingly neutral, objective vantage point that stands "above" or "outside" the social order, watching, preserving, safeguarding' (Nugent 2010: 683). In consequence, while often associated with lengthy and frustrating administrative procedures (Mathur 2016), tediousness, obscurity (Kafka and Bell 2009) and even stupidity (Graeber 2012), paperwork is a crucial, constitutive element of bureaucratic authority and of its 'social engineering' of populations (Bierschenk 2014).

In this context, it is important to emphasize the colonial script upon which state efforts to order, classify and control populations build. For instance, practices of fingerprinting were historically used by Western imperial states to identify, order and control 'unknown' imperial subjects, thus rendering them available for exploitation and enslavement (Cole 2009). These techniques were then transferred to the metropoles and used to identify and govern subordinate groups, including minoritized groups, vagabonds and the poor (see also Heyman 2009 on the connection between the looks of a person and the type of document they have, leading to various degrees of control). Contemporary efforts by Western states to govern the unwanted mobility of certain people similarly build on these colonially rooted practices – and, similarly to their historical precedents, their function is to render visible and legible to the state primarily poor, racialized groups in order to control, exclude and expel them from territories and resources (Anderson 2011). Documentation practices thus support state efforts to 'give unitary and unifying expressions to what are in reality multifaceted and differential historical experience of groups within society' (Corrigan and Sayer 1985: 4). Through processes of classification and simplification, they render individuals into legal subjects and reduce their position to singular identities as for example 'unwanted' or 'illegalized'. In this way, social inequalities become codified into law and bureaucratic documentation. As Philip Corrigan and Derek Sayer note, paperwork and other 'state forms are always animated and legitimated by a particular moral ethos' which supports and normalizes existing social inequalities that are structured 'along lines of class, gender, ethnicity, age, religion, occupation, locality' (Corrigan and Sayer 1985: 4). Paperwork, we contend, should therefore be understood as a complementary instrument to direct coercive practices for producing state power and maintaining an unequal social order (Gupta 2012; Sharma 2020). Documents thus 'uphold control' (Pigg, Erikson and Inglis 2018:

169): as such, '"paper shuffling" is the source of an essential power' (Latour 1988: 55; see also Vohnsen 2017).

In the past few decades, there has been a steadily growing interest among anthropologists and sociologists in bureaucracy as a form of organized power (Heyman 1995) and a site where societal inequalities are managed (and reproduced and contested). Researchers have demonstrated the central role of paperwork in enforcing and justifying these powers (Gupta 2012; Hull 2012). While far from all the work of bureaucrats follows formalized procedures (Heyman 2009), and while paperwork can be perceived as both constraining and enabling for bureaucrats, it is fundamental to the core function of bureaucracies: to render populations legible and to enforce order. Through bureaucratic simplification (Lipsky 1980) and the reduction of social identities and relations to forms and classification schemes, societal structures and their inequalities are managed and often sustained (Gupta 2012; Handelman and Leyton 1978). In the moment when documents are handed further, their circulation creates an official discourse which reinforces the 'state effect' (Dhupelia-Mesthrie 2014; Mathur 2016). Documentation practices further serve to depoliticize and obscure the violent nature of state interventions into the lives of those classified as unwanted, deviant or illegal (Canning 2017). While paperwork is daunting and at times despised among bureaucrats (Latour 1988), it is part of what enables street-level bureaucrats to distance themselves from the often violent consequences of their work – especially in the case of detainment and deportation, where the administrative framing of the bureaucratic decisions that underpin these measures stands in contrast to their often life-altering effects. Indeed, as argued by Michael Herzfeld in his study of national bureaucracy in Greece, the standardization and codification of state–(non)citizen encounters enables street-level officials to reject a 'common humanity' with their so-called clients and thereby renounce the ethical consequences of their own decisions and actions. This way, paperwork is key not only to the production of difference but also of social indifference (Herzfeld 1992). This arguably has particularly severe implications when coercive state power is mobilized against noncitizens and in particular illegalized persons, who generally hold weak rights claims on the state (Ellermann 2009; Vetters, this volume). Moreover, and as we will demonstrate in this chapter, paperwork both shapes and is the result of officials' perception of their own discretionary power (Pratt 2010) – that is, the possible range of actions or inactions available to them – even though the papers themselves are at times more important to the organization than to the officials putting them to work (see Heyman 2009). As such, paperwork becomes a tool for reifying the power and the 'truth' of the state, for its multiple possible interpretations and for its contestation (Eule et al. 2019).

Documenting the Swedish Deportation Regime

The research underpinning this chapter was conducted at a time when the detention and deportation of illegalized and 'unwanted' noncitizens re-emerged as a political priority in Sweden and elsewhere in Europe (Rosenberger and Koppes 2018). The Swedish government's promise to increase the rate and speed of deportations in 2016 was followed by increased investments in the border police and the expansion of migration-related detention (Lindberg 2022). While this did not constitute a radical change from prior policy, the bureaucratic agencies enforcing the detainment and deportation of illegalized persons experienced an intensified politicization of their work (Lindberg and Borrelli 2019). Moreover, and like elsewhere in Europe, policy changes in Sweden also led to a proliferation of liminal legal statuses (see Horton 2020). As temporary legal status became the new norm, the looming threat of future deportation also came to encompass people who obtained legal residency (Philipson Isaac 2022), who subsequently also faced increased uncertainty, surveillance, bureaucratic control and pressure to document and prove their deservingness of continued right of residence.

In this context, officials tasked with enforcing border and migration-related policy measures also faced increased pressure – or, in some officials' view, moral and political authorization – to use their discretion to step up arrests, detention and deportations. Our research participants encompassed street-level bureaucrats (Lipsky 1980), including border police officers tasked with detecting, detaining and ensuring the expulsion (whether 'voluntary' or forced) of persons who received a deportation order, and civil personnel working in migration-related detention centres (administered by the Swedish Migration Agency). Detainment and deportation entail the use of violence, both direct and indirect; they cause significant harm to those affected (Canning 2017), regularly spark controversy among the public and provoke resistance from people threatened by deportation (Ellermann 2009; Gibney 2008). Bureaucrats were thus to balance political demands for more efficient enforcement with an ambivalent public opinion while also seeking to ensure the 'cooperation' of the people threatened by deportation and a 'smooth' deportation process. Therefore, bureaucratic agents had incentives to downplay the violent nature of these procedures, to ensure their smooth enforcement (Walters 2016) and to make up for their inherent 'legitimacy deficit' (Bosworth and Slade 2014). Given the welfare state's heavy reliance on bureaucratic inscription to both legitimate and question coercive state powers (Lindberg 2020), the Swedish deportation regime emerges as a critical site for examining documentation practices that mediate, enforce and challenge the operation of such powers. In this chapter, for reasons of space, we study paperwork in a relatively narrow sense: namely, as practices of writing (as opposed to an expansive understanding of bureaucratic inscription that encompasses biometric and other technologies for rendering populations legible; see Horton 2020). In the following four examples, we trace the ambiguous yet profoundly productive role of paperwork in deportation processes.

The Productive Power of Paperwork

Official documents are not just material manifestations but are also productive of the power of state actors, as they are the means through which the latter produce knowledge of populations – which, in turn, becomes a 'reference for truth or authenticity' (Navaro-Yashin 2007: 84). That authentication of knowledge goes via paperwork is true both for bureaucratic procedures as such and for (non)citizens standing before the bureaucracy. In the context of migration bureaucracy, paperwork supports bureaucrats in their work to record, classify and simplify information with a view to rendering a given population legible and governable (Gupta 2012; Scott 1998) as (temporarily) legalized or illegalized subjects. In our research, we found that the time that bureaucratic officials engage with the *person* in question (often via a translator) is marginal compared with the time they spend filing information and producing documents for their case file.

Lisa would often sit with the Swedish border police units in their offices after they had 'closed' a case (meaning brought the apprehended, illegalized individual to detention), because their work was not done. Office hours extended late, because of the reports that had to be written and filed; paperwork was often referred to as a burden that officials wished to be spared from (Borrelli's field notes, 2017). As such, the apparently 'action-rich' patrolling was always accompanied by a caesura of paperwork, and the time it would take for officers to process documents not only frustrated the officials but was also one of the causes why detained or illegalized people would spend a prolonged time in limbo (Cabot 2012), waiting for documents to arrive, anxious about what they would bring. This waiting time could be used strategically by both bureaucrats and migrants (Eule et al. 2019), as asking for or filing additional documents could buy them time to figure out alternative courses of action; yet prolonged bureaucratic procedures often had a disempowering effect on migrants.

For the person applying for permission to enter or remain, engaging in paperwork is both a necessity and a risky endeavour (see Coutin 2020). During an application procedure, they are asked to provide excessive paperwork to render their identity and claims on the state 'credible' (Tuckett 2018). Yet, migrants can also engage in practices of subverting, mimicking and appropriating documents with a view to enhancing their chances of navigating the often obscure and hostile bureaucracies they face (see Nakueira, this volume). However, documents may also betray the applicant's original intentions: for instance, the identity papers and other documentation that they are required to present can, in the case of an unsuccessful application, later be used to enforce their deportation. A train ticket, necessary to verify payment and the right to travel, can be used by migration authorities to deflect responsibility for a case onto another country (Borrelli's field notes, 2017). Once filed, documents acquire a life of their own: for instance, a caseworker's note in the case file of a person seeking asylum regarding their general behaviour towards bureaucratic authorities (e.g. 'non-cooperative', 'withdrawn' or 'aggressive') can be used as grounds for detention by other actors, such as the border police (Borrelli's field notes, 2017–18). At the same time, migration officials may voice doubts about certain paperwork and its validity. This might be based on internally shared information (again, another set of paperwork) that informs them about recently received passports or other documents which were identified as fraudulent. Consequently, certain nation-state documents will be seen as more or less valid than others (Borrelli's field notes, 2017).

Thus, not only 'formal' signifiers but also the affective traits and personal characteristics of individuals become inscribed into the bureaucratic red tape and might justify coercive bureaucratic action. Through the process of documentation, these ascribed and inscribed characteristics become fixed in time (often to the applicant's disadvantage) because 'papers, especially written and official documentation, bear the symbolism of permanence' (Navaro-Yashin 2007: 84). Moreover, and importantly, bureaucratic officials retain the authority to decide what information is relevant for the case, which as such constitutes a form of symbolic violence (Graeber 2012), and which might be used to enforce decisions that do further violence to the individual (e.g. detention or deportation). While documentation is often perceived as an essential component of 'fair', 'just' and 'rational' bureaucratic decision-making, it simultaneously reflects and reproduces power inequalities between noncitizens seeking the right to enter or remain, and the bureaucratic authorities processing their requests. Not only is this true because rules, procedures and requirements on documentation keep changing; the unpredictability and illegibility of decision-making processes are also used as a way of sustaining power inequalities. For instance, unpredictability is at times used consciously, when authorities seek to prevent applicants from gaining full insight into the grounds of decision-making, which would enable them to adapt their stories and documentation accordingly. This results from the (un)intended yet systematically differential application of law onto different cases (Eule et al. 2019).

The bureaucratic standards to which documents are required to conform also vary significantly depending on the identity of the traveller. For example, Swedish border police officers explained to Lisa that being a young Albanian man will trigger suspicion at the airport, since Albanian nationals are 'known' to want to travel further to the United Kingdom to find work. When entering the country, they need to present not only a hotel booking, sufficient funding, a return ticket and knowledge about the places they want to visit; they will also need the signature of a financial guarantor. Such bureaucratic demands are directed towards 'suspicious' travellers, who are compelled to provide excessive documentation to 'prove' the authenticity of their identity and intentions. These demands create substantial paperwork hurdles and can be instrumentalized by state actors as a deterrence strategy (see Grinberg 2018). This example also demonstrates how paperwork hurdles target particular groups whose mobility is considered suspicious by default (Borrelli, Lindberg, and Wyss 2021). Here, nationality, class and race, as well as gender, intersect and create the 'need' for officers to control, whereas in other cases there is less action taken and less documentation required (see also Heyman 2009).

State authorities also hold discretionary power to decide which documents can be produced and mobilized under different circumstances. This can be used strategically to ensure the docility of those facing deportation. For instance, during a formal meeting between a border police case officer, a detained person and his lawyer, the border police revealed that documents had been produced which allowed for a detained man's deportation. The man was surprised and shocked that this could be done without his knowledge or signature (Borrelli's field notes, 2017), while the border police now hoped that he would accept the deportation order. This 'surprise' mobilization of documentation pushed the deportable man to react – to accept the deportation order or to enter into the bureaucratic game by producing further paperwork that attested his inability to travel (e.g. through medical certificates), or by appealing the deportation on new grounds. The deportation process here becomes a race for the right paperwork.

Paperwork practices thus both create assertiveness of the bureaucratic apparatus and uncertainty for those standing before it. Indeed, documentation practices are profoundly productive, as Talal Asad has pointed out, 'because only documents can confirm the required facts needed [to access e.g. legal residency or citizenship]' (2004: 284). More paperwork is required to eliminate the suspicion that is inherent to documentation procedures; more institutional structures, regulations and bureaucratic agents are required to enforce the procedures; and so on. At the same time, bureaucratically created paperwork accrues higher trustworthiness than documents produced or handed over by those facing detention or deportation.

Paperwork is thus profoundly productive of a state power that operates through an 'unstable interplay of truth and illusion' (Taussig 1984: 492). Contrary to the promises of guaranteeing equality before the law and predictability in legal procedures, excessive documentation practices often aggravate the uncertainty for people making rights claims on the state, and for noncitizens in particular (Cabot 2012; Eule et al. 2019). However, as we will explore in the next section, paperwork can also appear as obscure to the bureaucrats producing it.

The Illegibility of Documentation Practices

As Josiah Heyman contends, bureaucracies order and routinize what he calls 'thoughtwork'; as a result, bureaucrats are faced with the conundrum of being compelled to 'think for themselves because of the nature of their tasks, yet they must be controlled as thinkers in order to ensure the regular production of control duties' (Heyman 1995: 263). At times, however, the formalized order materialized in documents and protocols is also illegible to the bureaucrats putting it to work. To illustrate this, the next example follows border police officers at a police station in a large city in Sweden.

Lisa attends one of the regular meetings of the Swedish border police unit that she has been following during her fieldwork. It takes place at the 'conference hub', where the border police reconvene to exchange information on recent events – including (statistical) information on how many people have been apprehended by the mobile unit roaming the streets or at the airport, how many people were detained and who are to be deported. Participants also discuss more general issues, such as collaboration with other state agencies and internal communication. Usually, the head or deputy head of the police station guides these meetings – in which, ideally, all the heads of the subunits participate (there are mobile units, a unit for investigation, one for case processing and one for manhunts, as well as someone in charge of strategic planning and communication). At this meeting, the officers bring up a collaboration meeting that took place in the autumn, in which all agencies participated. They then return to a discussion on workplace inspections and how these should be conducted. The inspections can be planned or randomly conducted by the mobile units, who search workplaces where people are suspected to work unauthorized; other units will then take over the rest of the investigation. Yet, there is little communication between the units and, besides a general procedure on how to record cases, no clear written guidelines exist.

Sven,[2] responsible for strategic planning and analysis, argues, 'Each group works on their own island. They are all a little bit sovereign, but that does not work'. Regarding the manhunt and mobile units, he adds, 'They have the same orders and assignments and should inform each other'. Two other officers agree: 'It is weird, actually, because they have the same assignment'. Martha (the head of investigation) mentions: 'They [mobile units] wonder what we write down, but we just take in what they hand over to us. The content is decided by [the mobile unit]. The people who do the investigative interviews are in the mobile unit [right after they apprehend an undocumented or deportable person]'. Martha explains that mobile units have at times been irritated with the work of the investigation unit and the outcome of its casework, while the latter was irritated with the mobile units since they did not give those working in the investigation unit enough documentation or the documentation was of bad quality, hindering them in doing their job in a satisfactory manner. Martha suggests deepening the competences of the mobile units and developing their skills regarding criminal investigations (*brottsutredning*). Her idea is that competence training will give mobile units a better understanding of what will hold (apply and be valid) in court and what will not, in order to write better reports. 'We do not see more than them; they often send us bad quality pictures, incomplete descriptions of situations or interrogations, and so on'.

Martha criticizes the information they receive from mobile police units besides the recorded data on the person found in their databases, including notes from the interview with the person apprehended and the short reports about what happened. She finds this material bundle of paperwork insufficient for her unit to be able to keep working with the cases.

The group generally agrees that the mobile units need to do their job more thoroughly and understand that their colleagues, the investigators who will follow up on the cases further, depend on their information. This means more paperwork, something which no one in the mobile unit is particularly fond of. Lisa's observation of this issue is later confirmed – especially since the technology is slow and computer programs not up to date. After some more discussion, Sven concludes: 'There is not a single sheet of paper telling us how we should behave. We work a lot on ad hoc basis, fast, quick, *zack-zack*. We do not go back and ask what we have learned from our previous jobs and experiences, but just start with a new task' (Borrelli's field notes, 2017).

In the meeting, we hear how bureaucrats demand better organization of the paperwork, especially in situations where their work depends on each other. The field note illustrates how the state, which dictates the production of documents (Hull 2012), is itself in need of documents to produce a sense of order in its operations. In the case described, the concern of the police was not with the documentation of illegalized persons (or lack thereof) but rather the lack of coherent documentation and guidance for their own work, which rendered the quality and standards of their own operation internally contested and the paperwork they produced unreadable to other police units. Despite an abundance of different forms to fill out (or to be filled out by those facing detention or deportation), there was, as Sven acknowledged, little formal guidance on how they should do their job. The officers contended that the documents they currently produced were not of much help; rather, documentation had become an end in itself (see also Pigg, Erikson and Inglis 2018). Indeed, the abundant paperwork that *was* produced was perceived as unsatisfactory, if not unreadable; meanwhile, there was an absence of documentation where the officials needed it. Yet, regardless of its quality, the paperwork was used as a basis for bureaucratic action. Hence, the lack of formalized guidelines, internal frictions and the uneven quality of bureaucratic paperwork does not undermine the efficacy of the state's operation. Even in cases where the officers in the field note struggled to follow the paper trails and make sense of their colleagues' documentation practices, they acted on the inadequate or incomplete information and carried out their decisions to detain and deport apprehended migrants. The deportation regime thus remains 'functional', regardless of its perceived internal dysfunctions.

The field note further demonstrates how paperwork serves to create an 'illusion of explanatory depth' (Rozenblit and Keil 2002; see also Pigg, Erikson and Inglis 2018) and an 'image of proof, stability and durability' (Navaro-Yashin 2007: 84), which allows bureaucratic agents to retain a sense of bureaucratic order even in situations where documentation practices make little sense to them. Just as argued in the previous section, the documents create their own 'truths', which become legitimated through their circulation among different bureaucratic agents and units and are eventually acted upon (see Navaro-Yashin 2007; Nugent 2010; Trouillot 2001). The literal paperwork – the labour put into the production of documents – thus allows officials to maintain a performance of rational power even in situations where there is, as the police officer Sven concluded, no formalized basis for this power (Hull 2012). This internal perspective on official uses of paperwork demonstrates its powerful function in bureaucratic work. The internal illegibility of paperwork experienced did not prevent officers from using it as a basis for decisions. Intelligible or not, the power of paperwork seems to lie in its mere existence, which is considered enough to inform, shape and legitimize actions.

Paperwork as Legitimation Work

In some cases, more paperwork is required to lend legitimacy to a certain state action. Such is the case for migration-related detention, which entails the forced deprivation of liberty of people for reasons related to their migrant status. Prior research has shown that while it is 'administrative' in nature, detention is often experienced as punitive by detained persons (Bosworth and Slade 2014). The Swedish detention regime, which is designed to ensure the 'humane and dignified return' (DeBono, Ronnqvist and Magnusson 2015) of deportable persons, is consciously designed to downplay the violent and punitive elements of confinement (Canning 2019; Lindberg 2022). Paperwork here served a crucial function in mediating and covering up for the violent nature of confinement.

In the detention centre where Annika conducted fieldwork in 2017, staff liked to see themselves not as anything akin to guards or prison officers but rather as social workers performing a caretaking job (see also Canning 2019). The role of staff was routinized and monotonous: detention officials had little or nothing to do with the detained persons' immigration cases and spent most of their work time tending to administrative or logistical tasks, which included registering new arrivals and deregistering those who were deported or released, conducting inspection rounds, lending personal-care items (such as scissors and shaving razors) to detained persons, serving meals and communicating administrative decisions. Importantly, all these actions required them to fill out sheets documenting that they had performed the task. Filling out forms and reports is 'the prototype of bureaucratic writing', as Akhil Gupta (2012: 144) notes. It makes bureaucratic work traceable, evidencing that 'something' has been done irrespective of what exactly has been done and of the effects of the action taken.

Of particular importance was providing records of every coercive action taken against a detained person, including confiscation of personal belongings, body visitation, visitation of rooms and belongings, and decisions on solitary confinement. For every such decision, two copies of each document were printed and the person concerned was asked to sign that they had understood why this action had been taken against them. According to staff, this was done to ensure correct procedures and to justify practices that often appeared highly invasive to those detained. Greta, a senior official, explained to Annika that practically all coercive actions could be justified with reference to a 'threat to order and security': 'It's a standard formulation we use here, anything can be excused with this reason' (Lindberg's field notes, 2017). Hannah, another detention official, said the paperwork was important in order to ensure that detained persons knew their legal rights were respected, even if they often experienced the detainment as such as unjust.

Frequently, detained individuals would refuse to sign the forms, but this did not change the outcome as the decision was still enforced. Among those detained, this only reinforced the impression that paperwork was a symbolic act that protected the system but did little to guarantee their rights (Lindberg's field notes, 2018). Mary Bosworth (2016) has made a similar observation regarding administrative power in the UK detention system, arguing that paperwork ultimately serves to protect staff rather than the people detained. Her interlocutors – much like the Swedish detention officials – would deplore the significant amount of paperwork they had to fill out, and told her, 'It's all just an exercise in cover-your-arse', or, 'We need to be able to show we did all the right procedures . . . so if there is a problem, they can see it wasn't our fault'. Hence, paperwork lends an air of legitimacy to tasks that are contested, discomforting and sometimes perceived as questionable even among the bureaucrats themselves.

Aside from its legitimating function, paperwork was also used to obscure the violence inherent in detention and to contain its harmful effects on the persons detained (Canning 2017). We turn to another example from our empirical material on suicide screenings. These were mandatory for detention staff to fill out for each detained person upon arrival. In order to assess whether the person in question was suicidal, staff had to follow a detailed protocol which included questions such as 'Have you ever attempted suicide? Have you ever been treated for depression?' and, 'Have you ever felt like life is not worth living?' Staff found it awkward and highly intrusive to ask these questions. The protocol, as Annika was told, had been developed by a detention official who had experienced a detained man dying by suicide during her work shift. It was, on the one hand, intended to prevent similar acts of self-harm, and any suspicious answer to the stated questions could result in the detained person in question being taken into solitary confinement under observation or moved to a psychiatric clinic. On the other hand, the protocol was intended to prevent detention officials – and the detention institution as such – from becoming liable in case a detained person died by suicide. In other words, it enabled officials to (literally) write themselves free of responsibility for some of the direct, violent consequences of detention (see Lindberg 2022). Nicolas Fischer (2015) has similarly pointed out how detention is itself often the cause of the anxiety and depression that provoke self-mutilation among detained persons in the first place, noting that the rigorous suicide programmes put in place to prevent detained persons from committing acts of self-harm enable the detention institution to present itself as a humanitarian rather than violent realm. What is more, the presumed protective piece of paperwork justifies expansive coercive powers, such as placing a person in solitary confinement based on speculations about their mental conditions.

Paperwork performances thus serve important legitimation functions and constitute a way for bureaucratic officials to deflect responsibility for violent state interventions and their harmful effects. In this case, the people detained were rarely aware of the practical or legal implications of putting their signatures on a visitation order (here, the implications were practically none) or their accounts of their own mental condition (in these cases, the consequences were considerable); meanwhile, the forms themselves gave bureaucrats expanded powers. The paper trails could, however, also be used to hold the institution accountable: some detention officials explicitly said they wished for more detained persons to legally contest their decisions so that the bureaucrats would 'know whether they were doing things right' (Lindberg's field notes, 2017). However, the belief in paperwork showing the way to 'right and wrongs' in officials' work presupposes that the information and the formalized procedures that generate them are free from bias, discrimination and other 'wrongs'. This is, as we demonstrate in the next section, often not the case.

Paperwork Squared: The Role of Documentation in Legitimizing and Maintaining Structural Discrimination

When Lisa joins the police on a day shift in 2017, she reads through a document listing the different 'hints' the police have received. 'Hints' are defined as information on suspicious events or persons shared with the border police by the public (e.g. private individuals or businesses such as hotels) or by other state agencies such as the tax office. All received hints are translated into forms. Based on these forms, officers plan to conduct raids or inspections in sites where illegalized persons are suspected to reside or work. Hints are generally sorted into categories, with 'B' being the 'mostly reliable' (reliability depends on the source of information and how detailed the description is, as well as whether the person giving the hint has shared their contact details). The description is followed by sections which mention the type of crime; for instance, involvement in narcotics, burglary or being an illegalized migrant who resides and works somewhere. It is followed by a table with three sections: notes, circumstances (*omständigheter*) and evaluation (1–4). In the form Lisa looks at, nothing is written in the first section, while the second one shows the source of the information (here external) – saying 'Afghan man [name redacted] smokes cannabis with friends'. The evaluation mentions that the source is not reliable, but that the relevance is evaluated as quite high. An attached appendix contains documents with further information on the man, including his dossier/case number and abbreviations (*BR*, *MR*, *snatteri*)[3] about his criminal record.

The mobile unit within the Swedish border police with which Lisa conducted research in 2017 had made it its major task to conduct workplace controls. It based its selection of control sites either on its own 'intuition' (which essentially meant it would visit low-paid workplaces such as hair salons, car workshops, small grocery stores and fast-food restaurants, especially those frequented and run by people with a 'non-Swedish background') or on the kind of hints outlined earlier. Lisa was told that hints from hotel staff usually pertained to suspected sex work, which the mobile unit planned to collect in a database in order to make better use of them; the same went for restaurant owners and tips from private individuals, who were sorted into more or less reliable sources. This way, the police came to mentally map the city and its day- and nightlife – and any 'suspected' sites, persons or activities – and noted where people had been apprehended.

Through hints and calls from third parties – thus, people who are outsiders with respect to the bureaucratic system – structural discrimination is supported and upheld as broader stereotypes and discriminatory attitudes become translated into calls to the border police, which sorts them according to relevance. As such, anyone can denounce anyone, yet given that hints were given to the border police, they involved assumed 'foreign nationals', often profiled by their assumed nationality and potentially becoming 'suspicious' due to their skin tone. Hints are translated into documents, which now become clues on which (non)action is taken (see also Heyman 2009). This translation process into documents then allows for discrimination and legitimizes controls which might have been purely based on racial stereotypes in the first place.

> During a shift with the mobile unit, the team plans to follow up on some hints it had received about two to three 'dark-skinned women' (the term was written by the police as a direct translation of the 'hint' they had received from a private individual) who had raised 'suspicion' because of where they were located in the city. The police suspect they run a brothel in an industrial area, because for them it seems unlikely that someone would live there. It remains unclear to what extent their skin colour plays a role in their decision to follow up on this hint, until one officer says, 'They are surely Nigerians'. According to the officers, sex work is often done by women from the former Soviet Union and Nigeria (as much as Nigerian men were 'known' for selling drugs). It is discussed when officers should check this address as it will take time, and it is decided they might check after lunch. Some other hints are received but discarded because of their vagueness (being about a person selling coffee on the streets) and the address being far out of town. (Borrelli's field notes, 2017)

As such, suspicion is an essential part of police work (O'Brien-Olinger 2016) – and of migration bureaucracies (Borrelli, Lindberg and Wyss 2021) – yet supported and legitimized through paperwork and documentation. The field note illustrates the process whereby suspicion amongst the public informs the police, and the police, in turn, translate it into documentation that is mobilized as 'evidence' for their own suspicions. Once translated into official forms and documentation, this 'evidence' becomes the grounds upon which police decide where and whom to control – and whom not to control (indeed, decisions on 'when and on whom not to act' form an equally important part of police and other forms of bureaucratic power; see Heyman 2000). The reports based on public 'hints' thus become technologies of power – both through their content and material form, and through the powers they extend to the police (Pigg, Erikson and Inglis 2018). Unsurprisingly, this means that popular attitudes and 'moral panics' (Cohen 2001) over illegalized migration inform the assumption of whose presence and behaviour in the city is problematized, if not criminalized, and who goes unnoticed. (For an account of the police's moral and emotional reactions to tasks that involve criminalizing people who are simultaneously potential victims of crime, see Borrelli 2020.) These suspicions, in turn, come to inform bureaucratic practice and co-produce spaces of criminalization; illegalization; and, ultimately, potential arrest and deportation.

The field note further shows how these suspicions are based on gendered and racial tropes. In this example, it was the skin colour, gender and 'suspicious' location of the persons in question that raised mistrust among members of the public, which was in turn confirmed by the police officers. Since the police officers were acting on pre-existing documentation, they were further able to denounce criticism for racial profiling; they were not the ones initiating the searches but were simply following up on existing 'evidence' (see Parmar 2018, 2019). The police whom Lisa followed recalled having been criticized by shopkeepers in certain areas of the city, who felt discriminated against as their shops were regularly targeted by police controls due to their location and 'multicultural' clientele. During one patrol, one shopkeeper suggested the police officers should conduct workplace controls in larger supermarkets and other areas instead. Yet, the officers insisted they would not find 'those we are looking for' anywhere else besides the area where the shopkeeper worked (Borrelli's field notes, 2017).

The shopkeeper's criticism highlights the racial discrimination embedded in the police's gaze, and the officer's response suggests that their mapping of the city and its people into ordinary/deviant, legal/illegal also takes place irrespective of the 'hints' from the public. The interaction further shows how the police, through their reporting and controls, produce notions of 'deviant' and suspicious parts of the city as well as the dis-belonging of inhabitants and commercial actors in these neighbourhoods: as the shopkeeper pointed out, their racialized bodies are rendered suspect not only of criminal activity but also of being 'foreign', illegalized migrants. The field note thus also demonstrates how public suspicion against illegalized migration, which as such relies on racialized (and gendered, and class) stereotypes, becomes codified through documentation and distributed among state agencies. This distribution of information, in turn, allows for a collective sense-making throughout the administrative body (see Hull 2012) and a reproduction of racialized suspicion codified into 'objective' knowledge through paperwork (see also Pratt 2010).

Conclusion

Sarah Bronwen Horton speaks of 'bureaucratic inscription' as 'social and material dynamics though which migrants are inscribed into official bureaucratic systems at various scales of government' (Horton 2020: 3). We have taken up this interpretation of inscription and expanded on it by studying how documentation works upon and affects migrants' and bureaucrats' subjectivities alike – and how contradictions inherent to policies, but also forms of harm, are inscribed in such documentary practices. In our chapter, we have traced the role of paperwork in producing and legitimating bureaucratic power and enabling coercive state action within the field of migration control in Sweden. Drawing on our ethnographic research with various bureaucratic actors involved in the deportation process, we identified four distinct functions and uses of paperwork. First, and in line with previous research (see, e.g. Scott 1998), we detailed how documentation practices are fundamental to rendering people legible and classifiable as (il) legal (or liminally legal, see Horton 2020). At the same time, bureaucratic paperwork is supposed to render the practices and decisions of the state legible and accountable to the public; yet we found that documents are unreliable artefacts, often taking on a life of their own in the bureaucratic process as bureaucrats hold the power to decide how they are interpreted and when and how they are acted upon. Hence, we showed how documentation practices render state power obscure and, indeed, 'illegible' for migrants (Das 2004; see also Eule et al. 2019).

In our second example, we demonstrated how documentation practices may also appear as unreadable for bureaucratic officials – yet the documents produced, no matter their quality, nevertheless constitute the basis for decisions that have life-altering consequences for migrants. At the same time, paperwork does important legitimation work for bureaucrats, allowing them to show that they have done *something*, and in some cases enables them to (literally) write off personal responsibility for bureaucratic actions that are intrusive or violent.

Using examples from Swedish migration-related detention, the third example showed how documentation practices protected staff from being ascribed responsibility for the harms that incarceration inflicts on detained persons.

Finally, we used examples from border police work to show how documentation practices render suspicion – on the part of the police, but also emanating from the public – into 'evidence' against supposed criminalized and illegalized people. The 'evidence' that police officers would act upon drew on and reproduced racialized and gendered borders of the city and contributed to the symbolic, if not juridical, criminalization and illegalization of people's presence in certain places. This example also underscored how paperwork is not an isolated task of bureaucracy but co-produced by non-state actors, who partake in the 'internal bordering' (and ordering) of society (see Yuval-Davis, Wemyss, and Cassidy 2018). These bordering practices not only render certain people, behaviours and areas as suspicious, deviant and illegal but simultaneously produce a framework for the trustworthy and normative citizen, who is distinguished by the privilege of '[b]eing the beneficiary of non-action' (Heyman 2009) and non-recording by state authorities. Hence, bureaucracy does not act upon but co-produces and enforces an unequal social order along the lines of race, class, nationality; (il)legality is but one of several classification systems whereby this order is enforced.

To conclude, our examples all highlight the crucial yet often overlooked role of paperwork in the enforcement and legitimation of coercive state powers such as the policing; detainment; and, ultimately, deportation of illegalized persons. For anthropologists and other scholars studying bureaucracy, notably those concerned with coercive state functions, it is of vital importance to understand documentation practices as an essential – albeit relatively obscured – part of what puts this state violence to work. Importantly, while we have given examples of how paperwork can take on a life of its own, this does not cancel out individual bureaucrats' agency or responsibility for their practices. On the contrary, paper trails can expand the range of actions and inactions made available to bureaucrats.

We thus concur with the calls by researchers on bureaucracy to not accept the 'truths' produced through bureaucratic paperwork (Graeber 2012). Despite – or also because of – its corrective systems, bureaucratic classification ultimately remains reductive if not 'incompatible with humane social life' (Handelman and Leyton 1978, 136). Therefore, rather than forging a closed system, bureaucratic practice is made up of a multitude of interpretive actions; therein lies its power, but also the possibility for contestation. Indeed, our findings underscore how documents, rather than signalling a form of 'permanence' (Navaro-Yashin 2007), are continuously reinterpreted, reconfigured and acted upon. Our chapter has shown how this open-endedness of paperwork can facilitate unpredictable and arbitrary uses of power within states' deportation regimes.

Acknowledgements

This research was supported by the Swiss National Science Foundation (under project 153225) and the National Center of Competence in Research nccr – on the move (51NF40-182897).

Annika Lindberg is a researcher at the School of Social Work at HES-SO Valais-Wallis and at the Centre for European Research, University of Gothenburg. Her research concerns deportation regimes, state power and bureaucracy in Northern Europe. Email: Annika.lindberg@gu.se

Lisa Marie Borrelli works as an Associate Professor at the HES-SO Valais-Wallis and as a lecturer at the University of Basel. Her research explores border and deportation regimes, organizational sociology, social policies and state power across Europe. Email: lisa.borrelli@hevs.ch

Notes

1. Lisa Borrelli conducted fieldwork for four months in one of seven Swedish border police units, supported by fifteen semi-structured interviews and four field visits at a second border police unit with seven semi-structured interviews (2016–17). Annika Lindberg conducted ethnographic fieldwork with detention officials inside one of Sweden's six migration-related centres (one month, 2017) and additional field visits to three detention centres, including thirty semi-structured interviews (2017).
2. All names of interlocutors are pseudonyms.
3. Short for *brottsregister* (criminal record), *misstankeregister* (directory of suspected criminal activity) and shoplifting.

References

Anderson, B. (2011), 'Migration: Controlling the Unsettled Poor', OpenDemocracy, 1 August. Retrieved 12 February 2024 from https://www.opendemocracy.net/en/5050/migration-controlling-unsettled-poor.

Asad, T. (2004), 'Where Are the Margins of the State?' in V. Das and D. Poole (eds), *Anthropology in the Margins of the State*. Santa Fe, NM: School of American Research Press, pp. 279–88.

Bierschenk, T. (2014), 'From the Anthropology of Development to the Anthropology of Global Social Engineering', *Zeitschrift für Ethnologie* 139(1): 73–98.

Borrelli, L. M. (2018), 'Whisper Down, Up and Between the Lane – Exclusionary Policies and Their Limits of Control in Times of Irregular Migration', *Public Administration* 96(4): 803–16, https://doi.org/10.1111/padm.12528.

——— (2020), 'Whom to Punish? – Street-Level Dilemmas within the Swedish Border Police', in Jake Philips, Jamie Waters, Chalen Westaby and Andrew Fowler (eds), *Emotional Labour in Criminal Justice and Criminology.* Oxfordshire: Routledge, pp. 196–207.

Borrelli, L.M., D. Hedlund, L. Johannesson and A. Lindberg (2023), 'Border Bureaucracies: A Literature Review of Discretion in Migration Control'. Working Paper, nccr – on the move, 32. Retrieved 12 February 2024 from https://nccr-onthemove.ch/wp_live14/wp-content/uploads/2023/01/WP32_Borelli-et-al.pdf.

Borrelli, L.M., A. Lindberg and A. Wyss. (2021), 'States of Suspicion: How Institutionalised Disbelief Shapes Migration Control Regimes', *Geopolitics* 27(4): 1025–41, https://doi.org/10.1080/14650045.2021.2005862.

Bosworth, M. (2016), 'Paperwork and Administrative Power in Detention', Oxford Law Faculty Blog, 13 June. Retrieved 12 February 2024 from https://www.law.ox.ac.uk/research-subject-groups/centre-criminology/centreborder-criminologies/blog/2016/06/paperwork-and.

Bosworth, M. and G. Slade (2014), 'In Search of Recognition: Gender and Staff–Detainee Relations in a British Immigration Removal Centre', *Punishment & Society* 16(2): 169–86, https://doi.org/10.1177/1462474513517017.

Bosworth, M., A. Parmar and Y. Vázquez (eds) (2018), *Race, Criminal Justice, and Migration Control: Enforcing the Boundaries of Belonging.* Oxford: Oxford University Press.

Cabot, H. (2012), 'The Governance of Things: Documenting Limbo in the Greek Asylum Procedure', *PoLAR: Political and Legal Anthropology Review* 35(1): 11–29, https://doi.org/10.1111/j.1555-2934.2012.01177.x.

Canning, V. (2017), *Gendered Harm and Structural Violence in the British Asylum System.* London: Taylor & Francis.

——— (2019), 'Keeping up with the *Kladdkaka*: Kindness and Coercion in Swedish Immigration Detention Centres', *European Journal of Criminology* 17(6), https://doi.org/10.1177/1477370818820627.

Cohen, S. (2001), *States of Denial: Knowing about Atrocities and Suffering.* Oxford: Wiley.

Cole, M. (2009), 'A Plethora of "Suitable Enemies": British Racism at the Dawn of the Twenty-First Century', *Ethnic and Racial Studies* 32(9): 1671–85, https://doi.org/10.1080/01419870903205556.

Corrigan, P. and D. Sayer (1985), *The Great Arch: English State Formation as Cultural Revolution.* Oxford: Blackwell.

Coutin, S.B. (2000), *Legalizing Moves.* Ann Arbor: University of Michigan Press.

——— (2020), 'Opportunities and Double Binds: Legal Craft in an Era of Uncertainty', in Sarah Bronwen Horton and Josiah McConnell Heyman (eds) *Paper Trails: Migrants, Documents, and Legal Insecurity.* Global Insecurities. Durham, NC: Duke University Press, pp. 130–52.

Das, V. (2004), 'The Signature of the State: The Paradox of Illegibility', in V. Das and D. Poole (eds), *Anthropology in the Margins of the State*. Santa Fe, NM: School of American Research Press, pp. 225–52.

Das, V. and D. Poole (eds), *Anthropology in the Margins of the State*. Santa Fe, NM: School of American Research Press.

DeBono, D., S. Ronnqvist and K. Magnusson (2015), *Humane and Dignified? Migrants' Experiences of Living in a 'State of Deportability' in Sweden*. Malmö: Malmö University.

Dhupelia-Mesthrie, U. (2014), 'Paper Regimes', *Kronos* 40: 10–22.

Drotbohm, H. and I. Hasselberg (2015), 'Deportation, Anxiety, Justice: New Ethnographic Perspectives', *Journal of Ethnic and Migration Studies* 41(4): 551–62, https://doi.org/10.1080/1369183X.2014.957171.

Ellermann, A. (2009), *States Against Migrants: Deportation in Germany and the United States*. Cambridge: Cambridge University Press.

Eule, T.G., L.M. Borrelli, A. Lindberg and A. Wyss (2019), *Migrants Before the Law: Contested Migration Control in Europe*. London: Palgrave Macmillan.

Fischer, N. (2015), 'The Management of Anxiety: An Ethnographical Outlook on Self-Mutilations in a French Immigration Detention Centre', *Journal of Ethnic and Migration Studies* 41(4): 599–616, https://doi.org/10.1080/1369183X.2014.960820.

Gibney, M.J. (2008), 'Asylum and the Expansion of Deportation in the United Kingdom', *Government and Opposition* 43(2): 146–67, https://doi.org/10.1111/j.1477-7053.2007.00249.x.

Graeber, D. (2012), 'Dead Zones of the Imagination: On Violence, Bureaucracy, and Interpretive Labor – the Malinowski Memorial Lecture, 2006', *HAU: Journal of Ethnographic Theory* 2(2): 105–28, https://doi.org/10.14318/hau2.2.007.

Grinberg, O. (2018), 'Facsimileing the State: The Bureaucracy of Document Transmission in Israeli Human Rights NGOs', *Anthropologica* 60(1): 259–73, https://doi.org/10.3138/anth.60.1.t24.

Gupta, A. (2012), *Red Tape: Bureaucracy, Structural Violence, and Poverty in India*. Durham, NC: Duke University Press.

Handelman, D. and E. Leyton (1978), *Bureaucracy and World View: Studies in the Logic of Official Interpretation*. Social and Economic Studies, no. 22. St. John's, NL: Institute of Social and Economic Research, Memorial University of Newfoundland.

Herzfeld, M. (1992), *The Social Production of Indifference*. Chicago: University of Chicago Press.

Heyman, J. McC. (1995), 'Putting Power in the Anthropology of Bureaucracy: The Immigration and Naturalization Service at the Mexico–United States Border', *Current Anthropology* 36(2): 261–87.

——— (2000), 'Respect for Outsiders? Respect for the Law? The Moral Evaluation of High-Scale Issues by US Immigration Officers', *Journal of the Royal Anthropological Institute* 6(4): 635–52.

——— (2009), 'Trust, Privilege, and Discretion in the Governance of the US Borderlands with Mexico', *Canadian Journal of Law and Society / Revue Canadienne Droit Et Société* 24(3): 367–90.

Horton, S.B. (2020), 'Introduction. Paper Trails: Migrants, Bureaucratic Inscription, and Legal Recognition', in Sarah Bronwen Horton and Josiah McConnell Heyman (eds), *Paper Trails: Migrants, Documents, and Legal Insecurity*. Global Insecurities. Durham, NC: Duke University Press, pp. 1–26.

Horton, S.B. and J. McC. Heyman (eds) (2020), *Paper Trails: Migrants, Documents, and Legal Insecurity*. Global Insecurities. Durham, NC: Duke University Press.

Hull, M.S. (2012), *Government of Paper: The Materiality of Bureaucracy in Urban Pakistan*. Berkeley: University of California Press.

Joppke, C. (1998), 'Why Liberal States Accept Unwanted Immigration', *World Politics* 50(2): 266–93, https://doi.org/10.1017/S004388710000811X.

Kafka, F. and A. Bell (2009), *The Castle*. Oxford: Oxford University Press.

Latour, B. (1988), 'Drawing Things Together', in Michael Lynch and Steve Woolgar (eds), *Representation in Scientific Practice*. Cambridge, MA: MIT Press, pp. 19–68.

Lindberg, A. (2020), '*Minimum Rights Policies Targeting People Seeking Protection in Denmark and Sweden*', in D. Abdelhady, N. Gren and M. Joormann (eds), *Refugees and the Violence of European Welfare Bureaucracies*. Manchester: Manchester University Press, pp. 85–102.

——— (2022), *Deportation Limbo: State Violence and Contestations in the Nordics*. Political Ethnography. Manchester: Manchester University Press.

Lindberg, A. and L.M. Borrelli (2019), 'Let the Right One In? On European Migration Authorities' Resistance to Research', *Social Anthropology* 27(S1): 17–32, https://doi.org/10.1111/1469-8676.12659.

Lipsky, M. (1980), *Street-Level Bureaucracy: Dilemmas of the Individual in Public Services*. New York: Russell Sage Foundation.

Mathur, N. (2016), *Paper Tiger: Law, Bureaucracy and the Developmental State in Himalayan India*. Delhi: Cambridge University Press.

Navaro-Yashin, Y. (2007), 'Make-Believe Papers, Legal Forms and the Counterfeit: Affective Interactions between Documents and People in Britain and Cyprus', *Anthropological Theory* 7(1): 79–98, https://doi.org/10.1177/1463499607074294.

Nugent, D. (2010), 'States, Secrecy, Subversives: APRA and Political Fantasy in Mid-20th-Century Peru', *American Ethnologist* 37(4): 681–702, https://doi.org/10.1111/j.1548-1425.2010.01278.x.

O'Brien-Olinger, S. (2016), *Police, Race and Culture in the 'New Ireland': An Ethnography*. London: Palgrave Macmillan.

Parmar, A. (2018), 'Policing Belonging: Race and Nation in the UK', in M. Bosworth, A. Parmar and Y. Vázquez (eds), *Race, Criminal Justice, and Migration Control: Enforcing the Boundaries of Belonging*. Oxford: Oxford University Press, pp. 108–26.

——— (2019), 'Arresting (Non)Citizenship: The Policing Migration Nexus of Nationality, Race and Criminalization', *Theoretical Criminology* 24(1): 28–49.

Philipson Isaac, S. (2022), 'Temporal Dispossession through Migration Bureaucracy: On Waiting within the Asylum Process in Sweden'. *European Journal of Social Work*, Waiting In and For the Welfare State, 25(6): 945–56, https://doi.org/10.1080/13691457.2022.2077317.

Pigg, S.L., S.L. Erikson and K. Inglis (2018), 'Document/Ation: Power, Interests, Accountabilities', *Anthropological Quarterly* 60(1): 167–77.

Pratt, A. (2010), 'Between a Hunch and a Hard Place: Making Suspicion Reasonable at the Canadian Border', *Social & Legal Studies* 19(4): 461–80, https://doi.org/10.1177/0964663910378434.

Riles, A. (ed) (2006), *Documents: Artifacts of Modern Knowledge*. Ann Arbor: University of Michigan Press.

Rosenberger, S. and S. Koppes (2018), 'Claiming Control: Cooperation with Return as a Condition for Social Benefits in Austria and the Netherlands', *Comparative Migration Studies* 6(1), https://doi.org/10.1186/s40878-018-0085-3.

Rozakou, K. (2019), '"How Did You Get in?" Research Access and Sovereign Power during the "Migration Crisis" in Greece', *Social Anthropology* 27(S1): 68–83, https://doi.org/10.1111/1469-8676.12620.

Rozenblit, L. and F. Keil (2002), 'The Misunderstood Limits of Folk Science: An Illusion of Explanatory Depth', *Cognitive Science* 26(5): 521–62, https://doi.org/10.1207/s15516709cog2605_1.

Salter, M.B. (2006), 'The Global Visa Regime and the Political Technologies of the International Self: Borders, Bodies, Biopolitics', *Alternatives: Global, Local, Political* 31(2): 167–89.

Scott, J.C. (1998), *Seeing Like a State: How Certain Schemes to Improve the Human Condition Have Failed*. New Haven, CT: Yale University Press.

Sharma, N. (2020), 'The "People Out of Place": State Limits on Free Mobility and the Making of Im(Migrants)', in Sarah Bronwen Horton and Josiah McConnell Heyman (eds), *Paper Trails: Migrants, Documents, and Legal Insecurity*. Global Insecurities. Durham, NC: Duke University Press, pp. 31–52.

Stoler, A. (2004), 'Affective States', in David Nugent and Joan Vincent (eds), *A Companion to the Anthropology of Politics*. Oxford: Blackwell, pp. 4–20.

Taussig, M. (1984), 'Culture of Terror – Space of Death: Roger Casement's Putumayo Report and the Explanation of Torture', *Comparative Studies in Society and History* 26(3): 467–97.

Trouillot, M-R. (2001), 'The Anthropology of the State in the Age of Globalization: Close Encounters of the Deceptive Kind', *Current Anthropology* 42(1): 125–38, https://doi.org/10.1086/318437.

Tuckett, A. (2018), *Rules, Paper, Status: Migrants and Precarious Bureaucracy in Contemporary Italy*. Stanford, CA: Stanford University Press.

Vohnsen, N.H. (2017), *The Absurdity of Bureaucracy: How Implementation Works*. Manchester: Manchester University Press.

Walters, W. (2016), 'The Flight of the Deported: Aircraft, Deportation, and Politics', *Geopolitics* 21(2): 435–58, https://doi.org/10.1080/14650045.2015.1089234.

Yuval-Davis, N., G. Wemyss and K. Cassidy (2018), 'Everyday Bordering, Belonging and the Reorientation of British Immigration Legislation', *Sociology* 52(2): 228–44, https://doi.org/10.1177/0038038517702599.

3

Municipal Undocumentedness

Paperwork and the Performativity of Population Registers in Italy

Enrico Gargiulo

Introduction

All migrants who are legally authorized to stay in Italy have the right to obtain enrolment in the population registers of the municipality in which they live, under the same conditions as Italian citizens. Achieving municipal registration is highly important, as it is the prerequisite for actually exercising the rights to which individuals are entitled according to national laws – particularly, social assistance and public housing, enrolment in the country's national health service, acquiring citizenship and voting in local elections.

However, the right to obtain the status of local residents – *residency* – is often denied. Local governments and bureaucracies often carry out formal or informal strategies aimed at impeding registration. Basically, since municipalities pay a part of the costs of welfare and the welfare benefits and services are granted only to residents, local governments are strongly incentivized to limit social expenditure by avoiding paying for those who are in need and thus relying on state support. Denying registration, therefore, is tantamount to trying to save the money that would be spent on poor people, who often are migrants (especially refugees and asylum seekers) (Gargiulo 2017).

Furthermore, in recent years, national governments have changed national laws and regulations on registration in order to restrict the right to obtain enrolment in population registers. A ban on taking up residency in occupied dwellings was introduced, and people who are without fixed abode or homeless and want to be registered are required to prove the effective reality of their domicile. As a consequence of these actions, migrants – who often live in precarious dwellings, in illegally occupied buildings or even on the street, and hence are not able to meet the requirements for registration – are particularly subject to exclusion from access to benefits and services.

In regulating registration procedures, paperwork is crucial. In Italy, it is found both at the central and municipal level. At the national level, laws and regulations are clarified, detailed and concretely implemented through guidelines and circulars issued by the Ministry of the Interior and the National Institute of Statistics (ISTAT). At the local level, people are asked to fill in specific forms which are uniformly produced by the central authorities. But paperwork is also crucial to restricting or denying the right to registration. Frequently, the forms employed by municipal authorities are modified in order to serve exclusionary purposes. In this chapter, I will show the 'double-edged' nature of paperwork: it can be used to further registration but also – and above all – to restrict the right to registration. In Italy, paperwork is therefore a contested item: as the research presented in this chapter shows, it is necessary for concretely carrying out registration procedures, but at the same time it is a device which can restrictively manage enrolment in population registers when it is altered in order to make formal requirements more restrictive.

The misuse of registration through paperwork has a political meaning and follows a political logic which perverts the function of population registers: instead of *monitoring* the people who live within municipal territories, they are used as devices for *selecting* 'deserving' and 'desirable' local citizens. When this happens, a process of deliberately asymmetric construction of social reality takes places. Population registers thus unveil their performative nature – that of devices which do not represent but do perform the population. If this is true of population registers in general, it is even truer when they are used in a selective way. The difference is that when registers are used to monitor individuals, their performativity is unintentional: those who use them seek to merely "see" the population and not to alter it. On the contrary, when registers are employed to select, their performativity is intentional: those who (mis)use them explicitly desire to shape the local community.

By stressing how paperwork concerning registration is a field of tensions and conflicts between various actors and how it produces *performative* effects, this chapter aims at focusing on the construction of 'municipal undocumentedness'. This is a condition of lacking registration, which *de jure* and *de facto* involves many migrants who are authorized to stay in Italy and thereby have the right to be registered. Municipal undocumentedness affects the lives of those who are excluded from registration as it implies the impossibility of concretely exercising many fundamental rights.

By focusing on how this condition is constructed through paperwork, this chapter refers to concepts borrowed from studies on identification (Horton and Heyman 2020; Noiriel 1998; Torpey 2019) and on documents (Freeman and Maybin 2011; Goody 1986; Scott 1990; Weisser 2014). Moreover, by proposing a typology of paperwork and analysing in depth how the various types ambiguously relate to legal norms which regulate registration and often subvert them, this chapter aims to speak to anthropological research on law (Borrelli and Andreetta 2019; Cabot 2012; Heyman 1995, 2012; Hull 2008, 2012; Handelman and Leyton 1978; Mathur 2016; Pratt 2005; Riles 2006; Tuckett 2018; Vetters 2019) and to foster a more interdisciplinary approach to the study of the performativity of administrative power. More specifically, this chapter adds new, empirical elements to social and anthropological research on law as it shows the concrete functioning of paperwork in a field (municipal registration) that is not widely explored – especially as compared with other fields of bureaucracy and migration studies, where more research is conducted. This chapter also adds theoretical elements to the same literature as it furthers the reflection on paperwork as a documentary item that holds a performative power which has various facets that have not yet been deeply explored in the social and anthropological research on law.

The analysis conducted in this chapter relies on a path of research focused on registration and its uses and misuses. I have pursued this path for more than ten years, employing several methodological strategies: the analysis of political discourses; document analysis of legal norms and various kinds of administrative texts and paperwork; interviews; the collection of data from municipalities; and participant observation in professional courses, conferences and meetings addressed to registry officers and lawyers. Specifically, over the years and on different occasions, I have interviewed lawyers, activists, members of nongovernmental organizations (NGOs), trade unionists, experts, civil servants (belonging to municipal registry offices and prefectures) and occupiers. Moreover, in recent years I have had the occasion to participate, in the twofold guise of scholar and activist, in some paths of research/action aimed at contrasting the exclusionary practices of the authorities of some Italian cities.

These experiences have led to the writing of some chapters of NGO reports (MEDU 2019, Naga 2019). More recently, I began further research/action experience as part of a group of political activists, NGO members, lawyers and scholars who are committed to a double objective: combatting the discriminatory actions of the Municipality of Rome and trying to push the Italian Constitutional Court to declare Article 5 of the Housing Plan illegitimate. This experience has allowed me to collect more ethnographic, documentary and discursive data. It has also given me the opportunity to analyse migrants' interactions with municipalities and their reactions to registration practices, as well as to appreciate how resisting paperwork is part of a broader and conflictual process of construction of municipal undocumentedness, which can be better explained by resorting to the categories proposed by Albert O. Hirschman: exit and voice.

Access to fields such as occupations, housing struggles and combatting discrimination has not presented significant challenges for me, thanks to my prior relationships with various occupiers, activists and legal professionals. These connections have allowed me to build trust with the individuals with whom I have taken legal and political action. Additionally, I have changed all their names to ensure anonymity. Moreover, my research has supported the subjects under investigation, and on multiple occasions I have shared the research findings with the individuals I interviewed or with those who were involved in the occupations or had been excluded from residency. Access to institutional fields, on the other hand, has proven to be more challenging. Specifically, obtaining data from municipalities has been a hurdle. Out of the ninety-five municipalities I contacted, only forty-five provided the requested data – which included information on the number of rejected registration applications, the origin and citizenship of the applicants, the reasons for rejection and the documentation used for verification. However, I encountered no issues when conducting interviews or participating in professional courses, conferences and meetings geared towards registry officers and lawyers.

Varieties of Paperwork

Paperwork is intimately connected with the production and implementation of legal norms. It plays a role in the activity of legislation, both in the preparation of legal texts and in their subsequent enactment (Eule 2014; Eule et al. 2019; Gjergji 2013; Hing, Chacón and Johnson 2018). Basically, paperwork is itself a kind of *document* which, like other objects (Latour 2000), holds normative power.

According to the *Oxford Dictionary*, a document is 'an official paper, book or electronic file that gives information about something, or that can be used as evidence or proof of something'. More precisely, a document is a material or immaterial artefact (Riles 2006) that over the course of time has begun to connote 'proof' and is connected with collective memory and its public uses (Le Goff 1978). It is a structural element of social reality as it belongs to the category of 'institutional facts', which exist only within human institutions and arise when an empirical fact is assigned a function (Searle 1995). Indeed, a document not only certifies something but also contributes to shaping the social world. It allows interactions and activities, becoming a key aspect of daily life. It is the product of institutional acts, and is therefore the 'effect of practice', but at the same time it has 'effects of practice', meaning that it is performative (Weisser 2014: 47). Documents are the essential infrastructure of bureaucracies (Vismann 2008). Bureaucrats who produce documents and case files collect, select and densify information according to their relevance criteria as 'they [the documents] are drafted to create coherence between observations and its bureaucratic processing' (Bierschenk 2019: 116). Basically, they order the fragments of the state where they are produced and link it to other 'fragments' (Andreetta 2019), and also control clients as well as bureaucrats themselves (Vetters 2019).

Paperwork comprises documents that have different characteristics and functions. Its power depends on its relationship with law. In fact, paperwork is not law in itself but is rather only the material support on which law is written and through which it works. As an infrastructural object which aims to facilitate the implementation of legal norms, paperwork is not supposed to directly hold power but rather merely to exercise the power that the law confers on it. However, paperwork often works as if it were a law and exerts a power that theoretically it should not hold – in this way producing effects that go beyond its formal tasks and capabilities. Paperwork, moreover, plays a strategic role in the implementation of laws and decrees: forms that must be filled out are widespread and are at the base of the functioning of a bureaucracy, as they are essential to carrying out the bureaucratic procedures connected to the implementation of legal norms.

When paperwork works as a legal norm, it can take two different forms. The first is that of *soft law*. In legal literature, this term denotes instruments with extralegal binding effect – namely, principles, rules, and standards which do not stem from one of the sources of law enumerated in a certain legal framework (Baxter 1980; Terpan 2014). The use of soft law is widespread at the European level, where European Union (EU) institutions try to persuade national governments to act in a certain way in fields in which they do not have any direct power. However, it is also relevant at the state level, where, in order to more 'informally' regulate specific phenomena, governments issue plans or 'coloured' 'books' or papers and technical institutions release guidelines and manuals. In both cases, soft law has an ambiguous status: while formally it stands outside of the perimeter of the law (meant *stricto sensu*), still it has an actual and effective legal normative power that is capable of deeply affecting several social issues. Documents which are often issued to regulate certain kinds of conduct are presented and depicted as being binding and mandatory. Such a kind of camouflage effect is fostered by the procedure through which they are issued. Even though they are deployed by technical actors, such as experts and specialists, they are made effective by political actors, who legitimize them by attributing a certain role to them.

Paperwork takes up its second form when it works as a legal norm as that of *infra-law*, namely, of disciplines and regulatory commands which act within, or beneath the surface of, the law (Costa-Lascoux 1989; Carbonnier 1978). Infra-law devices are more or less compatible with the law: while they theoretically aim to clearly define the content of laws and decrees, in some cases giving 'flesh and blood' to too many abstract and generic legal prescriptions, in reality they often change the content of such prescriptions from within, *de facto* 'creating' new law. The Italian case is quite exemplary: even though ministerial guidelines and circulars are supposed only to make clearer what a law or decree states, practically they are often used to take advantage of the genericity of the law and replace it with extralegal decisions. Like soft law, and probably more so than soft law, infra-law has an ambiguous status: even though it should remain within the perimeters of the law, it actually oversteps them.

Both when used in place of a law or decree and when employed to apparently clarify the meaning of legal norms, paperwork is a device of governmentality (Dean 1991; Foucault 2008), as it works as an instrument which aims to discipline and shape human conduct (Lascoumes and Le Gales 2007). In doing so, it is not explicitly regulatory but rather it works through persuasion or by quietly and obliquely modifying regulations.

When paperwork has to do with carrying out administrative procedures which implement legal norms, it takes the form of *street-level bureaucracy*. Indeed, in their daily work, bureaucrats resort to various kinds of documents (Dubois 2014; Hull 2008, 2012; Lipsky 2010; Mathur 2016). Besides dealing with legal norms and implementation devices, they get in touch with their users through forms that must be filled out. These forms in some cases are arranged by a central authority, while in other cases are directly provided for by the street-level bureaucrats. Clearly, depending on the different situations, the degree of discretion changes, being lower in the first kind of cases and higher in the second (Gargiulo 2021). However, even when the forms are arranged by the central authorities, and hence are received by bureaucrats as something 'ready-made', it can happen that they are intentionally altered to serve purposes that are different from those for which they should be formally used.

The dynamics of paperwork are exemplified by the case of the Italian registration system. As will emerge in more detail below, paperwork here works as if it were a legal norm in two ways. First, it is used in the place of laws or decrees. When this happens, it produces the same regulatory effect even though it has a different legal status, as it is located in a lower position in the hierarchy of legal sources or even stands completely outside of that hierarchy. Guidelines issued by the ISTAT to regulate registration procedures are quite illustrative in this regard. Technicians who write down the texts of guidelines *de facto* act as if they have a political role and have been formally charged with the task of determining the content of a legal norm.

Second, paperwork is used to clarify the meaning of a law or decree. The guidelines and circulars issued by the technical staff of a ministry are asked to give a correct interpretation of a given legal norm. In so doing, they should implement this norm without changing its sense. However, circulars frequently 'innovate' with respect to the laws and decrees they are called on to simply clarify. Even in this case, technical actors play a major role – acting as *de facto* lawmakers.

Moreover, the forms used in registration procedures are an interesting kind of paperwork. Legally, they should be uniformly provided by the central authorities while local authorities are merely appointed to follow the instructions coming from above, and hence are not allowed to change the aspect and content of the forms or to bend their purposes. Yet, municipalities often autonomously arrange their own forms, which differ from the official ones. In most cases, they do this in order to prevent people who belong to certain social groups from obtaining registration.

Contextualizing Paperwork in Immigration Law

Paperwork plays a major role in the government of human mobility, in all the three forms mentioned above – namely, when it pretends to be a law or decree, clarifies the meaning of a law or decree, or acts as a form to be filled out. Indeed, it can replace – by standing for or 'clarifying' – the legal norms that regulate both the movement of people between different states and the paths of individuals' inclusion in host societies. It is also involved in the bureaucratic procedures concerning stay permits, registration with national and local authorities, and integration programmes.

Paperwork as soft law is often issued at the EU level. Indeed, over the last few decades, the European Union has been a key actor in producing law-like documents which are not legally binding but able to influence national politics and policies. Documents of this kind are used in fields where the direct power of the EU institutions is quite limited, and aim at persuading states to act in a certain way by spreading 'best practices' and trying to foster shared views of how to manage certain phenomena.

This has happened especially in the field of immigration, where guidelines try to promote changes in the beliefs and expectations of domestic actors and then to obtain a greater policy convergence in the long term (de la Porte 2002; Borrás and Jacobsson 2004). The integration of third-country nationals (TCNs) is an issue which particularly concerns EU institutions, to such an extent that a Framework for the Integration of TCNs in the EU has been proposed. Within it, several documents have been released. Probably, the best known is represented by the *Common Basic Principles*, issued by the European Commission (EC) in 2004. Even though these principles are formulated in a rather general way and do not push member states in a clear manner towards particular immigrant-integration programmes (Jacobs and Rea 2007), they do show how the EC plays a coordinating role in the exchange of national practices and experiences on the integration of TCNs among member states representatives (Carrera and Wiesbrock 2009).

At the state level, paperwork is widespread both as soft law and infra-law. In many countries, the government of immigration, besides laws and decrees, *de facto* hinges on documents such as guidelines and circulars, which do not hold the actual status of legal norms but play a major role in fields such as, for instance, entry and stay permits, family reunification and recognition of international protection. In the hierarchy of the sources of law, guidelines and circulars are not present, or, if present, occupy its lowest rungs. Generally, they are formally conceived as internal provisions of a general character or declarations of the intent of an administrative body. In Germany, for instance, *administrative guidelines* appear under a range of different designations such as directive, decree, administrative circular, internal instruction or procedural guidance (Vetters 2019: 76). In Italy, circulars are often issued by a ministry in order to clarify the contents of a legal norm for those bureaucrats who are called on to implement and apply them.

As such, guidelines and circulars are issued by a higher administrative authority and are addressed to subordinate authorities with the aim of providing guidance on how to implement relevant laws and carry out tasks. Theoretically, they are binding only internally: that is to say, they do not have to be obeyed by people who are external to the administration. Yet, they deeply affect the government of immigration and the lives of migrants. In Germany, guidelines are meant by those who use them as simply a means to counter the complexity of legal norms (Vetters 2019: 78). However, they play a more complex role, being a device of standardization and constituting 'an attempt by astute bureaucrats to codify their practical norms and to shield them from external challenges by inserting them into the space that the larger web of public law doctrine provides for bureaucratic margins of interpretation' (Ibid.: 82). In Italy, circulars, before the first law on immigration was issued in 1990, had for a long time been playing the role of actual laws. Subsequently, they were theoretically understood as documents merely aimed at interpreting and explicating the contents of a legal norm. Despite appearances, circulars have actually designed immigration politics and policies, and therefore have had the character of a 'device': even when they seem to limit themselves to giving a correct interpretation of a legal norm, they *de facto* alter the times and modalities of its application (Gjergji 2020: 332). For this reason, even though in Italy the legal condition of migrants, according to Article 10 of the Italian Constitution, is subject to a 'legal reserve' – namely, it has to be regulated by the law in conformity to norms and international treaties – it is *de facto* affected by circulars.

Paperwork as a form or document involved in bureaucratic procedures is highly important both at the state and the local level. Generally, the importance of documents for the working of bureaucracies and the relations of power they allow is well known in the study of discretion (Dubois 2014; Lipsky 2010) and in anthropological research on law (Heyman 1995, 2012; Hull 2008, 2012; Handelman and Leyton 1978; Pratt 2005; Riles 2006). The role of documents in the relationship between noncitizens and the institutions of the country in which they reside, or through which they transit, is a more specific topic – one, in turn, deeply analysed in many studies. Heath Cabot, for instance, has stressed the role of documents 'as regulatory technologies that enact control and legibility over both citizens and "aliens"' (Cabot 2012: 11). Anna Tuckett has talked about a 'documentation regime' – namely, a 'nexus of documents, paperwork, and legal and bureaucratic processes that migrants must engage with in their efforts to become and stay "legal," to bring family members into the country, and to attain citizenship' (Tuckett 2018: 4).

To people who have crossed the borders of a state they do not belong to, ordinary paperwork assumes new currency 'as it becomes valuable evidence of one's duration of residence, work history, or "moral character" (diligence, civic responsibility, compliance with the authorities)' (Horton and Heyman 2020: 11). More specifically, the interaction between migrants and the law of the host country, as it is mediated by 'mundane paperwork procedures, uncovers the diverse strategies that can be employed to bend the law to one's advantage' (Tuckett 2018: 15). This means that '"the state" – whether the local branches of government that issue these myriad documents or a centralized government authority – often assumes a greater presence in the lives and imaginations of precariously positioned migrants than it does in those of citizens' (Horton and Heyman 2020: 11). To the former, paperwork, being inserted within an opaque and not easily understandable system of governance, creates uncertainty and indeterminacy, making the existence of such persons precarious and at the same time affecting the work of low-level bureaucrats (Tuckett 2015).

Registration in Italy

In the countries where it is employed, registering fulfils various purposes. It allows state institutions first to track individuals who live in the various municipalities that compose the territory of a state and their movements – and hence, to understand the dynamics of internal mobility. It also permits them to know how the population is composed and distributed within the perimeters of the state, so as to foster surveillance and, at the same time, to better allocate public resources. In order to establish population registers and make them work, various kinds of paperwork are needed.

Italy is an interesting case study in understanding the role of paperwork in registration. In this country, devices aiming at gathering knowledge about the population had already been introduced around the time of state unification in 1861. Specifically, population registers or registers of the resident population (*registri anagrafici* or *registri della popolazione residente*) were established in 1862 on the basis of the first census, made the previous year. The intent was that of allowing institutions to see as clearly as possible all the different categories of people living or having interests within the diverse parts of the national territory. Technically, this means making the *de facto* population completely overlap with the *de jure* population.

In order to be efficient, accurate and detailed, population registers are conceived as administrative and statistical records which contain information about the people who habitually reside within a given municipality or who, being homeless or without fixed abode, have a certain kind of link with it. The act of registering (*iscrizione anagrafica*) produces as its output the formal recognition of a *legal status* called residency (*residenza*).

Registration in Italy is considered a matter of national importance. As such, it is defined and governed by a national law (Law 1228 of 1954) and its implementing regulation (Decree of the President of the Republic [DPR] 223 of 1989). According to these legal norms, the authority that confers residency is the state – even though, for exclusively practical reasons, the task of registering people is assigned to municipalities. Basically, the central authorities delegate their power to the local registry offices (*uffici anagrafici*), which are simply appointed to apply the national rules. As a consequence, even though municipal authorities are *de facto* autonomous in their work, they cannot rewrite or change the 'rules of the game' of registration. *De jure*, in fact, municipalities have but a limited and indirect 'sovereignty' over population registers. It is only the state that issues laws and regulations on registration, and it is only the state that has the authority to supervise the entire process and to revoke the delegation of powers to local registry offices at any time.

This articulation of powers between central government and peripheral local authorities, moreover, has been strengthened by the unification of the system of registration launched in 2005, with the issuing of Legislative Decree 82, called the 'Digital Administration Code'. This decree has introduced the *Anagrafe nazionale della popolazione residente* (National Register of the Resident Population – ANPR). It is a sort of national register collecting and connecting the different municipal registers in real time (Pelizza 2016).

As registration is crucial for state interests and is meant as a device to accurately monitor the territory, it is conceived so as to administratively and statistically cover the greater part of the resident population. Toward this end, it is extended to all Italian citizens, all EU citizens satisfying certain requirements and all non-EU citizens legally authorized to stay in Italy. For all these groups, registration is a duty: those who belong to them are legally obliged to declare their habitual dwelling (*dimora abituale*) to the municipal authorities or, should they be homeless or without fixed abode, the fact that they have decided to establish therein their domicile (*domicilio*) that is the centre of their affairs and interests. At the same time, the municipal authorities are expected to verify the accuracy of the declarations received and to register those who correctly declare their position.

For the same purpose of covering the population as completely as possible, registration is also a right: all the people who belong to one of these groups have to be registered by the local authorities. Moreover, this is the means to exercise other rights: social assistance, health assistance, public housing, the right to vote in local elections – for Italians and EU citizens – and many others all depend on registration. Even the acquisition of citizenship falls into this category: the regular presence in Italy of EU and third-country citizens is measured by the number of years they have been enrolled. Without residency, therefore, it is impossible to actually enjoy the better part of individuals' rights.

Governing Registration through Paperwork

Paperwork is essential for the functioning of the system of population registers. All the kinds of documents mentioned above are involved in designing and managing how registration works. They can act as soft law, by integrating the formal regulations and filling their lacunae; as infra-law, by specifying the content of legal norms and often changing their meaning and purpose; or as forms, which are necessary to complete the procedures of registration.

First, paperwork acts as soft law because national laws and regulations do not contain precise indications on all the aspects of registration. For instance, the concrete procedures for enrolling people who do not have a habitual dwelling are not provided for by legal norms. This gap is filled in by the Italian National Institute of Statistics (ISTAT), which is formally entrusted with the duty of overseeing the regular functioning of municipal registry offices.[1] In its operative guidelines, the ISTAT distinguishes two kind of people who do not have a habitual dwelling: those *with no fixed abode* and those who are *homeless*. The first, for professional or existential reasons, do not live in a stable way in a given municipality. The second conduct their existence within a certain municipal territory, but without having a proper living space and/or without dwelling constantly in a precise place. On the base of this distinction, the ISTAT invites 'the registry office to establish a street, territorially inexistent, but known with a conventional name given by the registrar (e.g. street. . . followed by the name of the municipality itself, Municipal House Street, etc.)' and to register both those who are homeless and those who are without fixed abode 'in this virtual street address, with progressive odd numbers' (ISTAT 1992: 45–46).

Second, paperwork plays the role of infra-law, as the ISTAT uses its guidelines and manuals not only to fill in the gaps of the law but also to clarify the meanings of the changes made to it. This happened, for instance, following the 'Security Package' (*Pacchetto sicurezza*) of 2009, a law that modified the requirements for the registration of those who do not have a habitual dwelling. This law established that they have to provide to the registry office all the elements for ascertaining the 'effective reality' of their declared domicile. Consequently, it risked increasing the confusion between the figure of the resident and that of the domiciled – namely, by giving rise to the idea that whoever wants to be registered as a person who is homeless or without fixed abode must demonstrate their physical presence. In order to clarify this question, the ISTAT, in its guidelines published in 2010, has stated that

> the assessment of domicile is different from that of residency as it does not presuppose the person's continual physical presence at the indicated address. Therefore the assessment by the Registry officer will regard the existence or non-existence of the principal base of the applicant's affairs and interests and not his/her physical presence, which is and will be, in such cases, an accidental element. (ISTAT 2010: 71)

A similar role was played by the circular issued by the Ministry of the Interior after Decree-Law n. 47/2014 – the so-called 'Lupi Decree' or 'Housing Plan' (*Piano casa*) – which states that '[a]nyone who abusively occupies a property without entitlement cannot ask residency or insertion in public services in relation to that property' (Art. 5). This circular states that those who dwell in abusively occupied property nonetheless have the right to be registered, and, since the general and prevalent criterion of the 'habitual dwelling' cannot be applied to them, no solution is possible other than registration 'by way of domicile', analogously to what happens with people without fixed abode.

Third, paperwork takes the form of bureaucratic forms, as these are essential for the administrative procedures that make registration concretely work. Specifically, two of them are important: the 'declaration of habitual dwelling' and the 'declaration of domicile'. The first is reserved for those who habitually reside in an accommodation of any kind (regardless of its material conditions and 'decency'). It contains the declaration of changing one's residence and several pieces of information concerning individuals and the space in which they live. Some of this information is mandatory while some is not, being simply of statistical interest. As a consequence of the issuing of Decree-Law n. 47/2014, anyone who declares their habitual dwelling must also prove their entitlement to occupy the accommodation in which they live. In order to ensure uniformity and consistency in the behaviour of the different local authorities, a circular issued by the Ministry of the Interior provided a standard form which asks the declarants to give – through a self-certifying process – all the relevant information and proofs.

The form reserved for those who do not have a fixed abode or are homeless contains instead the declaration about the lack of habitual dwelling and the address elected as domicile. As a consequence of the Security Package of 2009, it also asks them – again, mainly via self-certification – to provide all the elements which are necessary to prove the 'effective reality' of domicile.

With the introduction of the ANPR, moreover, access to registration depends even more on a system of nationwide digital identity, called SPID. As a consequence, the administrative process is gradually dematerialized, and the forms for enrolment are no longer paper made but go online.

Paperwork as an Institutional Battlefield

Despite the clarity of the legal norms and the indications stemming from the ISTAT and the Ministry of the Interior, there is neither agreement nor uniformity of behaviour in registering. Documents explaining the logic of enrolment in the registry office and allowing registration procedures therefore constitute a sort of battlefield, within which actors driven by different interests conduct their own strategies and conflict with each other. Basically, there are two kinds of conflict. The first involves the political and the technical level of the state apparatus: central governments attempt to tighten the right to registration through legal norms, the exclusionary effects of which civil servants and technicians attempt to ameliorate. The second sees state and local authorities facing off against each other: this happens whenever municipalities use registration improperly to the extent that they violate national regulations.

The first kind of conflict emerged especially in 2009 and 2014, when changes made to the legal norms which regulate registration started to become a problem, and in some way a challenge, to the civil servants of the Ministry of the Interior and the ISTAT. From their perspective, population registers are a strategic tool for monitoring a territory and the people who live and circulate in it. For this reason, any restriction put on registration is perceived as an impediment to the capacity to fully and accurately 'see' what happens in the state space. The guidelines produced by the ISTAT and the circulars issued by the Ministry of the Interior are an attempt to limit the power of those political actors who aspire to use population registers as a selective and not as a monitoring device. Restrictions to registration are perceived as impediments to seeing the territory by other state apparatuses – for instance, the Constitutional Court, as emerged on the occasion of its judgment about the legitimately of the decree on Security and Immigration, the so-called 'Salvini Decree'. Issued in 2018 under the pretext of protecting security, it denied the right to municipal residency to asylum seekers. According to the Constitutional Court, the decree was illegitimate, since, 'by preventing certain migrants from being registered, it has impeded the authorities from monitoring the territory and knowing exactly what people live and circulate in it'. In this way, the Salvini Decree has created insecurity by making it impossible to track migrants, and thus causing them to remain administratively invisible.

The fact that the first kind of conflict is conducted by technical actors does not mean that it is not 'political', for two reasons. First, because it involves the capacity of drawing the borders separating those who can exercise their rights from those who cannot despite being physically present in, or however linked to, a municipal territory. Controlling registration is therefore a highly political act as it implies deciding who deserves to be fully recognized and included in the local community. Second, on some occasions ministerial circulars have been used by political actors as a means to indirectly intervene in the political arena. The circulars following Decree-Law n. 47/2014 are an interesting case in point. The issuing of this norm triggered some tensions within the governing majority, composed of both centre-left and centre-right parties. Some members of the centre-left proposed amendments meant to alleviate the consequences of exclusion from registration. The proposals were voted down, but in the following months the 'dissident' members of the governing majority put pressure on the technical staff of the Ministry of the Interior to intervene with circulars that fulfilled the same purpose.

The second kind of conflict, on the other hand, has repeatedly emerged over the years, whenever municipalities have violated national laws and regulations on registration. Indeed, over the decades, local authorities have frequently refused to stick to national indications and have preferred, rather, to use registers as a selective device. In many cases, they have systematically avoided registering individuals of the lower classes and persons living at the margins of society who are likely to require social protection and who are, often, recently immigrated. More specifically, their targets have changed through time. If, up to the 1990s, it was mainly homeless Italian individuals, Roma or those with criminal records who were to be excluded from population registers (Kazepov 1997; Sigona 2002), later, increasing migratory movements and the politicization of the migratory issue made noncitizens as such the most excluded ones (Gargiulo 2021). To fulfil their purposes, local authorities have frequently issued formal acts, mainly ordinances and circulars, which tighten the requirements provided for by law or add new ones – for instance, holding a job contract, having a decent dwelling place, the absence of any criminal record (Lorenzetti 2009).

On many occasions, municipalities have fulfilled their selective aims by resorting to the forms used for the registration procedures. Misinformation contained in them or on websites – for instance, requiring a job contract or the absence of criminal records – exercises a dissuasive influence over people by confusing or pushing them to declare conditions and facts that might adversely affect their registration. Moreover, municipalities have taken advantage of the change in the registration procedures made by the Security Package of 2009 and the Housing Plan of 2014. In the first case, the request to provide all the elements which are necessary to prove the effective reality of domicile is arbitrarily and univocally interpreted as an obligation to get in touch with social services. The case of two large Italian cities, Florence and Milan, is quite representative in this regard: there, social workers are called to act as 'filters', able to select the 'deserving' migrants (MEDU 2019; Naga 2019). In the second case, instead of asking for a self-certification of the entitlement to occupy the accommodation in question, the authorization of the landlord is mandatorily requested – and, in some cases, that of the tenants as well, if they are already present within the dwelling. Here, another large Italian city, Rome, makes an interesting case: people who declare their habitual dwelling there are expected to have their landlord and the other tenants fill out the form that, according to the law, only they should fill out (Actionaid 2021; Nonna Roma 2022).

All these municipal behaviours are illegal. Formally, it is the Ministry of the Interior which has a steering and coordinating function in the field of registration, supporting the prefectures and local administrations and monitoring their conduct. Legally speaking, the latter are subordinate to the former: the mayor is the final link in the 'chain of command' proceeding from the Ministry of the Interior all the way through its territorial articulations. For this reason, in the matter of registration, the mayor acts as a government official and not as the head of an administration (a role that he/she plays in other areas).

Over the years, the Ministry of the interior has tried to contain the exuberance of local governments by issuing several ministerial circulars. In 1985, for instance, a circular exhorted them to register those Roma people who live within their territories. Over the following decade, two circulars, issued in 1995 and 1997, clarified that it is not permitted to request as a requirement for any registration documentation which demonstrates things such as having an occupation or the absence of criminal records, and specified that the nature of a dwelling – for example, a building without licensed habitability or one which does not obey urban specifications (caves, caravans, etc.) – shall not be considered an obstacle to enrolment in the population registers.

The introduction of the ANPR and the digitalization of the registration procedures, furthermore, risks paving the way for new forms of exclusion. In the current intentions of central institutions, access to registration will depend on SPID as a digital identity. The possibility of holding it, however, hinges on the availability of an ID card – which, in turn, presupposes registration. The choice to digitalize the procedures for being registered, therefore, on the one hand simplifies the procedures and turns paper forms into online forms; on the other hand, however, it triggers a form of Catch-22: being registered is the beginning and, at the same time, the end of the registration process.

Resisting Paperwork

People who are exposed to exclusion from registration are not always aware of the injustice and discrimination they suffer. From the perspective of lay people, the complexity of the rules is a barrier preventing full comprehension of what is going on. Paperwork appears as something inscrutable and indisputable. Conforming to the obligations contained in it is considered natural, even when they lie completely outside of the law. People I have interviewed who live in an illegal occupation in Rome offered statements like the following: 'They always ask you for a rent contract; without that, you can't get residency'; 'If you don't have residency, the police headquarters won't renew your stay permit, and they won't do it even if you only have a virtual residency'. Substantially, they think that the requests contained in paperwork (or simply asked verbally) are as such legitimate. This depends on the fact that such requests are so widespread as to seem 'normal', in the sense of conforming to legal norms. In this regard, the informational asymmetry between institutional actors and the users of the registry office certainly plays a strategic role.

In other cases, people are aware of the injustice and discrimination they suffer, but they decide not to respond. When this happens, paperwork is perceived as an impenetrable barrier: it is considered wise to forgo trying to overcome it, rather than starting a battle which one is bound to lose. Adopting the categories proposed by Hirschman (1970), this attitude is a form of *exit*.

However, some people decide to circumvent the requirement contained in the paperwork by simply pretending to be able to meet them (Gargiulo 2021). For instance, if they live in an abusively occupied dwelling they declare they are resident in another place, one in which they actually do not live. This other dwelling is made available by a friend or is obtained by paying for it.

On the other hand, there is also *protest*: in this case, paperwork, as well as the entire registration procedure within which it plays a strategic role, is explicitly contested. Requirements requested by the institutions are labelled illegitimate and unfair. Politically, paperwork containing them is considered to be a device conveying and symbolizing all the abuse and prevarication carried out by the local and national authorities. As such, actions to show how it is discriminatory and oppressive are taken. These actions are a form of *voice*: movements, unions and NGOs organize mobilizations aimed at emphasizing the exclusionary aspects of the device of registration (Ibid.).

These kinds of organized protest are part of broader struggles for migrants' rights and the right to the city which, over the last few decades, have been conducted in Italy jointly by migrants and Italian activists. Within these protests, the condition of the undocumented person, the *sans-papier*, has often been considered emblematic of a political and economic system that resorts to documents in order to raise barriers against undesired individuals and social groups. Claims for fair and easily accessible documents have been made against the international and national institutions that use paperwork as immaterial borders which contain and constrain migrants' lives. In recent years, these claims have been intertwined with those at the local level, and specifically for enrolment at municipal registry offices as a means for exercising rights.

In contesting the exclusionary ways local authorities use documents, the right to housing has played a major role – especially as a consequence of the economic crisis of 2008 and the resulting austerity policies. Migrants have been the main actors in many housing movements, in terms of both numbers and organizational capacity (Mudu 2014; Nur and Sethman 2017). They have contributed to proposing different repertoires and strategies of action, and have framed the protest in terms of counter-racialization (Oliveri 2018).

More generally, Italian and non-Italian urban dwellers and activists, given the lack of top-down organization of urban services, have developed autonomous organizational practices of survival. In creating networks of resistance and solidarity, these practices have also expressed the capacity to denounce the fact that while institutions refuse to provide even basic infrastructure, such as drainage systems and electricity supply, they are at the same time inflexible in asking for documents and use paperwork as a tool of selection (Grazioli and Caciagli 2018).

Besides protests, the struggle against exclusive registration paperwork is sometimes conducted through judicial proceedings – even though, for several reasons, this is not an easy path. When paperwork takes the form of soft law or infra-law, it is practically exempt from judicial control – in the first case because it is apparently a mere suggestion and not a prescription, while in the second case because it is formally internal to an administration. When paperwork takes the form of an Act issued at the local level, on the other hand – for instance, a mayor's ordinance or circular – appealing to administrative and civil courts is easier. In this case, additional – and, as such, illegitimate – requirements have been explicitly added through a formal act, or are contained in a registration form which has been altered by the local authorities and differs from the original one issued by the ministry. If, on the contrary, requirements are only verbally asked for, appealing to a court is quite difficult as there is no clear and formal proof of illegitimate action. To make it possible to initiate legal action, the denial of registration has to be formalized in a written text. Only in this way are there administrative traces of what actually happened, such as might be used as proof in a trial (Morozzo della Rocca 2017).

The Performativity of Paperwork

Registration is a technology through which states make societies legible and more easily governable (Scott 1998). Like other written forms of knowing and tracking individuals, it contributes to reducing the complexity of a society and standardizing administrative procedures, making possible a more modern and efficient management of the state's core activities (Goody 1986). Paperwork such as documents and certificates has historically contributed to the increase of a government's intellectual capacity to exercise logistical power and engage in territorial governance (Mukerji 2011). From this perspective, registration contributes to providing *individual identification* by allowing states to make each person administratively classifiable and knowable (About, Brown and Lonergan 2013; Caplan and Torpey 2001;

Higgs 2011; Noiriel 1998; Torpey 2019). This is especially true in the case of migrants: towards them, it acts as a form of *bureaucratic inscription* through which information about their characteristics and immigration status is incorporated into official state registers (Horton and Heyman 2020: 5) and is specifically linked to a given municipal territory (Gargiulo 2023).

Registration processes in Italy add particular and strategic aspects to this bureaucratic inscription. They produce a *legal status* which is equivalent to the formal recognition of being 'local citizens' in a municipality. The legal rationale and rules governing how this status is attributed clearly reflect the importance of population registers for the Italian central state apparatuses. Those who meet the requirements for being registered have a subjective right to registration, not merely a legitimate interest in it. More specifically, residency is a *declarative*, and not a constitutive, condition: a person does not become resident because she/he is discretionarily registered, but rather has to be *ipso facto* registered as she/he finds her/himself in the material condition of being a resident.

In more theoretical terms, legal recognition does not turn an individual into a formal resident but simply constitutes the legal declaration of her/his material condition: that of being a resident. Since the system is designed in this way, the rules on registration try to facilitate the administrative and statistical 'capture' of those who are linked to a territory. In other words, population registers are meant to be devices that can produce a detailed 'picture' of those living within Italian borders and keep track of the different 'categories' to which they belong (Gargiulo 2021).

Registration, from the perspective of the institutions which have invented and realized it, constitutes the mere *representation* of the people linked to a territory and of how they move. According to the ISTAT (1992), population registers strive to bring the *de jure* population to correspond exactly to the *de facto* population. In these terms, the act of registering does not affect the reality it is called on to accurately 'describe'.

Yet, instead of merely certifying a material condition, registration shapes a legal population which conforms to certain institutional rules, rather than simply reflecting how people live and dwell in a territory. Since people who declare their residence or domicile have to fit into well-defined categories, they are substantially pushed to live and dwell differently from how they would if they were free to decide for themselves. Their decision to settle and the ways they manage their lives in the territory are somehow conditioned. At the same time, people who are materially resident but fall outside the legal categories through which population registers work are neglected and made invisible. As underlined by James Scott regarding other fields of state action, the concepts and legal notions employed by institutional actors often become categories that organize people's daily experience precisely inasmuch as they are embedded in state-created institutions which are able to structure that experience (Scott 1998: 82–83).

Registration, therefore – like other demographic devices such as censuses, which have been deeply analysed by literature coming from Science and technology studies (STS) (Curtis 2002; Ruppert 2007, 2011) – is a *performative* device: by attributing a legal status, it confers an *administrative existence*. This materializes in the documents released by local authorities: in Italy, registration is required before obtaining an ID card, which is not mandatory but is concretely necessary in interacting with the public administration, conducting private transactions and facing police control – particularly for non-Italians.

Avoiding registering people who live or have the centre of their interests in a municipal territory consequently means making them *administratively invisible* to the state: they are 'administrative ghosts', being unregistered in the place in which they live or to which they are somehow linked. It also means exercising a specific kind of performative power, which is *intentional* rather than unintended: registers are used with the aim not of obtaining a detailed picture of the population but of altering its representation by selecting its 'deserving' components.

The power paperwork holds within registration procedures is a genus of the broader species of *identificatory* power characterizing modern states and their establishment process. As stressed by Gérard Noiriel, the 'identificatory revolution', which involved many European states towards the end of the nineteenth century, marked the advent of papers and codes and made distinctions introduced for administrative ends a central element of the government of populations and territories (Noiriel 1991). This formally decreed the affirmation of the legal statuses of the 'regular' and the 'irregular' migrant. Since then, therefore, the identity of noncitizens, more than that of citizens, has been broadly determined by legal and administrative procedures, and specifically moulded by the documents and practices of registration (Noiriel [1988] 1996: 45). Basically, this means that the documentation of foreign nationals makes it possible for governments to record and formally recognize individuals, and in the end to produce the status of being authorized/unauthorized (Horton and Heyman 2020: 111).

The choice of registering or not registering those who live in a municipal territory, particularly if they are non-Italians, produces huge effects not only on their lives but also on the population as a whole – especially considering the fact that the status deriving from registration is not a simple right but is rather a right which allows one to concretely exercise other rights. The lack of registration is therefore the lack of formal recognition, and consequently of rights. Those who are 'present yet not registered' are 'local non-citizens' (Gargiulo 2017). Among them, some are residents elsewhere while others completely lack registration. 'Municipalityless' people are seldom Italians, being composed mostly of non-Italians who have arrived in the Italian territory for the first time. Those who are local noncitizens but are residents elsewhere are less vulnerable than the 'municipalityless': the former can at least exercise their rights in a municipality different from that in which they live, while the latter cannot. Thus, 'municipalityless' people lack any kind of local recognition, and thereby resemble stateless persons.

Conclusion

As shown throughout this chapter, paperwork can take three different forms – all of which are exemplified in the procedures for registration. It can work as: a soft law, which tries to standardize the behaviours of the local authorities; an infra-law that clarifies/changes the content of legal norms, in an attempt to reduce the exclusionary effects of political choices or to intensify discriminatory acts at the local level; or a bureaucratic form through which enrolment in registry office is eased or, on the contrary, impeded.

In Italy, as has emerged throughout the chapter, there is a structural gap between the theory and practice of registration. Rules are systematically violated by local authorities. Moreover, in recent years, central governments have modified them in order to turn registration from a monitoring device into a selective one. Within this strategy of transformation, paperwork has played different roles. It has therefore constituted a sort of battlefield: the interpretations of the rules of registration, as well as of the documents which have tried to explain and correct them, have been at the centre of a conflict involving different state apparatuses. Moreover, forms of resistance against a certain use of paperwork have been carried out by those who are excluded from population registers, and often have had as their target the forms to be filled out for registration.

Paperwork therefore is 'paper "at work"' – namely, 'a set of practices and processes through which power circulates, and identities and boundaries are produced and materialise' (Borrelli and Andreetta 2019: 4). As such, it is the basis for the functioning of the state, as it produces 'legitimacy and establishes "truths" upon which bureaucrats as well as migrant individuals act' (Ibid.: 3).

Moreover, this chapter has shown that the power of paperwork for registration can be exercised both unintentionally and intentionally. In the first case, the act of registering performs a population even though those who use registers wish to merely represent it. In the second case, the same act is made just to shape the population in a desired manner. The power of paperwork, therefore, can be apparently technical or can be explicitly political. In any case, it is able to deeply affect the lives of migrants by making them municipally undocumented and hence impeding them from exercising the rights they are entitled to.

Enrico Gargiulo is Associate Professor of Sociology at the Department of Political and Social Sciences of the University of Bologna since 2019. He is the author of three books – *L'inclusione esclusiva. Sociologia della cittadinanza sociale* (FrancoAngeli, 2008), *Appartenenze precarie. La residenza tra inclusione ed esclusione* (Utet, 2019) and *Invisible Borders. Administrative Barriers and Citizenship in the Italian Municipalities* (Palgrave, 2021).

Note

1. As specified by Art. 12 of Leg. 1228/1954 and by Arts. 52–55 of DPR n. 223/1989.

References

About, I., J. Brown and G. Lonergan (eds) (2013), *Identification and Registration Practices in Transnational Perspective: People, Papers and Practices.* Basingstoke: Palgrave Macmillan.

Actionaid (2021), *L'anagrafe respingente. Una fotografia di Roma in emergenza.* Rome: Actionaid.

Andreetta, S. (2019), 'Writing for Different Audiences. Social Workers, Irregular Migrants and Fragmented Statehood in Belgian Welfare Bureaucracies', *Journal of Legal Anthropology* 3(2): 91–110.

Baxter, R.R. (1980), 'International Law in "Her Infinite Variety"', *International and Comparative Law Quarterly* 29(4): 549–66.

Bierschenk, T. (2019), 'Postface. Anthropology, Bureaucracy and Paperwork', *Journal of Legal Anthropology* 3(2): 111–19.

Borrás, S. and K. Jacobsson (2004), 'The Open Method of Co-Ordination and New Governance Patterns in the EU', *Journal of European Public Policy* 11(2): 185–208.

Borrelli, L.M. and S. Andreetta (2019), 'Introduction. Governing Migration through Paperwork', *Journal of Legal Anthropology* 3(2): 1–9.

Cabot, H. (2012), 'The Governance of Things: Documenting Limbo in the Greek Asylum Procedure', *PoLAR: Political and Legal Anthropology Review* 35(1): 11–29.

Caplan, J. and J. Torpey (eds) (2001), *Documenting Individual Identity: The Development of State Practices in the Modern World.* Princeton, NJ: Princeton University Press.

Carbonnier, J. (1978), *Sociologie juridique.* Paris: PUF.

Carrera, S. and A. Wiesbrock (2009), *Civic Integration of Third Country Nationals: Nationalism versus Europeanisation in the Common EU Immigration Policy*. Brussels: CEPS.

Costa-Lascoux, J. (1989), *De l'immigré au citoyen*. Paris: La Documentation francaise.

Curtis, B. (2002), *The Politics of Population: State Formation, Statistics, and the Census of Canada, 1840-1875*. Toronto: University of Toronto Press.

Dean, M. (1991), *The Constitution of Poverty: Toward a Theory of Liberal Governance*. London: Routledge.

De la Porte, C. (2002), 'Is the Open Method of Co-Ordination Appropriate for Organising Activities at European Level in Sensitive Policy Areas?' *European Law Journal* 8(1): 38–58.

Dubois, V. (2014), 'The State, Legal Rigor and the Poor: The Daily Practice of Welfare Control', *Social Analysis* 58(3): 38–55.

Eule, T. (2014), *Inside Immigration Law: Migration Management and Policy Application in Germany*. Farnham: Ashgate.

Eule, T., L. Borrelli, A. Lindberg and A. Wyss (2019), *Migrants Before the Law: Contested Migration Control in Europe*. London: Palgrave Macmillan.

Foucault, M. (2008), *The Birth of Biopolitics. Lectures at the Collège de France, 1978-1979*. Basingstoke: Palgrave Macmillan.

Freeman, R. and J. Maybin (2011), 'Documents, Practices and Policy', *Evidence & Policy* 7(2): 155–70.

Gargiulo, E. (2017), 'The Limits of Local Citizenship: Administrative Borders Within the Italian Municipalities', *Citizenship Studies* 21(3): 327–43.

——— (2021), *Invisible Borders. Administrative Barriers and Citizenship in the Italian Municipalities*. Basingstoke: Palgrave Macmillan.

——— (2023), 'Registration as a Border: Shaping the Population at the Local Level in Italy', *Geopolitics* 28(1): 439–63.

Gjergji, I. (2013), *Circolari amministrative e immigrazione*. Milano: FrancoAngeli.

——— (2020), 'Immigrazione e infra-diritto: dal governo per circolari alla Twitter-governance', *Etica & Politica / Ethics & Politics* 22(3): 323–39.

Goody, J. (1986), *The Logic of Writing and the Organization of Society*. Cambridge: Cambridge University Press.

Grazioli, M. and M. Caciagli (2018), 'Resisting to the Neoliberal Urban Fabric: Housing Rights Movements and the Re-appropriation of the "Right to the City" in Rome, Italy', *Voluntas* 29(4): 697–711.

Handelman, D. and E., Leyton (1978), *Bureaucracy and World View. Studies in the Logic of Official Interpretation*. Newfoundland Social and Economic Studies No. 22. St. John's: Memorial University of Newfoundland.

Heyman, J. (1995), 'Putting Power in the Anthropology of Bureaucracy: The Immigration and Naturalization Service at the Mexico-United States Border', *Current Anthropology* 36(2): 261–87.

——— (2012), 'Deepening the Anthropology of Bureaucracy', *Anthropological Quarterly*, 85(4): 1269–1277.

Higgs, E. (2011), *Identifying the English. A History of Personal Identification 1500 to the Present*. London: Bloomsbury.

Hing, B.O., J. Chacón and K.R. Johnson (2018), *Immigration Law and Social Justice*. New York: Wolters Kluwer.

Hirschman, A.O. (1970), *Exit, Voice, and Loyalty. Response to Decline in Firms, Organisations, and States*. Cambridge, MA: Harvard University Press.

Horton, S.B. and J. Heyman (eds) (2020), *Paper Trails: Migrants, Documents, and Legal Insecurity*. Global Insecurities. Durham, NC: Duke University Press.

Hull, M.S. (2008), 'Ruled by Records: The Expropriation of Land and the Misappropriation of Lists in Islamabad', *American Ethnologist* 35(4): 501–18.

——— (2012), 'Documents and Bureaucracy', *Annual Review of Anthropology* 41: 251–67.

ISTAT (1992), *Anagrafe della popolazione. Legge e regolamento anagrafico (legge 24 dicembre 1954, n. 1228, D.P.R. 30 maggio 1989, n. 223), avvertenze, note illustrative e normativa AIRE*. Rome: Istituto nazionale di statistica.

——— (2010), *Guida alla vigilanza anagrafica*. Rome: Istituto nazionale di statistica.

Jacobs, D. and A. Rea (2007), 'The End of National Models? Integration Courses and Citizenship Trajectories in Europe', *International Journal on Multicultural Societies (IJMS)* 9(2): 264–83.

Kazepov, Y. (1997), 'Senza casa e senza diritti. Le politiche locali contro l'esclusione sociale e abitativa dei senza fissa dimora', in P. Guidicini, G. Pieretti and M. Bergamaschi (eds), *Gli esclusi dal territorio. Comunità e politiche di welfare di fronte ai percorsi di impoverimento*. Milan: FrancoAngeli, pp. 153–90.

Lascoumes, P. and P. Le Gales (2007), 'Introduction: Understanding Public Policy through Its Instruments—From the Nature of Instruments to the Sociology of Public Policy Instrumentation', *Governance: An International Journal of Policy, Administration, and Institutions* 20(1): 1–21.

Latour, B. (2000), 'The Berlin Key or How to do Words with Things', in P.M. Graves-Brown (ed), *Matter, Materiality and Modern Culture*. London: Routledge, pp. 10–21.

Le Goff, J. (1978), 'Documento/Monumento', in *Enciclopedia Einaudi*, vol. V. Turin: Einaudi.

Lipsky, M. (2010), *Street-Level Bureaucracy: The Dilemmas of the Individual in Public Service*. New York: Russell Sage Foundation.

Lorenzetti, A. (2009), 'Il difficile equilibrio fra diritti di libertà e diritto alla sicurezza', in A. Lorenzetti and S. Rossi (eds), *Le ordinanze sindacali in materia di sicurezza pubblica e sicurezza urbana. Origini, contenuti, limiti*. Naples: Jovene, pp. 191–205.

Mathur, N. (2016), *Paper Tiger: Law, Bureaucracy and the Developmental State in Himalayan India*. Delhi: Cambridge University Press.

MEDU - Medici per i Diritti Umani (2019), *Le residenze invisibili: Indagine sulle emergenze abitative a Firenze*. Florence: MEDU.

Morozzo della Rocca, P. (2017), *I luoghi della persona e le persone senza luogo (itinerari di diritto civile ed anagrafico)*. Rimini: Maggioli.

Mudu, P. (2014), '"Ogni sfratto sarà una barricata": Squatting for Housing and Social Conflict in Rome', in Squatting Europe Kollective (eds), *Squatters' Movement in Europe: Commons and Autonomy as Alternatives to Capitalism*. London: Pluto Press.

Mukerji, C. (2011), 'Jurisdiction, Inscription, and State Formation: Administrative Modernism and Knowledge Regimes', *Theory and Society* 40(3): 223–45.

Naga (2019), *Senza (s)campo. Lo smantellamento del sistema di accoglienza per richiedenti asilo e rifugiati*. Un'indagine qualitativa. Milan: Naga.

Noiriel, G. (1991), *La Tyrannie du national. Le droit d'asile en Europe (1793–1993)*. Paris: Calmann-Lévy.

——— [1988] (1996), *The French Melting Pot: Immigration, Citizenship, and National Identity*. Minneapolis: University of Minnesota Press.

——— (1998), 'Surveiller les déplacements ou identifier les personnes? Contributions à l'historie du passeport en France de la Ier a la IIIe république', *Genèses: Sciences sociales et histoire* 30: 77–100.

Nonna Roma (2022), *Dalla strada alla casa. Un rapporto sui senza dimora a Roma*. Rome: NonnaRoma.

Nur, N. and A. Sethman (2017), 'Migration and Mobilization for the Right to Housing in Rome: New Urban Frontiers?' in P. Mudu and S. Chattopadhyay (eds), *Migration, Squatting and Radical Autonomy: Resistance and Destabilization of Racist Regulatory Policies and B/Ordering Mechanisms*. London: Routledge, pp. 78–92.

Oliveri, F. (2018), 'Racialization and Counter-Racialization in Times of Crisis: Taking Migrant Struggles in Italy as a Critical Standpoint on Race', *Ethnic and Racial Studies* 41(10): 1855–73.

Pelizza, A. (2016), 'Developing the Vectorial Glance: Infrastructural Inversion for the New Agenda on Governmental Information Systems', *Science, Technology and Human Values* 41(2): 298–321.

Pratt, A. (2005), *Securing Borders: Detention and Deportation in Canada*. Vancouver: UBC Press.

Riles, A. (2006), 'Introduction: In Response', in A. Riles (ed.), *Documents: Artifacts of Modern Knowledge*. Ann Arbor: University of Michigan Press, pp. 1–38.

Ruppert, E. (2007), 'Producing Population'. Cresc Working Paper Series, no. 37.

——— (2011), 'Population Objects: Interpassive Subjects', *Sociology* 45(2): 218–33.

Scott, J.C. (1998), *Seeing Like a State: How Certain Schemes to Improve the Human Condition Have Failed*. New Haven, CT: Yale University Press.

Searle, J. (1995), *The Construction of Social Reality*. New York: The Free Press.

Sigona, N. (2002), *Figli del ghetto. Gli italiani, i campi nomadi e l'invenzione degli zingari*. Civezzano: Nonluoghi Libere Edizioni.

Terpan, F. (2014), 'Soft Law in the European Union: The Changing Nature of EU Law', *European Law Journal* 21(1): 69–96.

Torpey, J. (2019), *The Invention of the Passport. Surveillance, Citizenship and the State*. Cambridge: Cambridge University Press.

Tuckett, Anna (2015), 'Strategies of Navigation: Migrants' Everyday Encounters with Italian Immigration Bureaucracy', *Cambridge Journal of Anthropology* 33(1): 113–28.

_______ (2018), *Rules, Paper, Status: Migrants and Precarious Bureaucracy in Contemporary Italy*. Stanford, CA: Stanford University Press.

Vetters, L. (2019), 'Administrative Guidelines as a Source of Immigration Law? Ethnographic Perspectives on Law at Work and in the Making', *Journal of Legal Anthropology* 3(2): 70–90.

Vismann, C. (2008), *Files: Law and Media Technology*. Stanford, CA: Stanford University Press.

Weisser, F. (2014), 'Practices, Politics, Performativities: Documents in the International Negotiations on Climate Change', *Political Geography* 40: 46–55.

4

Writing for Different Audiences

Social Workers, Irregular Migrants and Fragmented Statehood in Belgian Welfare Bureaucracies

Sophie Andreetta

Introduction

> 'They always say no the first time you ask for help', Marie explains about her local welfare administration. 'My lawyer told me that when they refuse my request, I can come back with the decision and we would take the matter to court'. (Excerpt from interview, 2019)

Marie moved to Belgium in 2012 in order to get medical treatment for a degenerative disease that couldn't be property treated in her home country, the Côte d'Ivoire. She travelled with a ten-day tourist visa but, as soon as she arrived, she was so sick that she had to be transported to the hospital directly from the airport. Three weeks later, her doctor advised her to contact her local welfare office – the Public Centre for Social Assistance (PCSA) – and ask for emergency medical assistance (EMA), so that they could cover the bills as well as her future treatments. Her request was denied on the grounds that her visa was delivered under the premise of sufficient resources. The social report leading to that decision also stated that Marie was consistently refusing to be truthful about the 'real' motives of her trip to Belgium, and that her visa had most likely been obtained under false pretences. Five months later, the court ruled in Marie's favour, ordering the administration to pay for her medical bills. Over the last six years, Marie has been to court (and won) three times against the welfare office.[1]

In Belgium, welfare administrations are tasked with delivering social assistance, which is meant to safeguard human dignity. It can take many shapes and forms: public centres for social assistance can help people pay for healthcare, they can give out furniture or household appliances, milk for new-borns, or nappies. They can also provide replacement revenue for those with no other source of income. Since 1996, however, social assistance has been limited to EMA for those without regular immigration status on Belgian territory – which is the case for Marie. Labour courts, which deal with all social-security matters including welfare, have, however, identified a series of exceptions based on human-rights principles such as the prohibition against torture and inhuman and degrading treatment. Thanks to one of these exceptions, in addition to her medical bills, Marie was also granted financial aid of €600 a month while she waits for immigration courts to settle her case.

In many European countries, recent welfare policies and administrative procedures have been intended to limit access to social assistance for those with a precarious immigration status (Pfirter 2019). However, in large cities especially, welfare bureaucracies are increasingly confronted with users without permanent residency, ranging from undocumented third-country nationals to European citizens with or without a registered address (Lafleur and Mescoli 2018), or people whose immigration claim is pending yet are considered 'undeportable' (De Genova 2002) for a variety of reasons. Building on the idea that states, public institutions and the work of civil servants can be understood by following the trail of paperwork, this chapter shows that while administrative procedures tend to effectively limit access to social assistance for those with a precarious legal status (Goldring, Berinstein and Bernhard 2009), in French-speaking Belgium social workers are still regularly taking special pains to facilitate migrants' access to emergency medical care and, sometimes, to financial social assistance despite the restrictions imposed by law and administrative guidelines. Based on ethnographic fieldwork conducted at welfare offices, legal clinics and labour courts, I demonstrate how social reports produced by the administration can not only become viable tools of contestations against the state in court but also offer a nuanced understanding of state-(non)citizens' (Tonkiss and Bloom 2015) relationships with public services.

When it comes to the welfare–migration nexus especially, scholars mainly investigate migrants' strategies outside of, or at the margins of, the state – highlighting the numerous obstacles in accessing public social-protection schemes (Sabates-Wheeler and Macauslan 2007; Alpes 2015; Chauvin and

Garcés-Mascareñas 2020). In parallel, civil servant's discretionary practices are often described as over-filtering (non)citizens claims and restricting access to public services (Spire 2008; Perna 2018, 2019; Eule, Loher and Wyss 2017). Against this backdrop, this chapter shows how welfare workers, when faced with claimants in particularly precarious situations, use state laws and documents in order to help further migrants' requests. These strategies of resistance against restrictive immigration/welfare policies illustrate the double-edged potential of state laws and documents. Social reports are produced by the state and contribute to welfare administrative practice, but they can also be used as evidence against the administration in court. State laws, through administrative guidelines, both restrict irregularized migrants'[2] access to social assistance and allow for contestations in court. The way documents are written, circulated and used as evidence within different parts of the state therefore eventually illustrates how the fragmented character of statehood offers potential for contestation and resistance within state institutions themselves, using state laws.

During the course of this research, I shadowed users, whom I usually met when they consulted legal clinics where they shared their difficulties or the reasons for their reluctance to ask for social assistance. I would accompany them to their local welfare office and act as a facilitator or a translator. Over a period of six months, in 2018 and 2019, I also shadowed social workers from four local welfare offices in Brussels and in Wallonia while they dealt with new requests, performed house visits, held interviews with beneficiaries and discussed cases with their colleagues. I read social reports; asked how they were written and for what purpose; and listened to the doubts, difficulties and pitfalls of doing social work for public-services agencies.[3]

As part of a field of research that studies the link between welfare bureaucracies and undocumented migrants, this chapter provides an analysis of the broader legal framework to shed new light on the emergence of restrictions on migrants' rights to social assistance over time. It also explores how welfare claims are filed and processed by the administration and delves into the significance of how documents are collected, circulated and processed by social workers. Finally, the chapter also focuses on the documentary evidence, such as reports, produced by social workers and shows how competing interpretations of law shape the content of these administrative documents. Understanding how documents are produced and utilized within and outside of welfare bureaucracies allows for insights into the ambiguities of civil servants' relationship to the state, and the tools available to them for dealing with conflicting loyalties – towards the administration as their employer, the beneficiaries as their 'clients' – and the ethical guidelines that frame and condition their professional identity.

Welfare Bureaucracies, Irregular Migrants and (Fragmented) Statehood

Inspired by Michael Lipsky's (1980) analysis of street-level bureaucracies, social scientists have generally widened the analytical lens on public institutions to include the practices of their civil servants (Maynard-Moody and Musheno 2000; Spire 2008; Bierschenk and Olivier de Sardan 2014; Thelen, Vetters and Benda-Beckmann 2017). These scholars approach bureaucracies from different yet overlapping angles. While some analyse interactions between front-desk civil servants and users (Heyman 1995; Spire 2008; Bierschenk and Olivier de Sardan 2014), others focus on paperwork (Hull 2012; Mathur 2016). Administrations were commonly studied as a way to understand statehood (Hull 2012; Bierschenk and Olivier de Sardan 2014), to analyse policy implementation (Spire 2008; Dubois 2010) or for the (often competing) understandings of law involved in state-(non)citizen interactions (Alpes and Spire 2014; Andreetta 2020). In studying the practices of street-level bureaucracies who are entrusted with the task of aiding migrants with a precarious legal status (Spire 2008; Cabot 2012; Perna 2018, 2019; Borrelli and Lindberg 2018), this chapter shifts the focus to the modes of producing, sharing and utilizing documents within and across public administrations in French-speaking Belgium. It draws on recent studies on paperwork and governance in Asia (Hull 2012; Gupta 2012) and on the idea that unpacking the discourses and practices of street-level bureaucrats is central to understanding statehood (Bierschenk and Olivier de Sardan 2014) – albeit, in this case, to the way migration continues to be governed beyond the purview of immigration desks.

Immigration desks and welfare offices were no exceptions in the study of public policy implementation by street-level bureaucrats (Evans 2010; Heyman 2009; Vetters 2019). Alexis Spire (2008) has shown that immigration bureaucrats often act as a first filter, taking it upon themselves to identify 'good', 'deserving' migrants. Vincent Dubois (2010), on the other hand, argues that contrary to immigration bureaucrats, welfare workers try to make bureaucratic processes more humane for those they consider most vulnerable. In a context where management models have increasingly been enforced in the public sector, others explore the influence of supervisors on the exercise of discretion by civil servants (Avril, Cartier and Siblot 2005; Evans 2010). Recent scholarship has also reflected on the role of affects and emotions in the work of street-level bureaucrats (Borrelli and Lindberg 2018). With respect to the aforementioned literature, the contribution of this study is threefold.

First, when it comes to the discretion of street-level bureaucrats, these scholars either looked at migration enforcement or at welfare desks (Evans

2010; Eule et al. 2019) – with the exception of quantitative studies assessing the 'deservingness' of various groups (Van Oorschot 2006; Jilke and Tummers 2018). While 'getting papers' is undeniably a key concern for irregular migrants, immigration desks are not the only public-service providers for migrants – especially those with a precarious legal status. This chapter, therefore, asks how welfare bureaucrats process the requests of those deemed both vulnerable and 'undesirable'.

Second, it proposes to study street-level bureaucrats not only through their interactions with users and with their superiors but also through the documentation they produce in the course of work. More recently, paperwork has been recast as being at the centre of bureaucracies, and as a vital artefact that offers insights into the manifestations of the state in its citizens' lives (Das 2004; Hull 2012; Gupta 2012; Mathur 2016). This contribution shows how documents can both limit access to social assistance (Gupta 2012) and, at the same time, help vulnerable groups fight for their rights. Reports written by and for the administration can indeed – and are sometimes meant to – be used 'against the state' in welfare court. As a consequence, negative decisions regularly serve as a first step in the long process of claiming financial assistance through litigation. Bureaucratic paperwork generated in the domain of social assistance, in this sense, illustrates the double-edged nature of official documents – that they can be used as a means for contestation not only by public-service users but also by the very civil servants who write and process them.

Third, the authors mentioned above mainly focused on civil servants' practices, especially on how they have exercised discretion and interacted with citizens. They analysed how laws were interpreted by the administration, highlighting the contingent nature of citizens' access to social or administrative rights, which partially relied on the person(ality) behind the desk – the way they saw their role, interpreted the law and implemented policies, which were often assumed to be coherent (Holm Vohnsen 2017: 16). The manner in which social assistance for irregular migrants is dispensed has put the spotlight on the dilemma of civil servants in the face of competing interpretations of laws and social policies – deriving from the courts, from federal administrations and from local hierarchies. At the same time, it facilitates an analysis of their daily responses to these competing interpretations.

This contribution, finally, reflects on the place and value of the state in the everyday work of civil servants – especially in their interactions with (non) citizens and, more specifically in the context of this study, with undocumented migrants (see also Spire 2008; Borrelli and Lindberg 2019). At the end of the 1990s, a small group of scholars pointed out the relevance of the street-level approach to studying statehood and governance (see Blundo and Olivier de Sardan 2007; Bierschenk and Olivier de Sardan 2014 Olivier de Sardan and De Herdt 2015). Within that framework, civil servants were not only investigated in terms of their interactions with citizens; their professional ethos and affective relationship with the state was also discussed in recent contributions (Verheul 2013; Lentz 2014; Andreetta and Kolloch 2018). This chapter builds on the idea that the practices of civil servants must also be analysed against the backdrop of their perception of and relationship to the state (Laszczkowski and Reeves 2018): in welfare administrations, social workers are paid by the state, they represent the state and are responsible for enforcing the policies of the state; yet, in some cases, which are key to this study, they also help people to litigate against the office that they work for.

In line with the aforementioned ideas, focusing on paperwork in welfare bureaucracies eventually reveals the fragmented (Bierschenk 2014) yet interconnected nature of statehood – in this case, of the Belgian state. With every request sent to the local welfare office, information is transmitted from and to various federal agencies – some responsible for funding local offices. The guidelines and instructions of these agencies can be challenged, and sometimes overturned, by state courts. Welfare administrations can produce documents rejecting a claim in compliance with federal regulations, while simultaneously arguing in favour of granting social assistance in the same instance in internal reports, which are eventually used for judicial appeals.

The Different 'Parts' of the State: Welfare Laws, Institutions and Funding Practices

Welfare laws and administrative guidelines have become increasingly restrictive over the years, especially when it comes to those with a precarious immigration status. Against this backdrop, labour courts have argued for the need to safeguard fundamental rights – in effect, creating situations such as Marie's, where migrants approach the administration expecting a negative outcome which their lawyer can subsequently challenge in court.[4] This section will detail the legal and the institutional framework within which social-assistance requests are assessed.

In line with the Belgian Constitution, which declares that 'everyone is entitled to live in conditions that conform to human dignity' (art. 23), in 1976, local welfare administrations, also called Public Social Assistance Centres (PSACs), were created to dispense social assistance to guarantee that people lived in humane conditions. They replaced the old Commissions for Public Assistance (CPA) that were created in 1925 and organized help for 'the poor' at the local level. The CPA's help was often arbitrary and associated with charity – rather than with the subjective rights that beneficiaries could claim (Martens 2019). In conjunction with the creation of CPAs, the Belgian Parliament also voted for the law on EMA,[5] the precise modalities of which were later defined in a royal decree (1965).

Far from being restricted to health emergencies in the strictest sense – in which case, people can immediately be treated in hospital – EMA covers both preventive and curative care, provided it is deemed necessary by a physician. It can, however, only be granted to irregular migrants who are in a 'state of need', thus excluding people with private health insurance or with social-security coverage from another European country as well as those owning sufficient resources to privately cover the costs of the treatment. When EMA is granted, people usually collect a 'medical card' from the welfare office, which allows them to go to a designated general practitioner (GP) to buy the prescribed medicine at the pharmacy and, if necessary, to designated specialists to get treatment for a specific disease. Medical cards, generally valid for three months, can be renewed through application.

From 1976 onwards, CPAs became PCSAs, which, aside from social assistance, were tasked with implementing a minimum income scheme for Belgian citizens with no other source of income: the *minimum de moyens d'exisentence* (1974); since 2002, the Social Inclusion Revenue (*Revenu d'Intégration Sociale*). Social assistance, on the other hand, could take many shapes and forms: PSACs could, and still can, help people pay for healthcare and give out furniture or household appliances, milk or nappies for new-borns. They could also provide financial assistance for non-Belgian nationals.

The 1976 law on Public Social Assistance initially did not include specific provisions regarding those without a regular immigration status, which meant that although they were disqualified from the minimum income scheme they could benefit from social assistance that included, but was not limited to, medical assistance. The 57th article of the law was modified for the first time in 1984, in an attempt to limit social assistance for 'illegal' migrants to the bare minimum; however, it still allowed administrations to grant them the same benefits as those given to Belgian citizens. In 1993, the same article was modified again, and limited 'illegal' migrants' social assistance to the (financial) help that was necessary to allow them to leave the country. In 1996, social assistance was limited to EMA.[6]

Labour courts, however, came up with a series of exceptions to enable social assistance to irregular migrants on a regular basis. The first kind of exceptions are linked to the impossibility of deporting people to their own country due to medical, administrative or family reasons, such as people who are severely ill or heavily pregnant, whose home country refuses to recognize them as their citizens or who are a parent to Belgian children.

More recently, the European Court of Justice[7] ruled that those who had applied for Belgian residency based on a severe medical condition and were denied their claim by the Foreign Office, forcing them to bring their case before immigration courts, could claim their right to an effective recourse against administrative decisions and also be granted financial assistance. In other words, deporting them to a country where they claim they could not get proper treatment, or leaving them without any resources on Belgian soil, would violate their fundamental rights. National courts, however, have to assess whether the basis for appeal is substantial and the medical condition serious enough.

Citizens and migrants who wish to benefit from social assistance – medical or otherwise – must file their request with the PSAC of their municipality. Based on a 'social inquiry' conducted by a caseworker, the administration examines whether the applicant meets the legal criteria. A decision is eventually made by the PSAC's council and the applicant is notified by post. When granted in compliance with the guidelines of the federal Public Planning Service for Social Integration (SPP IS), social assistance and minimum income are funded by the ministry. Those guidelines define, for example, what kinds of medical treatment constitute EMA – which means that the costs of other treatments must be assumed by the respective local office. Should they be unsatisfied with the outcome, people can either ask the PSAC's council for a hearing or take their case to court: both options are generally mentioned in the 'small print' of every decision.[8] If the judge finds against the administration, the costs are eventually covered by the federal state regardless of administrative guidelines.

This section, therefore, has illustrated the plurality of norms and institutions involved in the provision of social assistance and highlights the rising significance of the Belgian judiciary, specifically in the case of irregular migrants.

Making a Case for Social Assistance: Documents as Filters

This section explores how social-assistance requests are filed, and the necessary documentation constituted in local welfare offices based on documents requested from migrants, on the one hand, and the ones that social workers hand out to migrants, on the other. It shows how paperwork can both allow effective action against the administration and act as a filter to limit access to public assistance.

Although every local welfare office is organized slightly differently, generally, offices in larger cities process first-time applications with the help of a specific team composed of administrative staff or of social workers. These front-line workers are tasked with registering the claims, assessing whether or not people are in the right place and if their claim for social assistance is likely to be legitimate – in which case, they proceed to 'opening a case-file'. People who are deemed unlikely to qualify are either redirected to other public-services agencies or simply told that they do not meet the legal requirements for public assistance. Once they have successfully passed through this first filter, people are given an appointment, a list of documents they need to present and a receipt proving that their request has been filed with the administration. The welfare office then has thirty days to examine and reply to their request.

Those documents represent the second filter in accessing social assistance: in most welfare offices, claims will only be examined once the file is deemed 'complete' with all the requested documents, which conditions and limits access to social assistance – often beyond the legal provisions, as most offices systematically ask for bank statements, for example, while they are under no legal obligation to do so. Legal provisions only refer to the 'absence of resources' and the 'state of need', but do not stipulate how these should be assessed. As the following example illustrates, local bureaucracies often opt for a strict interpretation of legal principles, effectively limiting beneficiaries' access to public assistance (Gupta 2012).

> *14 March 2019, Brussels*: I'm accompanying Elizabeth, a 40-year-old woman from the DRC [Democratic Republic of the Congo], to the welfare administration in order to request emergency medical assistance. Elizabeth explains that she came to Brussels in order to work for her embassy and decided to stay on when her contract ended, although she had by then lost her legal immigration status. 'My kids have been going to school here for several years', she explains, 'in my country, they won't get any education. Besides, there is no unemployment benefits for me, no more work'. Two weeks ago, she tried to get EMA from anther office. When they told her that they would have to perform a house visit as a part of the social inquiry, she had to withdraw her request: she lives with a friend, also in a precarious legal situation. 'I begged her, but she does not want a civil servant to come into the house', Elizabeth explains.

The purpose of those visits is to verify the actual residency, which is one of the legal conditions for granting social assistance. Some social workers only check that the person is there; others ask to see the different rooms in the house and take notes of the belongings – or the absence thereof. Those visits are also, in theory, meant to help caseworkers[9] to further connect with the person and potentially identify other needs that the administration could help with – although when it comes to beneficiaries with a precarious legal status, 'help' is often limited to medical assistance. In practice, social workers generally focus on the first point, as demonstrated in this further account regarding Elizabeth:

We get to the PSAC. Elizabeth presents her passport at the front desk. Half an hour later, Mr. Paco, one of the social workers, shows us the way into this office. He sits behind the computer and asks: 'So, why are you here?' Elizabeth turns to me. 'We came to request emergency medical assistance', I explain. Mr. Paco asks for her passport and notices the old visa. He asks about the validity, and then explains: 'because the information you give us here can go to the foreign office'.

Elizabeth interrupts: 'I don't think you understand me. My passport is no longer valid, nor is my visa. I'm illegal here'. 'All right. So, where do you live then?' For over half an hour, Mr. Paco asks about where she stays, with whom, where she eats, where she does laundry, where and how her children go to school, how she pays for food and for the bus, where she buys phone cards. He also asks why she came to Belgium, how and when, what kind of applications she made for residency, why she stayed when her visa expired. Mr. Paco asks how she gets by, especially with two underage children. Finally, he asks about her health. She didn't bring a doctor's certificate, but she can bring one next week. He asks again about her living situation: Elizabeth explains that she left her friends' house and has been staying in a park for the last few weeks – this way, she places herself under the jurisdiction of this particular office. Mr. Paco highlights that given the fact that she has two children, this will raise questions from his superiors.

He eventually prints out a series of documents. The first one contains an appointment in two weeks: provided her file is complete, she can pick up her 'health card'. He gives her a receipt, and asks her to sign three other documents: one where she declares she has no resources in Belgium or abroad, a second one stating the duties of the beneficiary – informing their caseworker of any change in their administrative, professional, or private life, responding to the administration's request for information, meeting with their caseworkers when summoned – and a third one concerning her children. 'Here, you choose one box, and you sign', Mr. Paco states. Elizabeth turns to me. 'I don't know what this is'. Mr. Paco explains: 'This document tells you about the possibility of securing food and housing within a centre, because the state is concerned about children staying in the street. You can say you'd like the accommodation, but then you may eventually get deported, or you can refuse, it is your choice. Just tick the box and sign it'. Elizabeth hesitates. Some NGOs warn migrants against signing this form, which welfare offices' lawyers sometimes use in court to argue that people are not really in need of assistance, because they denied it when it was offered. I ask: 'Can we bring it back with the medical certificate next week?' 'No problem, but her file won't be complete until I have this', Mr. Paco explains, 'I can't give her medical assistance without it. It is a requirement from the ministry'. (Fieldnotes, March 2019)

Beyond the legal framework, welfare administrations are also bound by administrative guidelines from the ministry – the respect of which conditions federal reimbursements to the local administration. If those requirements are not met and requests are granted anyway, local offices lose a portion of their funding. The federal administration, however, performs checks only in cases where public assistance was granted. If local offices wrongly deny someone medical or financial assistance, no penalties will occur. These selective control practices often lead to a restrictive interpretation of administrative guidelines by welfare offices. In the case described above, administrative guidelines only request that welfare offices inform families with a precarious legal status of the possibility of being housed in a centre. Having people sign a document where they choose to accept or refuse public housing therefore effectively adds one condition – filling out the form and, most likely, denying the state's help beyond emergency medical care – that would qualify them for medical treatment. This condition can, furthermore, potentially limit people's ability to claim financial assistance later on.

The documents handed out, on the other hand, materialize the claim. With the receipt proving that a request was made, and remained unanswered, people can take their request directly to court if local offices do not make a decision within thirty days. Failure to issue such documents, makes it impossible for users to take their case to court. Front-desk workers – who interview visitors about their immigration status, their home accommodation and their resources – regularly inform them that they, unfortunately, might not qualify for any financial benefits. Those requests for social assistance are, therefore, never formally filed or examined, and the *de facto* negative decisions that result from the front-desk interactions make it impossible to challenge them as a consequence – because there is no (paper) evidence that a claim was filed and denied. People are also given copies of the documents that they were asked to sign at the time they filed their request. Those documents include a declaration of their resources and family status, whereby they commit to keeping their social worker informed of 'any change'. Most caseworkers explain that this involves a potential change of address, of immigration status or employment. Failure to volunteer such information can be considered fraud, and lead to the withdrawal of assistance as well as to financial penalties. When it comes to irregular migrants especially, those documents are usually presented as 'necessary for the case to be opened', never translated and hardly explained – unless people specifically ask. The way documents are handed out, therefore, results in 'illegible' administrative procedures (Eule, Loher, and Wyss 2017; Eule et al. 2019; Borrelli and Lindberg 2019), and their outcomes are impossible to challenge as a consequence.

In the first steps of assessing a claim for social assistance, paperwork therefore largely functions as a selection mechanism: those who do not have the right papers and those who cannot comply with the growing requests for documents and signatures are simply disqualified. However, because they help materialize the claims, the same documents are potent tools for contestation 'against the state' in court – when a request is denied or remains unanswered. The way files are constituted within welfare bureaucracies also helps depict legal and policy implementation as a sedimented and fragmented process (Bierschenk 2014; Gupta 2012), where, with each interpretative 'layer', access to public assistance becomes subject to a growing number of conditions.

Writing Social Reports: Professional Ethos, Conflicting Interpretations and Competing Loyalties

After a case file is deemed complete by the caseworker in charge, he/she has to 'do the case' (*faire le dossier*), which involves writing a report that summarizes the results of the investigation and recommends granting or denying the applicant's request. Once validated, the applicant is notified of the decision. Social reports are, in theory, meant to be read and shared within the administration and controlled by the ministry. Users never get to see them unless they formally make a request to read their files. Welfare decisions, on the other hand, are meant for the beneficiaries. They have to be justified by both law and facts, and can, if beneficiaries disagree, be challenged in court. In the case of irregular migrants, however, social workers sometimes anticipate or even encourage people to take their (negative) decision to court and adapt their report accordingly. These documents, thus, show how, beyond the influence of supervisors (Evans 2010), civil servants engage with competing instructions and interpretations of law – on the one hand, of the ministry, which restricts social assistance for irregular migrants; on the other, of state courts. How social workers finally write up their report illustrates their double-edged relationship with the state: social reports carry the 'signature of the state' (Das 2004) yet, at the same time, the very same reports are used to challenge the state's administrative decision.

Writing reports is a crucial part of the social workers' job and, in fact, accounts for more than half their workload. The reports generally summarize a range of issues, such as the person's administrative situation; the circumstances that led them to request welfare assistance; their journey as a migrant; and their education, professional experience and healthcare situation. Social reports also include a description of the person's home, after the social worker performs a home visit, and the recommendation of the respective caseworkers on the merits of the request.

While the wording of decisions is often described as too legalistic, and mainly based on templates, social workers often highlight the degree of autonomy and discretion they enjoy in writing reports.

> 'You can present things however you'd like', Romuald, a 33-year-old social worker explains, 'because even if your boss is going to read what you wrote, and check that you have all of the documents, in the end you are the only person who meets with beneficiaries'. (April 2019)

> 'You can really sway a case, influence its outcome, with the way you present things in your social report', Anne, 32 (June 2018), confirms.

Most agencies provide their employees with a template for the report, with sections earmarked for information on – as mentioned above – such aspects as identity, education, work history, family ties and health. Although reports are meant to be 'objective', social workers all agree that in presenting their client's situation they can either insist on the precariousness of their living conditions or of their health, or, on the contrary, indicate that people should be able to get by without help. Reports from social workers regularly describe the appearance of the person and their own impressions of them based on their most recent interview, and also whether or not their story seems 'credible'. Marie's[10] social worker, for example, wrote that she was not being truthful about the reasons for travelling to Belgium and about the manner in which she had obtained her visa. Her social report argued that it was likely that Marie was lying and, therefore, should be denied EMA. Such comments, however, rarely appear on official notifications. Thus, while the document that Marie received simply stated that this form of social assistance could not be granted to those holding a valid visa, the documentary evidence prepared by the social workers may serve as the main reason why requests are granted or denied. Administrative boards rely almost exclusively[11] on paper realities – what social workers write and describe in their reports – in order to decide on specific cases.

Supervisors, however, can request more details, or more (documentary) evidence. Social workers' practices, especially when it comes to documents, therefore, partly depend on their superiors (Evans 2010).

> 'I never used to have people sign at the bottom of my reports', Romuald remembers, 'then I had a new supervisor and he really insisted on it. He even blocked some of my cases because of that'. (March 2019)

Supervisors can also have a say in a case's outcome if they conclude that the conditions for social assistance have not been met or that more information needed to be provided, such as on the resources of relatives or potential possessions abroad.

Social workers, however, are careful to point out that their final recommendation, as ratified by the PSAC's council, is mostly contingent on administrative guidelines and the associated federal funding. On the one hand, the ministry's guidelines are based on a national administrative interpretation of welfare laws: irregular migrants are granted EMA on the condition that their visa has expired and they have no guarantors in the country. Labour courts, on the other hand, regularly find that withholding treatment to those carrying a visa would breach Article 3 of the European Convention on Human Rights (ECHR), or that financial assistance must be granted to those who are proven too ill to be deported. In such situations, social workers end up in a double bind – or, more accurately, are trapped in contradictory interpretations of the law.

In cases involving irregular migrants, social reports are, as a consequence, regularly at odds with the final decision, which is often drafted by the social workers themselves and validated by the supervisor and eventually by the PSAC's council. Although requests for financial assistance are almost always denied, social reports frequently describe situations where people have no source of income and very few possessions. At best, most are granted just the EMA. Other social workers, like Anne, remain committed to requesting financial help on behalf of their clients in their recommendations: she noted:

> I have this case, a woman and her children, they have no papers, and they really live in terrible conditions. Every time I do my 3-monthly report for EMA, I also ask for financial help. It's always denied. But I think my job is also to write all of that. (April 2018)

Welfare offices almost systematically reject requests that would involve payments not stipulated in the administrative guidelines, and therefore not state funded, for financial reasons. If they are ordered by welfare courts to do so, however, the amounts granted will be reimbursed by the ministry. Social workers who deal with irregular migrants are generally aware of this problem and write their social reports accordingly: most mention the need to carefully weigh their words in a document that could eventually be used as evidence in court proceedings. Some even write in the hope that their reports will be used in court, as Anne explains:

> I asked for social assistance on our own funds, and I knew it was going to be denied. But I'm thinking that if the lady's lawyer goes to court, and my report is in her favour, maybe the judge will decide in her favour too. (March 2018)

Helping or encouraging people to go to court, therefore, is sometimes the only strategy at hand to secure social assistance when local administrations are unable to afford it. Melissa, a 32-year-old social worker explains:

> We denied social assistance and gave them emergency medical care, and then we worked together with the lawyer because I wasn't 'against' this family. I did everything I could in my social reports, I explained how the family lived, I explained it was inhumane to leave children in conditions such as those: there was no food . . . the house was mouldy, there was no heat, no electricity and no water, it was living conditions like I rarely saw them. (May 2018)

On Melissa's advice, the family went to a pro bono lawyer and took the welfare office to court. Six months later, they were granted social assistance. In those situations, social workers often mention conflicting loyalties, to the state as their employer and to their *professional ethos* on the other, as Francine noted:

> There are rules, there are laws, and there are the bosses of the administration, but you are there to help people. My job is to help people, it is not to help my employer not to give money. (May 2018)

Cases like Melissa's are, however, the exception: mostly, irregular migrants only get access to emergency healthcare – on the condition that they agree to file a request supported by a medical certificate and endure a month's wait until their case is decided upon. Social workers only offer the tools favourable for litigation if they judge that the situation justifies it – 'living conditions like I've rarely seen' – and believe that their 'client' would have a chance to win. Getting someone to go before the court, thus, often involves explaining that a negative decision is expected but it is possible to sue the administration. Such a strategy is only used in favour of those identified as 'really needing it', in the same way that teachers tend to help students primarily on the basis of *needed deservingness* (Jilke and Tummers 2018). In welfare administrations, 'needed deservingness' is often established on an emotional basis – whereby social workers confess to being 'touched' or 'moved' by certain situations or conditions. Francine adds:

> Once, I even called the lawyer and coordinated with him; it was a women, her daughter had a very rare disease. The hospital was suggesting experimental treatment, and their insurance wouldn't cover it. Because they still had a visa, I couldn't grant EMA. I just couldn't tell them 'thank you, and goodbye'.

When it comes to irregular migrants, social workers constantly have to balance the stipulations of the state – or, more accurately, of the administration – with the interests of those who come to them for help. This section has also shown how documents meant to be written by and for the administration are sometimes intended for the judiciary, hence influencing the information selected or omitted in the drafting of those reports. Valérie (a social worker) explains:

> I now pay much [more] attention to the way I describe people's home after my visit, because I had a case where the judge questioned the people's state of need, because I wrote about the furniture, the TV, the clothes. The family had been living here for 10 years, of course there was a lot of stuff. When we write about home visits, we are trying to establish effective residency, so it made sense to describe all of that. Since then, I'm much more succinct in my reports.

Besides the fragmented nature of the Belgian state, social workers' strategies and writing practices eventually illustrate its interconnectedness: documents, although initially written for one purpose, are transmitted and utilized by several administrative sites to serve their own agendas. Those reports also act as spaces for contestation, not only for irregular migrants and their lawyers but also for social workers who manage to use administrative documents against the very administration that generates them. Contrary to the common assumption that street-level bureaucrats break or circumvent the law on a regular basis (Blundo and Le Meur 2009; Holm Vohnsen 2017), such bureaucrats, in writing for divergent audiences, use the law and official procedures to help migrants mount cases not so much against the state as against its most recent policies and modes of enforcement.

Conclusion

Foreigners in Belgium are entitled to different forms of social assistance. Depending on their immigration status, these range from emergency medical care to welfare benefits. But in a context where residence permits are constantly updated, re-examined or sometimes withdrawn by the administration, the relationship between irregularized migrants and the Belgian welfare state is at best tenuous.

Decisions on requests for financial or healthcare assistance are made on the basis of documentary evidence. Shifting the focus to the social effects of paperwork generated in the context of the Belgian welfare regime, various sections of this chapter have shown its deployment towards a more restrictive implementation of welfare laws – in line with the current political agenda.

Social workers in Belgium are, at the same time, at pains to create spaces for contestation against administrative practices. Contrary to Spire's (2008) immigration bureaucrats, Belgian social workers sometimes use their discretion to help further migrants' claims to social assistance. Rather than seeing their role as protecting the state, they regularly question the accuracy of the ministry's interpretation of national laws and highlight their ethical and professional commitment to help those in need.

The case of welfare for irregular migrants illustrates how street-level bureaucrats navigate between competing interpretations of law and policy guidelines and adapt their practices accordingly. Detailed ethnographic research helped show that welfare workers ensure that they comply with the administrative guidelines for financial reasons, while, at the same time, encouraging litigation against the administration by producing documents that can help the vulnerable groups win. This last point helps demonstrate that the fragmented nature of statehood – and the conflicting norms that state actors must reconcile on a daily basis as a result – simultaneously allows for increased control of (non)citizens and civil servants alike, and for acting against or beyond such control. Official documents, laws and administrative guidelines have the potential to both restrict and to further migrants' rights – depending on how they are worded, which forum they are brought before and how they are used.

Sophie Andreetta works as a FRS-FNRS Research Associate within the University of Liège. Her work focuses on the place, and the many potential roles/strategies of law in policy areas generally perceived as functioning based on informal logics. At the intersection of social–legal studies and the anthropology of the state, her publications use ethnographic methods to delve into (non)citizens' relationships with law and state institutions, and the concrete implementation of public policies. Email: sandreetta@uliege.be

Notes

1. Some of the facts of this case were altered in order to guarantee anonymity. All participants were given pseudonyms, as well as approximate ages and job titles.
2. This chapter refers to migrants who, under welfare law, are categorized as 'illegal'. Building on De Genova (2002) and Goldring Berinstein and Bernhard (2009), I also refer to them as irregularized or as holding a precarious immigration status.
3. After they graduate, social workers can choose between different fields: welfare, healthcare, the youth or the family sector, either within public institutions such as hospitals or PCSAs – the largest employer for social-work graduates – or in nongovernmental organizations (NGOs). Working 'for the state' as a social worker comes with specific obligations, not only with respect to the wellbeing of the beneficiaries but also in terms of complying with certain rules and being loyal to the state as well as to those using public services.

4. Organic Law of 8 July 1976 on Public Social Assistance Centres.
5. Law of 8 July 1964 on Emergency Medical Assistance, *Moniteur belge*, 25 July 1964; Organic Law of 8 July 1976 on Public Social Assistance Centres, *Moniteur belge*, 5 August 1976.
6. Organic Law of 8 July 1976 on Public Social Assistance Centres.
7 See CJEU Case C-562/13, Abdida, judgment of 18 December 2014, ECLI:EU:C:2014:2453.
8 Law introducing the 'Charter' of the social beneficiary, *Moniteur belge*, 6 September 1995.
9. In the context of welfare administrations, social workers are the caseworkers. The terms are used interchangeably.
10. See introductory vignette.
11. Except when people make use of their right to be heard – less than one case per month.

References

Alpes, M.J. (2015), 'Social Protection and Migration Control: the Case of Migrant Care Workers and Parisian Welfare Hotels', *Transnational Social Review – A Social Work Journal* 5(3): 1–16.

Alpes, M.J. and A. Spire (2014), 'Dealing with Law in Migration Control: The Powers of Street-Level Bureaucrats at French Consulates', *Social and Legal Studies* 23(2): 261–74.

Andreetta, S. (2020), 'The Symbolic Power of the State: Inheritance Disputes and Litigants' Judicial Trajectories in Cotonou', PoLAR: Political and Legal Anthropology Review 43(1): 5–20, doi:10.1111/plar.12341.

Andreetta, S. and A. Kolloch (2018), 'Money, Morality and Magistrates. Prosecuting and Judging in the Republic of Benin', *Journal of Legal Pluralism and Unofficial Law* 50(2): 145–66, doi: 10.1080/07329113.2018.1494407.

Avril, C., M. Cartier and Y. Siblot (2005), 'Les rapports aux services publics des usagers et agents de milieux populaires : quels effets des reformes de modernisation?' *Sociétés Contemporaires* 58(2): 5–18, Retrieved 7 March 2024 from https://www.cairn.info/revue-societes-contemporaines-2005-2-page-5.htm.

Bierschenk, T. (2014), 'Sedimentation, Fragmentation and Normative Double-Binds in (West) African Public Services', in Thomas Bierschenk and Jean-Pierre Olivier de Sardan (eds), *States at Work. Dynamics of African Bureaucracies*. Leiden; Boston, MA: Brill, pp. 221–49.

Bierschenk, T. and J-P. Olivier de Sardan (eds) (2014), *States at Work. Dynamics of African Bureaucracies*. Leiden; Boston, MA: Brill.

Blundo, G. and P-Y. Le Meur (eds) (2009), *The Governance of Daily Life in Africa. Ethnographic Explorations of Public and Collective Services*. Leiden: Brill.

Blundo, G. and J.-P. Olivier de Sardan (eds) (2007), *État et corruption en Afrique. Une anthropologie comparative des relations entre fonctionnaires et usagers (Bénin, Niger, Sénégal)*. Paris: Karthala.

Borrelli, L.M. and A. Lindberg (2018), 'The Creativity of Coping: Alternative Tales of Moral Dilemmas among Migration Control Officers', *International Journal of Migration and Border Studies* 4(3): 163–78. doi: 10.1504/IJMBS.2018.093876.

Borrelli, L. M., and A. Lindberg (2019), 'Paperwork Performances: Legitimating State Violence in the Swedish Deportation Regime', *Journal of Legal Anthropology* 3(2): 50–69. Retrieved 6 February 2024 from https://doi.org/10.3167/jla.2019.030204.

Cabot, H. (2012), 'The Governance of Things: Documenting Limbo in the Greek Asylum Procedure', *PoLAR: Political and Legal Anthropology Review* 35(1): 11–29, doi: 10.1111/j.1555-2934.2012.01177.x.

Chauvin, S. and B. Garcés-Mascareñas (2020), 'Contradictions in the Moral Economy of Migrant Irregularity', in S. Spencer A. and Triandafyllidou (eds), *Migrants with Irregular Status in Europe*. Cham: SpringerOpen, pp. 33–49.

Das, V. (2004), 'The Signature of the State: the Paradox of Illegibility', in D. Poole and V. Das, *Anthropology in the Margins of the State*. Oxford: James Currey, pp. 225–52.

De Genova, N. (2002), 'Migrant "Illegality" and Deportability in Everyday Life', *Annual Review of Anthropology* 31: 419–47, doi: 10.11146/annurev.anthro.31.040402.085432.

Dubois, V. (2010), *The Bureaucrat and the Poor: Encounters in French Welfare Offices*. Aldershot: Ashgate.

Eule, T., L.M. Borrelli, A. Lindberg and A. Wyss (2019), *Migrants Before the Law. Contested Migration Control in Europe*. London: Palgrave Macmillan.

Eule, T., D. Loher and A. Wyss (2017), 'Contested Control at the Margins of the State', *Journal of Ethnic and Migration Studies* 44(16): 2717–29. doi: 10.1080/1369183X.2017.1401511.

Evans, T. (2010), *Professional Discretion in Welfare Services: Beyond Street-Level Bureaucracy*. London, New York: Routledge.

Goldring, L., C. Berinstein and J. K. Bernhard (2009), 'Institutionalizing Precarious Migratory Status in Canada', *Citizenship Studies* 13(3): 239–65, doi: 10.1080/13621020902850643.

Gupta, A. (2012), *Red Tape : Bureaucracy, Structural Violence, and Poverty in India*. A John Hope Franklin Center Book, Durham, NC: Duke University Press.

Heyman, J. McC. (1995), 'Putting Power in the Anthropology of Bureaucracy: The Immigration and Naturalization Service at the Mexico–United States Border', *Current Anthropology* 36(2): 261–87.

——— (2009), 'Trust, Privilege, and Discretion in the Governance of the US Borderlands with Mexico', *Canadian Journal of Law and Society / Revue Canadienne Droit Et Société* 24(3): 367–90.

Holm Vohnsen, N. (2017), *The Absurdity of Bureaucracy. How Implementation Works*. Manchester: Manchester University Press.

Hull, M.S. (2012), *Government of Paper: The Materiality of Bureaucracy in Urban Pakistan*. Berkeley: University of California Press.

Jilke, S. and L. Tummers (2018), 'Which Clients are Deserving of Help? A Theoretical Model and Experimental Test', *Journal of Public Administration Research and Theory* 28(2): 226–38, doi: 10.1093/jopart/muy002.

Lafleur, J-M. and E. Mescoli (2018), 'Creating Undocumented EU Migrants through Welfare: A Conceptualization of Undeserving and Precarious Citizenship', *Sociology* 52(3): 480–96, doi: 10.1177/0038038518764615.

Laszczkowski, M. and M. Reeves (eds) (2018), *Affective States. Entanglements, Suspensions, Suspicions*. London, New York: Berghahn Books.

Lentz, C. (2014), '"I Take an Oath to the State, Not the Government": Career Trajectories and Professional Ethics of Ghanaian Public Servants', in Thomas Bierschenk and Jean-Pierre Olivier de Sardan (eds), *States at Work. Dynamics of African Bureaucracies*. Leiden: Brill, pp. 175–204.

Lipsky, M. (1980), *Street-Level Bureaucracy: Dilemmas of the Individual in Public Services*. New York: Russell Sage Foundation.

Martens, J. (2019), 'La dignité humaine comme mesure de l'aide sociale', in C. Bedoret and S. Gilson, *Les contours de l'aide sociale*. Limal: Anthemis, pp. 27–52.

Mathur, N. (2016), *Paper Tiger. Law, Bureaucracy and the Developmental State in Himalayan India*. Cambridge: Cambridge University Press.

Maynard-Moody, S. and M. Musheno (2000), *Cops, Teachers, Counselors: Stories from the Front Lines of Public Service*. Ann Arbor: University of Michigan Press.

Olivier de Sardan, J-P. and T. De Herdt (2015), *Real Governance and Practical Norms in Sub-Saharan Africa. The Game of Rules*. London: Routledge.

Perna, R. (2018), 'Re-Bounding EU Citizenship from Below: Practices of Healthcare for "(Il)Legitimate EU Migrants" in Italy', *Journal of Ethnic and Migration Studies* 44(5): 829–48, doi: 10.1080/1369183X.2017.1362977.

——— (2019), 'Bound between Care and Control: Institutional Contradictions and Daily Practices of Healthcare for Migrants in an Irregular Situation in Italy', *Ethnic and Racial Studies* 42(12): 2103–22, doi: 10.1080/01419870.2018.1533645.

Pfirter, L. (2019), 'Constructing "Unteachability" through Menacing Warnings', *Journal of Legal Anthropology* 3(2): 29–49, doi: 10.3167/jla.2019.030203.

Sabates-Wheeler, R. and I. Macauslan (2007), 'Migration and Social Protection: Exposing problems of access', *Development* 50(4): 26–32.

Spire, A. (2008), *Accueillir ou reconduire. Enquête sur les guichets de l'immigration*. Paris: Raisons d'agir.

Thelen, T., L. Vetters and K. Benda-Beckmann (2017), *Stategraphy. Towards a Relational Anthropology of the State*. New York, Oxford: Berghahn Books.

Tonkiss, K. and T. Bloom (2015), 'Theorising Noncitizenship: Concepts, Debates and Challenges', *Citizenship Studies* 19(8): 837–52.

Van Oorschot, W. (2006), 'Making the Difference in Social Europe: Deservingness Perceptions among Citizens of European Welfare States', *Journal of European Social Policy* 16(1): 23–42, doi: 10.1177/0958928706059829.

Verheul, S. (2013), '"Rebels" and "Good Boys": Patronage, Intimidation and Resistance in Zimbabwe's Attorney General's Office after 2000', *Journal of Southern African Studies* 39(4): 765–82, doi: 10.1080/03057070.2013.858544.

Vetters, L. (2019), 'Administrative Guidelines as a Source of Immigration Law?: Ethnographic Perspectives on Law at Work and in the Making', *Journal of Legal Anthropology* 3(2): 70–90. doi: 10.3167/jla.2019.030205.

5

Governing through Paperwork

Examining the Regulatory Effects of Documentary Practices in a Refugee Settlement

Sophie Nakueira

Introduction

Documents are a crucial part of any bureaucracy (Hull 2012), but only recently have scholars of anthropology taken an interest in the study of bureaucracy or documents (see Hull 2008, 2012; Riles 2006; more recently, see Horton and Heyman 2020). Sarah B. Horton posits that identity documents, in particular, expose 'power dynamics between migrants and the state in traditional immigrant-receiving countries' (Horton 2020: 1). Extending these scholars' assertions, I argue that in refugee contexts, bureaucratic documents (beyond migrant identity cards) reveal the regulatory power between multiple actors at various levels within and beyond the state. Thus, in the context of resettlement programmes, documents are a crucial site for exploring how the mobility of refugees is governed and what 'thought-work' drives interactions between humanitarian street-level bureaucrats and refugees (Heyman, 1995, see also Burris, Drahos and Shearing 2005 on 'mentalities' or 'ways of thinking'). Studies on bureaucracy that have examined documents have centred either on their organizational aspects – the extent to which they bring about order in organizations (Hull 2012) – or on 'state governance as material practice' (Hull 2008: 501).

Another body of scholarship, on the analysis of documents by anthropologists, has focused mainly on 'their role as regulatory technologies that enact control and legibility over both citizens and "aliens"' (Cabot 2012: 11). The regulatory effects of documents in the context of a humanitarian setting in the Global South is largely missing from these studies (for exceptions, see Sandvik 2008; Thomson 2018). This chapter shows how documents are mobilized by refugees seeking resettlement to countries in the Global North *and* the resulting regulatory effects. Thus, I consider documents as regulatory tools that, as Heath Cabot posits, 'reinforce and undermine attempts to make persons governable' (2012: 11). I focus on the production, procurement and circulation of documents such as letters, medical certificates, bureaucratic forms, decisions and reports through various forms to demonstrate the regulatory effects of documentary practices in a Ugandan refugee setting. In doing so, I reveal the conflicting 'thought processes' inscribed in humanitarian organizations' forms and refugees' use of these forms – thereby showing how documents function as sites of 'struggle' that contain contradictory worldviews that humanitarian organizations and refugees each hold about the other (Heyman 1995: 264).

This chapter, based on ethnographic data, argues 'that documents are not simply instruments of bureaucratic organizations' (Hull 2012: 253) but are also technologies of governance (Burris, Drahos and Shearing 2005), through which refugees seek to make themselves 'legible' (Scott 1998) to and within a humanitarian system – and through which mobility to third countries is regulated in the context of the resettlement programme. I posit that although the resettlement scheme is meant to protect the most vulnerable refugees by resettling them in countries outside the refugee settlements, documents themselves – as well as the processes through which refugees seeking resettlement go through to procure these documents – act as regulatory mechanisms which constrain rather than enable mobility outside their country of asylum. I consider a conceptualization of the manner in which papers are produced, deployed and circulated in the selection of vulnerable refugees using the bureaucratic machinery of a humanitarian setting as an example of 'governance beyond the state' or governance 'at a distance' (Rose and Miller 1992: 179; see also Burris, Drahos and Shearing 2005; Crawford 2003; Shearing and Stenning 1981). With such a conceptualization, I argue that humanitarian workers as implementors of resettlement policies should be viewed as the gatekeepers of mobility to resettlement countries (traditionally, developed countries in the Global North). This conceptualization becomes all the more important because humanitarian street-level bureaucrats (protection officers) exercise discretion on whether or not to act. Josiah Heyman's work on how discretion and non-action function in the policing of the Mexico–US border is particularly important as it stresses the effects of non-action at the initial stage of policing (2009: 368). In the context of resettlement, the exercise of discretion in deciding whether or not to forward a refugee's case at the first stage has important implications for human-rights protection generally and mobility specifically, as it constrains or enables resettlement applications to move forward. I consider the provision of aid services or the exercise of bureaucratic functions in Nakivale refugee settlement as 'fragmented' (Crawford 2003) or 'diffused', given that it is run under diverse auspices and by divergent providers (Bayley and Shearing 2001) of protection services (see also Burris, Drahos and Shearing 2005; Crawford 2003; Shearing and Stenning 1981). As I will show, refugees' efforts to procure documents attesting to diverse narratives of suffering (Sandvik 2008) subjects them to 'fragmented and plural forms of control' (Crawford 2003: 480).

Access through Paperwork

I came to understand the centrality of documentary practices not just by listening to accounts of interlocutors but also by reflecting on my personal dealings with the bureaucracy of Nakivale refugee settlement.[1] I had to follow a specific procedure which entailed submitting a copy of my research permit to the Office of the Prime Minister (OPM) at different governmental levels before commencing fieldwork. Thus, it is not just refugees' movements that are governed through documents but also researchers' mobility in and out of humanitarian spaces and bureaucracies. Horton and Heyman argue that documents are a great lens through which to understand 'the power dynamics between migrants and the state' (Horton and Heyman 2020: 4). I extend this argument to the state's role in governing researchers' entry into humanitarian spaces, thereby effectively regulating what type of research can be done and who can do it. Letters were submitted to the OPM, a state agency that oversees the affairs of refugee settlement alongside the United Nations High Commissioner for Refugees (UNHCR). I found that documents regulated the movement of those who moved within the settlement irrespective of whether they were refugees – especially if they sought to engage with the humanitarian bureaucratic system.

However, I also came to learn that my positionality as a Black researcher in the settlement meant I needed more than the 'right' documents to negotiate access to refugees. Racialized assumptions about the aid industry were prevalent, as refugees perceived anyone White as a 'saviour' and capable of influencing their resettlement case. What follows is a brief background of the location of the settlement and how it is constituted spatially and nationally, to provide some context on the great lengths that refugees who live at a relative distance from aid agencies must travel just to procure and circulate documents.

Navigating the Settlement's Bureaucracy

The road to Nakivale refugee settlement is isolated and distant from urban areas. This road was as hard to navigate in the wet season (when vehicles often get stuck in the mud) as it was in the dry season (when the dust engulfs every part of passengers or pedestrians on this road). I equated navigating the road to Nakivale settlement on a rainy day to its bureaucratic system. Both impressions were conjured up by refugees' explanations of the resettlement process in terms of images or feelings of being stuck, frustrated and anxious. Located near the border of Tanzania and Uganda, Nakivale provides refuge to asylum seekers and refugees from Somalia, Eritrea, Ethiopia, the Democratic Republic of the Congo, Rwanda, Burundi, South Sudan, Sudan and other countries. Comprising seventy-nine villages, Nakivale is a vast space of constant flows of people. New arrivals from conflict-ridden countries seeking asylum and refugees seeking aid services, or those seeking resettlement in North America or Europe, means that agencies are abuzz with aid workers taking notes or filling in forms or taking a break from filling in forms. As Heyman argues, much of what street bureaucrats do is 'thought-work' (1995). In the case of humanitarian bureaucrats in Nakivale, thought-work entailed interpreting and documenting solutions or organizational responses to refugees' complaints or services they (the bureaucrats) had provided.

The overwhelmingly large number of refugees that aid workers attend to on a daily basis gradually led me to conclude that note taking or form filling were often routinized activities for some, and that such documentation did not always achieve the refugee-protection goals sought because of the large amount of paperwork that had to be filled in and circulated. This corroborates Heyman's assertion on how the concept of thought-work is valuable for investigating the ways in which 'bureaucracies generate chronic struggles and, indeed conduct violence' (1995: 278). However, I argue that in the context of Nakivale refugee settlement this was not a result of aid agencies' negligence but rather symptomatic of the limited resources available to follow up on each claim in a timely manner. Aid offices in the settlement were often understaffed, and aid workers had to attend to refugees all day long while manually filling in forms to record the particulars of numerous clients that came through their doors. Often, refugees had to retell their stories when files got lost, which was very common given the rudimentary storage systems of some agencies. For many aid workers (some of whom were themselves refugees), capturing the stories of refugees was as far as their mandate went. Capturing stories of variegated suffering in the camp and recommending solutions that were all but satisfactory to those seeking resettlement could be interpreted as a routine to which many aid agencies had become accustomed.

In Uganda, refugees are, by law, granted freedom of movement – but in practice, they need written permission to leave the settlement. Therefore, documents play an important role in regulating the mobility of refugees within the country, whether it is for travel to the capital city for medical treatment or for verifying their status as refugees in Uganda. By examining the paperwork (official records from aid agencies, hospitals or other state institutions) of refugees seeking resettlement, I discovered they had acquired permission from the OPM to leave the settlement. This was specifically the case for refugees who were referred for medical services outside the settlement. However, it cannot be said that refugees who wanted to travel to the trading centres outside the settlement had sought or had the required documentation.

Governing Everyday Life through Paper

I arrived at the settlement in September 2017, when a second verification exercise was taking place for those who had missed the first one. Verification is a form of census that confirms one's status as a 'refugee'. Upon verification, a valid refugee attestation card is issued, which entitles the holder access to various aid services. This card lists the age, sex, family size and marital status of refugees (factors that are considered in resettlement cases). Without it, a refugee cannot interface with aid agencies. Thus, in the everyday lives of refugees, documents play an important role not only in accessing aid services but also, at a minimum, in their self-identification to aid officers. However, refugees perceive a bigger role for documents for the purposes of getting resettlement. On this basis, they collect as much paperwork or leave as many paper trails (Andreetta and Borrelli, this volume) as they can so as to qualify as vulnerable refugees. Resettlement, as my data showed, was one of the most discussed topics that intersected with many conversations in the daily lives of refugees. Many refugees I spoke to – irrespective of their country of origin – always raised the issue of resettlement in conversations or interviews. This was in the form of either complaints about being excluded from the resettlement process or indirect and outright requests for help to expedite their resettlement cases.

UNHCR (2016) regards resettlement as an important protection mechanism in countries of asylum where refugees' rights are at stake. It is against this backdrop that many refugees sought resettlement – mostly citing incidents of insecurity in the camp. For refugees in Nakivale, the quest for resettlement was predominantly motivated by the wish to get away from what they described as a hard life and a place where they envisioned no future. Programmes aimed at providing durable solutions for refugees in protracted situations, and stories from refugees who had been resettled overseas about their great lives in these new places, fuelled the desire to leave.

Although many refugees are eligible for resettlement, only a few are resettled because few countries participate in the resettlement programme. Less than 1 per cent of refugees are actually resettled to a third country, so by focusing on resettlement many refugees get stuck in limbo or in what others describe as 'permanent temporariness' (Grayson 2017: 453; Sandvik 2008). Repatriation is often not a viable solution for refugees from countries experiencing ongoing conflict, while integration is often a solution some refugees do not consider – especially those who lived in cities or urban areas in their countries of origin.

Forum Shopping in the Quest for Resettlement

Many refugees I spoke to knew about the criteria for resettlement by observing trends of people who had been resettled or through aid workers, but they did not quite understand how the selection process worked. Refugees who were fixated on getting out of Nakivale resorted to using diverse strategies. One of them was engaging with the agencies that were most likely to refer them for resettlement or rephrasing their problems for other agencies when they did not achieve the desired result. Such actions were intended to increase the chances of their cases being submitted to the UNHCR for consideration for resettlement. These strategies represent instances of 'forum shopping' and 'forum shifting'. These terms are used in law to describe a phenomenon whereby litigants choose jurisdictions that will be likely to grant them favourable decisions. Nakivale refugee settlement is structured in such a way that no agency works on its own. In total, seventeen agencies cater to diverse aspects of refugees' needs. These agencies use UNHCR guidelines as well as their own. Each relies on referrals from other agencies, which identify refugees' needs and direct them to the one best suited to handle the problem. Protection officers identify cases for referral to the UNHCR for resettlement.

The bureaucratic composition of aid agencies is so diverse that, within any one agency, aid workers exercise distinct but complementary tasks aimed at addressing refugees' protection needs. For instance, several agencies have protection officers and/or psychosocial workers, or offer educational skills specific to their mandate. In executing these mandates, aid agencies generate a lot of paperwork. As Annelise Riles (2006) argues, bureaucrats at times compete by displaying their 'knowledge practices'. As my findings demonstrated, this 'display of practical know-how' by diverse agencies in the settlement is often captured through documents (Pouliot 2016: 2). Paperwork generated by different aid agencies includes forms distributed to those refugees seeking their assistance. Most aid agencies had official forms on which refugees' problems were captured. Aid workers ticked predetermined boxes indicating how the problem was addressed. Explaining the effects of such documentation practices and how they take place in international organizations, Vincent Pouliot notes:

> At heart, then, practice entails a politics of competence. This politics plays out in the clash of practices and the competing authority claims that come with them. Willingly or not, players fight to establish the competence of their ways of doing things over that of others. By the simple fact of playing the game, they jockey for position in and through practice. (2016: 55–56)

Without suggesting this as a deliberate practice on the part of aid agencies in Nakivale, I view this as problematic for refugee protection in a bureaucratic structure where aid agencies' performance is measured or audited through paperwork. My field data, based on participant observations and conversations with aid workers, showed that aid workers' performance or competence was measured not only by the content of these documents but also by the number of documents they produced. The emphasis on dispensing solutions and documenting them on paper, and the insistence on documentary evidence in every aspect of the daily affairs of the camp, have led to the proliferation of a paper regime in which both refugees and aid agencies produce and circulate paperwork for different and sometimes opposing purposes (Cabot 2012).

Because of the large number of refugees in the settlement who need basic services such as psychosocial support, medical attention or other forms of protection, the limited number of aid staff attending to such large populations may compromise the capacity of aid agencies to attend to refugee needs. Moreover, in the context of resettling the most vulnerable refugees, these documentary practices invariably constrain the mobility of refugees by stalling the very process meant to expedite their removal from the camp for their protection overseas. Refugees often expressed feeling 'stuck' (Nakueira 2019) in the process, because they were referred to different agencies but none of the agencies recommended resettlement. This lack of recommendation rested on how agencies exercised discretion in discerning whether refugees were telling the truth before offering a solution within their mandate. Marnie Jane Thomson argues that in the context of resettlement, this 'shifts humanitarian attention in the camp from refugee assistance to one of evaluation' (2018: 225). I refer to this process as gatekeeping: in doing so, aid agencies' decisions impact on who gets to *go further* in the process.

I noted that at times documents were mobilized for opposing goals by refugees and some aid agencies. Since their goals at times sit at opposing ends of the broad spectrum of protection, refugees were anxious about a system whose internal functioning they did not fully understand. For instance, not all agencies deal with resettlement matters. Thus, refugees spent valuable time collecting documents from agencies whose testimonies added little or no weight to the resettlement process. An examination of the different documents procured by various interlocutors suggested the humanitarian system produces two types of documents: bureaucratic documents (which are acquired formally) and non-bureaucratic imitations of the formal documents. The latter were often acquired informally (from brokers) by those trying to circumvent the arduous bureaucratic machinery. These imitations were sold by fellow refugees trying to capitalize on an abundant market of desperate refugees seeking to leave the settlement.

Criteria for Resettlement Eligibility

To qualify for resettlement, refugees must fit preconceived vulnerability UNHCR (2011) categories stipulated in the High Commissioner's *Resettlement Handbook*. A person must be 'determined to be a refugee by UNHCR'. All possibilities for durable solutions must have been exhausted, and resettlement determined by the assessors as 'the most appropriate durable solution'. A refugee must fall into one or more of the prescribed categories to be considered for resettlement: legal and/or physical protection needs, survivors of violence and/or torture, medical needs, women and girls at risk, family reunification or children and adolescents at risk. This demonstrates governance through documents, as one requires a valid attestation card to be considered a refugee by the UNHCR. Further, it helps explain why in evaluating refugees' cases aid workers recommend other solutions first as opposed to resettlement.

Many refugees easily fall into one or more of the vulnerability categories as they are survivors of violence and torture, or sexual violence. Because of the many conflicts, a great number of children and adolescents, as well as women and girls, fit the 'at risk' categories. Through these categories, the humanitarian system classifies who is deserving of resettlement. My data showed how specific bureaucratic actions create a situation where refugees try to fit into as many categories as possible to increase their chances for resettlement. This relates to Matthew Hull (2012: 259), who notes that eligibility criteria result in 'bureaucratic determinations of what sort of person fits into them'. Documents then become vital in efforts to construct or prove claims of multiple forms of vulnerabilities. The assessment of vulnerability claims transforms the humanitarian system from a system of protection into what Hull has described as a 'bureaucracy of regulation' (Ibid.: 260). I argue that through their assessments, aid workers from diverse agencies become *de facto* regulators of an externalized border who screen and sort those who are more and less deserving for migration to third countries. The following example of a refugee, Nadine,[2] is only one of the many filing vulnerability claims, and illustrates the role of her collected documents in articulating or negating these claims.

Constructing Vulnerability

On a hot, dusty day in October 2018, I sat in one of the shelters at Base Camp as some refugees waited to show me their documents. I had come to learn that since I was often in the company of aid workers, some of the refugees thought I had the potential to influence their resettlement cases. On that particular day, several refugees explained, in harrowing detail, the traumatic events that had led to their fleeing the Democratic Republic of the Congo and the continuing persecution they faced in the camp, while many more waited on a bench. Each insisted that I take copies of their documents, which upon examination were testimonies of their vulnerability in the settlement. They held these documents like prized possessions. Refugees were visibly oblivious to the fact that many of the documents – like hostile witnesses – actually betrayed them because they contradicted their claims. This was the case for a large number of the refugees who were not yet in the resettlement process but were seeking to interface with the UNHCR to make a resettlement claim.

Nadine's story stood out. Unlike other refugees who claimed they were being persecuted by 'unknown persons' in the settlement, Nadine sought resettlement because, as a single woman, life in the camp was hard. She explained she had unknowingly had an affair with a married man and that his wife had threatened to kill her. She also complained of the medical complications she endured in the camp, and showed me a letter in broken English supposedly written by women from the DRC who were threatening to kill her. Nadine could speak only French and Lingala and, in our interview, the translator had relayed her story to me through these languages. Thus, I concluded that the letter, which was addressed to her in English, must have been written by a broker for the benefit of Ugandan aid workers who would assess her case. In the letter, Nadine was addressed as 'Dear Sir or Madam' and was accused of sleeping with married men whose wives threatened to kill her. There were inconsistencies in the letter and in other documents she gave me.

Accounts by several refugees of brokers who sell resettlement stories to new arrivals revealed not only a thriving industry of fake stories (on 'crafted' stories in Nyarugusu camp [Tanzania], see Thomson 2018) and fake supporting documents but also the agency of refugees, whose inability to get formal documents from aid agencies had not stopped them from resorting to informal means to support their claims. Horton argues that documents are a 'potent site for resistance' because they are prone to being fabricated, imitated or misused (Horton 2020: 4). Formal and illicitly acquired documents were often lumped together by refugees, who perceived any forms obtained from aid agencies or brokers as powerful testimonies to their vulnerability. These were unlike the 'clean fake' documents used by Kazakh migrants that were hard to differentiate from official ones, as Madeleine Reeves (2013: 508) has noted. Most of the supporting documents in Nakivale gave away the illicit nature of how they had been acquired. Since English is the official language of Uganda, it was easy to detect documents that were not written by native speakers based on the errors in the document.

Nadine's formal medical report – which gave her a clean bill of health – was lumped in the same folder with other 'fake' testimonies on a medical form with no official letterhead, and signed by a doctor who could neither spell nor sign his name consistently on the pages of the medical letter recommending that she be referred for treatment 'outside the country of asylum'. Along with other medical records, Nadine provided documents with the same diagnosis for the different illnesses she was supposedly inflicted with. Stipulated in these documents, riddled with typos and inconsistent spelling of the name of the national referral hospital, was the same recommendation that she be treated 'outside the country of asylum'. Nadine was in fact vulnerable. She just was not vulnerable in accordance with the UNHCR categories, and had sought to circumvent the resettlement process by procuring fake documents to construct an identity that was legible to the vulnerability and documentary sensibilities of the humanitarian system. She was addressing a system in which a clean bill of health would render her immobile by providing fake documents which suggested the contrary.

In narrating their stories of persecution, refugees appeal to the emotive aspects in their tales in efforts to enlist pity, both orally and materially, through documents. This appeal to affects, as Hull notes, is intended to circumvent, 'conventions of emotionally evacuated bureaucratic discourse'. However, as my data showed, it sometimes achieves the opposite effect. For instance, an examination of some files or documents submitted by refugees whose resettlement claims were rejected or who were seeking audience with aid agencies to make resettlement claims demonstrated that documents acted as hostile witnesses to that which was alleged, thus attesting to the manner in which documents 'contradict one another on heterogenous institutional terrains' (Hull 2012: 255).

However, owing to language barriers, many of the refugees (who did not speak or read English) were unable to discern that some of the documents they had painstakingly acquired from aid agencies, or illicitly through brokers, most likely constituted the reason their resettlement claims had been rejected. Rejection letters were not always explicit, and were masked through checked boxes offering other alternatives to resettlement such as 'counselling'. Sometimes aid workers simply referred the claimant to other aid agencies, especially in matters outside their mandate. A noteworthy aspect of the formally acquired forms was that once a refugee's claim for resettlement was denied, the refugee in question had no way to appeal the decision. As Thomson (2012: 199) also notes in her work in Nyarugusu refugee camp in Tanzania, refugees seeking resettlement did not have a specific point of contact once their cases were rejected, arguing that there is an inherent contradiction in the performative aspects of the 'collective' (see also Boyer 2003). She notes that although the 'production, collection, storage, and sharing of files allow bureaucratic actors to garner a sense of collective agency', the paradox is that in executing their respective assignments every bureaucrat fulfils a particular duty for each file in a manner that denounces any appearance of unity (Thomson 2012: 199).

I argue that this diffusion of power in the execution of specific tasks has regulatory effects that constrain the achievement of specific goals for refugees seeking to make resettlement claims. In the context of a refugee setting, such 'silos' result in aid workers continuously referring refugees to another department or agency altogether – with frustrating effects for the refugees. For example, an examination of many of the documents that were formally acquired by refugees from diverse agencies showed that these forms recommended alternative solutions to resettlement or simply said the refugee in question had been attended to or that they had been referred to another agency. Rarely did the authors of the formal documents ever recommend the refugee be resettled, even though it was one of the solutions listed on some of the agency's forms. This suggests the aid worker, having assessed the refugee's claim, had not deemed them eligible for resettlement, or having attended to the refugee thought there were alternative solutions to resettlement as per the guidelines in the resettlement handbook. This was in sharp contrast to documents acquired illicitly, which often recommended that the only 'durable solution' for the refugee was to be taken 'outside the country of asylum' – using the grammar of the humanitarian system.

It is unsurprising, then, that aid workers mostly distrusted vulnerability claims by refugees seeking resettlement even when they presented supporting documents. Aid workers often said that refugees would do or say anything to get resettled. Some aid workers refused to give out forms in cases where they distrusted refugees' narratives, or simply refused to acknowledge the legitimacy of the contents of documents provided by particular agencies, received from refugees as evidence of their vulnerabilities. Refuting the validity of documents presented is, as Tobias Kelly (2006) posits, a form of bureaucratic control. In Nakivale, certain documents (such as those provided by the police or medical records) were deemed by some aid agencies as easily acquired through bribery. The rampant distrust of refugees reveals the worldviews (Heyman 1995) of street-level humanitarian bureaucrats and the resulting impact of thought processes on refugee protection. My observation was that the worldviews of aid workers I spoke to were at once conflicting and paradoxical because, on the one hand, they exhibit 'publicly visible' (Ibid.: 261) service provision and attention to refugees while, on the other hand, distrust of refugees effectively enhances refugees' vulnerability as it prompts inaction (Heyman 2000: 641) on the part of aid workers on refugees' claims. In his research on policing the Mexico–US border, Heyman found that the longer border officials had been at the job, the less sympathetic they were towards illegal migrants. This prompted him to ask, 'why would tenure on the job lead to a more critical rather than sympathetic view?' (2000: 642). He found that the critical view of migrants was driven by extensive information about their techniques and aims as well as their weaknesses (Ibid). Many aid workers I spoke to confessed that the first few months on the job were difficult for them due to the secondary trauma of listening to refugees' experiences. However, the longer they stayed, the more they learned of refugees' strategies and illicit efforts to get into the resettlement process. The material lies refugees tell are akin to those told by migrants at the US border, thus constructing street-level humanitarian bureaucrats as a form of immigration police of an internally invisible border to countries in the Global North. A focus on the associations engendered by the 'production and circulation of documents can help us understand the contested processes that oscillate between the inside and the outside of offices' (Robert Oppenheim, cited in Hull 2012: 258).

In the context of Nakivale settlement, the apparent distrust associated with documents produced by some agencies is also telling of the distrust between these aid agencies. The contested processes of procuring valid documents must be considered in terms not so much of what these show about the relationship between these aid agencies but of how these processes draw attention to the likely effects of such contestations in the assessment and selection of vulnerable populations – this, in particular, for third-country resettlement and, in general, for refugee protection. Moreover, as Thomson (2018) notes, the humanitarian system positions aid workers as objective evaluators of vulnerability claims in the selection of resettlement candidates that 'responsibilises' (O'Malley and Palmer 1996) the refugee to provide proof of vulnerability. However, as argued by Heyman, bureaucrats have their own worldviews and differing interpretations based on their own experiences and values, and therefore such assemements can never be objective and are often 'embodied in organizational world views' (Heyman 1995: 261). Thus, despite specific guidelines stipulated in the resettlement handbook on screening resettlement claims, the system implicitly favours those who can tell the most convincing narratives of persecution in ways that appeal to the emotions of protection officers and can provide credible documents, as well as those whose values do not contradict those of the street-level bureaucrat involved.

However, the 'trust' accorded to refugees is usually exercised discriminately and selectively in an environment where distrust not only is mutual but also represents the norm. My numerous conversations with local aid workers brought out the fact that refugees are the least trusted within humanitarian settings (see also Sandvik 2008). This suggests that to evaluate or assess vulnerability claims in such a context, the burden of proof shifts to refugees to prove their vulnerability. This is in sharp contrast to border police at the US–Mexico border, who were the subject of Heyman's study and who rely on visual cues (such as race and class) to decide whether or not to act or enforce migration control (Heyman 2009). Without discounting the necessity of evaluating claims, the shifting of evidentiary burden to refugees in the context of a humanitarian setting whose very existence is premised on protecting vulnerable populations presents an interesting paradox. While refugees rely on documents and performative forms of suffering, some aid workers largely draw on their instincts or emotions in evaluating refugees' vulnerability claims.

This may be related to Max Weber's point that 'bureaucracy develops more perfectly, the more it is "dehumanised", the more completely it succeeds in eliminating from official business love, hatred, and all purely personal, irrational, and emotion elements' (cited in Hull 2012: 255). This is paradoxical in the way the humanitarian system functions, particularly so regarding the successful selection of resettlement applicants. Given that the resettlement programme is intended to select the most vulnerable refugees (according to the UNHCR's criteria), the bureaucratic system in practice mostly relies on one's ability to appeal to the assessor's or aid worker's emotions. This is a key insight, as while many studies have centred on affect from the perspective of the subjects of documentation (i.e. those who are documented or undocumented), not much research exists on affect with respect to 'those doing the documenting' – particularly in the case of aid workers. Focusing solely on documents was not usual in this settlement, where attestations to suffering could easily be acquired illicitly. Refugees and aid workers admitted that most of the people who were seeking resettlement were in possession of either fake documents or illicitly acquired bureaucratic documents. Refugees who were frustrated by the arduous procurement process associated with acquiring formal documents from the relevant agencies complained about the resettlement process even as they engaged with the bureaucratic aid system that produces these documents. Some refugees enlisted the help of brokers to bypass the formal process of production and circulation of documents. These document brokers claimed to have contacts within specific agencies. As observed elsewhere by Francis Cody, even in this refugee settlement, the production and circulation of documents engenders 'document brokers' (cited in Hull 2012: 258).

In the context of a humanitarian setting, this perpetuates a vicious cycle of mutual distrust between the producers of documents and the subjects of documents within the system in which these documents are circulated. Further, refugees notably often resorted to such tactics not because of prescribed ideas of vulnerability but because of views about it being more efficient to bypass the otherwise long process of procuring formal documents to support claims of 'accepted' forms of vulnerability. As the research discussed here shows, governance in the implementation of the resettlement programme engenders practices that shape the protection of refugees towards what Cabot describes as 'overlapping, conflicting or even unrelated ends' (2012: 22). At the centre of these governance practices are documents which play a vital role in refugees' efforts to prove eligibility for resettlement, thus exposing the regulatory nature of the bureaucratic aid system. In Nakivale, as in Nyarugusu refugee camp, refugees go to great lengths to procure them from aid agencies (Thomson 2018: 229).

'In Process' of Resettlement

While most of the documents I examined were from refugees who were waiting 'to get in process' or whose claims had been denied, I encountered many refugees whose documents showed they had already undergone the resettlement interviews and orientation and were waiting for their visas to be resettled to the United States, Canada or other developed countries. Those who had been accepted and were waiting to go to North America were just as fearful as those who were not 'in process'. Having undergone the resettlement interviews several years earlier, they were now nervous of having been forgotten. The documents they held no longer provided the initial relief and joy as first experienced when they became part of the selected few among many eligible refugees who had been submitted to the UNHCR. For many, such as those who had qualified on medical grounds, the problems for which the resettlement had been granted persisted. As one elderly Congolese refugee asked me as I examined his file, 'But what about the sick child? I am worried that he will die while we are still here'. He had been approved for resettlement based on the medical needs of one of his dependents. Several years later, they were still waiting to get a US visa.

He was not the only one. Many of the refugees who had been approved for resettlement to the United States were in lengthy waiting processes which created uncertainty and ambiguity, and at times caused accusations of witchcraft (Nakueira 2019). The waiting processes from the time of approval to time of departure are often longer than that ideally recommended under UNHCR priority categories of 'emergency', 'urgent and 'normal'. Thus, refugees go to aid agencies repeatedly to find ways of expediting their departure, with very little success. Cabot notes the same about refugees in Greece who are seeking pink cards (a resident permit that temporarily allows holders to stay and work legally in Greece as well as free movement in the Schengen countries), and posits that the 'arbitrary, even mysterious qualities of procedures . . . increase anxiety and fear among those waiting, who come back week after week in the hopes (but never in the certainty) of acquiring the pink card' (2012: 16). This is not dissimilar to the anxiety experienced by refugees waiting for visas after gaining approval by third states for resettlement, obtained after first undergoing the strenuous screening processes by the aid bureaucrats. Some refugees awaited their visas for years (such as those waiting to go to the United States) and some for several months (such as those waiting for visas to Canada, Australia or some Schengen countries). This shows the 'temporal controls' (Anderson, 2020: 54) inscribed within mobility regimes in humanitarian contexts, and how they function to enhance the anxieties of those selected for resettlement and documented as being extremely vulnerable.

Considering that resettlement slots are granted to the most vulnerable refugees, some of whom having been approved based on medical needs, these long waiting periods inflicted more anxiety and sometimes fear that the sick person might die before being resettled. Interviews with the International Organization for Migration and the UNHCR revealed the limits of the aid bureaucratic system. While aid agencies conduct the initial processing, submission and orientation programmes, the final say on who is selected depends on the receiving countries. Through these processes, aid agencies become conduits of governance who facilitate third states screening vulnerable refugees eligible for resettlement. This 'governance at a distance' (Osborne and Gaebler 1992) by third-country states through the bureaucratic aid machinery positions aid workers as 'the new police' and documents as mediating objects (Hull 2012). Viewed from a governance perspective, resettlement countries are regulators that regulate the humanitarian regime at a global level (on meta-regulation, see Ayres and

Braithwaite 1992). The phenomena of new actors in migration governance have also been observed elsewhere outside refugee contexts. For instance, Horton notes that in the US, state officials are working with 'new bureaucratic agents in immigration control' such as police officers and workers in the Department of Motor Vehicles (2020:2). She also notes that in the United Kingdom, new actors such as 'landlords, professors and truckdrivers' have been enrolled in immigration control by the state (Ibid). What the enrolment of new actors within and outside humanitarian contexts reveals is a broader agenda manifesting itself in the intensification of migration control globally. This corroborates Heyman's argument that 'organisations employ techniques of power for specific ends in contexts wider than the bureaucracy itself' (1995: 261).

'Governance beyond the State'

Although some scholars have likened humanitarian governance to types of occupations (Fox 2008) in which global institutions exercise sovereign power on state territory, I argue the complexity of humanitarian governance remains to be further developed in the existing scholarship to better demonstrate the entanglement of interests at play in this governance network. Heyman argues that bureaucracies expose the political dynamics at play through 'subtle means' or 'hidden evidence' (1995: 264). He proposes an examination of key decisions, what issues bureaucrats focus on and the financial resources allocated in order to understand the politics at play. At the time of data collection, the emphasis was on expediting the resettlement of LGBTQIA+ refugees – illustrating the current power of the LGBTQIA+ movement and contemporary politics. The operation of the resettlement scheme rests on participating third states, whereby refugees seek to become legible to a system based on specified vulnerability categories. As a UNHCR representative explained to me, the UNHCR can advocate for more refugee slots but cannot force resettlement countries in the issue of which refugees to take.[3] Controlling migration through the resettlement scheme has been a successful endeavour from a purely governance perspective, but at great cost to achieving the protection goals of the resettlement programme. As the data showed, an inherent design principle of the humanitarian bureaucratic system in Nakivale is the collaborative execution of tasks.

This follows up on Clifford Shearing's (2015) point about how such tasks can steer governance functions through diverse nodes. Through documentary practices, diverse agencies such as 'auspices' and 'providers' (see also Bayley and Shearing 2001) execute different but complementary protection mandates. In the nodal governance lexicon, aid agencies are 'sites of capacity, knowledge and resources relevant to "shaping the flow of events"'

(Holley and Shearing 2017: 165; Parker and Braithwaite 2003: 119). In a humanitarian context, this means keeping refugees from moving by fulfilling their protection needs inside the current country of asylum. This is corroborated by Alexander Betts and James Milner (2006), who argue that African countries have cautioned about this externalization process: instead of 'burden sharing', Western states were engaged in 'burden shifting' by offering paltry sums of money to keep refugees in Africa and limiting their migration to the Global North at the cost of protection goals.

Conclusion

This chapter has examined how refugees seeking to make themselves legible to the resettlement process are regulated through the documents and discretionary practices of aid bureaucrats. This involves a type of governance whose bureaucratic procedures for delivering humanitarian goals relies more on conforming to the processes of issuance than on achieving those goals (see also Reeves 2013: 508). I have argued that bureaucratic practices effectively constrain the mobility of refugees through processes that run counter to the aims of the resettlement process, illustrating through my data how a heavy reliance on documents and discretionary practices runs the risk of excluding vulnerable refugees who lack persuasive performative emotions of suffering. However, I have shown that documentary practices constraining resettlement also stem from the procurement of fake documents by refugees, as this makes aid workers suspicious of the validity of their claims. Paradoxically, the same system that values documentary evidence also renders some formal documents worthless because of suspicion over how they were acquired. In effect, the humanitarian-aid bureaucratic machine in practice performs regulatory functions for external governments by redirecting the resources of humanitarian bureaucracy towards specific governance objectives (Nakueira 2014). The result is that discretionary processes and documentary practices further constrain the migration or mobility of refugees from the Global South to the Global North.

Acknowledgements

This research was funded by the department 'Integration and Conflict' at the Max Planck Institute for Social Anthropology.

Sophie Nakueira is a Research Associate at the Global Risk Governance Programme at the Faculty of Law, University of Cape Town. She has worked in various capacities as a researcher, visiting scholar, guest lecturer and consultant in Uganda, South Africa, Australia, Belgium and Germany.

Notes

1. I chose to conduct my research in Nakivale because of its greater composition of refugees from diverse countries around the region in comparison with other settlements. Access was gained through a recommended legal-aid agency following my interest in understanding the implementation of law/policies in refugee settings. I carried out an ethnographic study which included engaging in sensitization programmes, community meetings and workshops organized by various aid agencies. I closely observed how aid workers executed their mandates and how refugees reacted to or interacted with aid programmes. Semi-structured interviews with aid workers brought out their understanding of their roles within the broad protection goals of the settlement without confining them to strict responses. Un-structured interviews in some instances often occurred where an aid worker or refugee initiated a conversation.

   In conducting interviews with refugees, I spoke English and used the services of interpreters. Some refugees insisted on using their own interpreters, who were often not fluent in English. Language limitations were addressed through data triangulation: for instance, I cross-checked the verbal responses with the documents refugees had given me to see if they were consistent. I clarified ambiguities by conducting follow-up questions. I noticed a pattern in the answers of refugees from diverse countries – for instance, in the procedure of procuring certain documents or accessing certain aid agencies.

   Documentary analysis of photos, letters and official records from state and non-state agencies, such as forms that were given to me by refugees, were usefully assessed in my work. An analysis of agencies' forms enabled follow-up questions on trends which followed in the solutions dispensed. For security reasons, I was advised not to reside in the camp and therefore drove to the settlement on various field visits. On these trips, aid workers and refugees requested lifts to the nearest town, adding to the spaces for informal conversations. During these conversations, aid workers or refugees recommended other people I could interview. This snow-balling exercise led to access to key interlocutors as well as to high-profile meetings with key agencies.
2. For confidentiality purposes, I do not mention the names of the aid agencies. All names of interlocutors are pseudonyms.
3. However, it should be noted that while states cannot be forced to receive refugees, they have legal obligations in accordance with international law and the refugee conventions. These obligations are not discretionary for states, which allows for a breach of international humanitarian law where such international obligations are unfulfilled.

References

Anderson, B. (2020), 'About Time Too: Migration, Documentation and Temporalities', in J. Heyman and S. Horton (eds), *Paper Trais: Migrants, Documents and Legal Insecurity*. Global Insecurities. Durham, NC: Duke University Press.

Ayres, I. and J. Braithwaite (1992), *Responsive Regulation: Transcending the Deregulation Debate*. New York: Oxford University Press.

Bayley, D.H. and C.D. Shearing (2001), *The New Structure of Policing: Description, Conceptualization, and Research Agenda*. Washington, DC: National Institute of Justice.

Betts, A. and J. Milner (2006), 'The Externalisation of EU Asylum Policy: The Position of African States'. Working Paper no. 36. Oxford: COMPAS (Centre on Migration, Policy and Society).

Boyer, D. (2003), 'Censorship as a Vocation: The Institutions, Practices, and Cultural Logic of Media Control in the German Democratic Republic', *Comparative Studies in Society and History* 45(3): 511–45.

Burris, S., P. Drahos and C.D. Shearing (2005), 'Nodal Governance', *Australian Journal of Legal Philosophy* 30: 30–58.

Cabot, H. (2012), 'The Governance of Things: Documenting Limbo in the Greek Asylum Procedure', *PoLAR: Political and Legal Anthropology Review* 35(1): 11–29.

Crawford, A. (2003), 'Contractual Governance of Deviant Behaviour', *Journal of Law and Society* 30(4): 479–505.

Fox, Gregory H. (2008), *Humanitarian Occupation*. Cambridge: Cambridge University Press.

Grayson, C.-L. (2017), '*Refugees in Extended Exile: Living on the Edge* Jennifer Hyndman and Wenona Giles' [book review], *International Review of the Red Cross* 99(904): 453–57. Retrieved 8 October 2019 from https://doi.org/10.1017/S181638311700073X.

Heyman, J. (2020), 'Introduction: Paper Trails: Migrants, Bureaucratic Inscriptions, and Legal Recognition', in Josiah Heyman and Sarah B. Horton (eds), *Paper Trails: Migrants, Documents, and Legal Insecurity.* Durham, NC: Duke University Press, pp. 1–30.

——— (1995), 'Putting Power in the Anthropology of Bureaucracy: The Immigration and Naturalization Service at the Mexico–United States Border' (download available), *Current Anthropology* 36(2): 261–87.

——— (2000), 'Respect for Outsiders? Respect for the Law? The Moral Evaluation of High-Scale Issues by US Immigration Officers' (download available), *Journal of the Royal Anthropological Institute* (N.S.) 6(4): 635–52.

——— (2009), 'Trust, Privilege, and Discretion in the Governance of the US Borderlands with Mexico' (download available), *Canadian Journal of Law and Society / Revue Canadienne Droit Et Société* 24(3): 367–90.

Holley, C. and C. Shearing (2017), 'A Nodal Perspective of Governance: Advances in Nodal Governance Thinking', in P Drahos (ed.), *Regulatory Theory: Foundations and Applications*. Canberra: ANU Press, pp. 163–80.

Horton, S.B. (2020), 'Introduction. Paper Trails: Migrants, Bureaucratic Inscription, and Legal Recognition', in S.B. Horton and J. Heyman (eds) (2020), *Paper Trails: Migrants, Documents, and Legal Insecurity*. Global Insecurities. Durham, NC: Duke University Press.

Horton, S.B. and J. Heyman (eds) (2020), *Paper Trails: Migrants, Documents, and Legal Insecurity*. Global Insecurities. Durham, NC: Duke University Press.

Hull, M.S. (2008), 'Ruled by Records: The Expropriation of Land and the Misappropriation of Lists in Islamabad', *American Ethnologist* 35(4): 501–18.

——— (2012), 'Documents and Bureaucracy', *Annual Review of Anthropology* 41: 251–67.

Kelly, T. (2006), 'Documented Lives: Fear and the Uncertainties of Law during the Second Palestinian Intifada', *Journal of the Royal Anthropological Institute* 12(1): 89–107.

Nakueira, S. (2014), 'New Architectures of Governance: Transnational Private Actors, Enrolment Strategies and the Security Governance of Sports Mega Events', Ph.D. dissertation. South Africa: University of Cape Town.

——— (2019), 'The Politics of Accusations Amidst Conditions of Precarity in the Nakivale Resettlement Camp', *Cambridge Journal of Anthropology* 37(2): 39–56. Retrieved 9 October 2019 from https://doi.org/10.3167/cja.2019.370204.

O'Malley, P. and D. Palmer (1996), 'Post-Keynesian Policing', *Economy and Society* 25(2): 137–55. Retrieved 9 October 2019 from https://doi.org/10.1080/03085149600000007.

Osborne, D. and T. Gaebler (1992), *Reinventing Government*. New York: Penguin Press.

Parker, C. and J. Braithwaite (2003), 'Regulation', in P. Cane and M. Tushnet (eds), *The Oxford Handbook for Legal Studies*. Oxford: Oxford University Press, pp. 119–45.

Pouliot, V. (2016), *International Pecking Orders: The Politics and Practice of Multilateral Diplomacy*. Cambridge: Cambridge University Press.

Reeves, M. (2013), 'Clean Fake: Authenticating Documents and Persons in Migrant Moscow', *American Ethnologist* 40(3): 508–24. Retrieved 10 October 2019 from https://doi.org/10.1111/amet.12036.

Riles, A. (2006), *Documents: Artifacts of Modern Knowledge*. Ann Arbor: University of Michigan Press.

Rose, N. and P. Miller (1992), 'Political Power beyond the State: Problematics of Government', *British Journal of Sociology* 43(2): 172–205.

Sandvik, K.B. (2008), 'The Physicality of Legal Consciousness: Suffering and the Production of Credibility in Refugee Resettlement', in R.A. Wilson and

R.D. Brown (eds), *Humanitarianism and Suffering: The Mobilization of Empathy*. Cambridge: Cambridge University Press, pp. 223–44.

Scott, J.C. (1998), *Seeing Like a State. How Certain Schemes to Improve the Human Condition Have Failed*. New Haven, CT: Yale University Press.

Shearing, C.D. (2015), 'Reflections on the Nature of Policing and Its Development', *Police Practice and Research* 17(1): 84–94. Retrieved 8 October 2019 from https://doi.org/10.1080/15614263.2015.1109390.

Shearing, C.D. and P.C. Stenning (1981), 'Modern Private Security: Its Growth and Implications', *Crime and Justice* 3: 193–245.

Thomson, M.J. (2012), 'Black Boxes of Bureaucracy: Transparency and Opacity in the Resettlement Process of Congolese Refugees', *PoLAR: Political and Legal Anthropology Review* 35(2): 186–205. Retrieved 10 October 2019 from https://doi.org/10.1111/j.1555-2934.2012.01198.x.

——— (2018), 'What Documents Do Not Do: Papering Persecution and Moments of Recognition in a Congolese Refugee Camp', *Anthropologica* 60(1): 223–35.

UNHCR (2011), *UNHCR Resettlement Handbook*. Geneva: UNHCR.

——— (2016), 'UNHCR Projected Global Resettlement Needs', 22nd Annual Tripartite Consultations on Resettlement, Geneva, 13–15 June.

6

Refugees in the Making

Durable Marks of the Nansen Passport in Contemporary Humanitarian Governance

Hanna Berg

–We had agreed to leave together.
–To Belarus?
–Yes, to Belarus, but the problem is that I should have left a long time ago. But do you know what stopped me from leaving?
–Your dossier?
–Our dossier. I thought that I could wait since I would travel with my family to America. But it doesn't seem like that will happen . . .

—Conversation with Said in Amman, October 2021[1]

During the autumn of 2021, Belarus, in response to European Union (EU) sanctions, started issuing tourist visas to migrants, encouraging illegal border crossing into Europe (Adams 2021; Walsh 2021). In Jordan, thousands of Syrian asylum seekers, having waited for several years for third-country resettlement, seized the opportunity, which pushed the United Nations High Commissioner for Refugees (UNHCR) in Jordan into proclamation. Except for strongly advising 'against travelling through irregular and informal routes such as those to Europe through Belarus' on its official Facebook page on 4 October 2021, on 17 November that year the UNHCR also published a 25-minute video information session on irregular mobility (*l-tanaqqul gheyr l-muntaẓim*). Alongside stressing the dangers of such mobility, the UN agency explained that, in contrast to third-country resettlement – organized and coordinated in collaboration between states and the UNHCR, thus ensuring refugee protection – irregular mobility was 'a personal choice to leave through illegal paths and expose oneself to problems and risks'.[2] Further, the UNHCR repeatedly stressed that leaving Jordan for, for example, Belarus meant losing the internationally recognized refugee status,[3] and the protection and assistance that this secured – including third-country resettlement (UNHCR Jordan 2021).

Conducting ethnographic research in Jordan that autumn, studying how humanitarian bureaucratic artefacts mediate both spatial and temporal (im)mobility for Syrian asylum seekers, I witnessed how the topic of Belarus intensified among my interlocutors, on social media and in news media. Everyone knew someone who had travelled – and many wanted to leave themselves, but not everyone did. The friends Said and Ashraf had long considered leaving Jordan together, although, in the end, only Ashraf did so. I met them for the first time in 2016, when my research project was yet to take form. At the time, I was working as an interpreter at a rehabilitation centre in Amman for Syrians who had been injured as a consequence of the brutal violence that followed the Syrian revolution 2011. They were also working there, informally (Lenner and Turner 2019), helping out with various administrative tasks and daily business such as buying food, cleaning and helping those who resided there. Said and Ashraf were, like most Syrians in Jordan, registered at the UNHCR. Since the Jordanian government is not a signatory of the 1951 Refugee Convention, they were not recognized as refugees, but as asylum seekers (*ṭālibīn lujū'*) – despite the absence of any tangible asylum law in the country (Stevens 2013). In Jordan, Syrians and other refugees cannot enter any process of asylum, which immobilizes their lives in various ways both spatially and temporally. In my larger research, I examine the role of bureaucracy in (re)producing and maintaining aftermaths of humanitarian emergencies.[4] Approaching bureaucratic procedures not only as cogs in the humanitarian machinery (Dunn 2012; Gatter 2023; Nakueira 2019) but also as a condition through which certain ways of 'knowing and doing' are produced, my interest lies in how epistemologies of humanitarian governance are (re)produced both in navigations of everyday bureaucratic 'street-level' practices (Andreetta 2019; Cabot 2012, 2013; Gatter 2023; Heyman 1995; Tuckett 2018) and in institutional trajectories through which they become conditioned (Riles, 2006). How Syrians' everyday documentary practices affect and (re)shape their own spatiotemporal (im)mobility is one object of observation in this regard.

Locating 'refugees' and 'migrants' 'at opposite ends of the political spectrum' (Crawley and Skleparis 2018: 49) generates an imaginary distinction between vulnerable and non-vulnerable humans, one that justifies the differentiation of not only legitimacy for the international protection of people in displacement but also mobility. Considered the only legitimate 'humanitarian corridor' for refugees, third-country resettlement is a bureaucratic power technique within a larger, global system through which resettlement states attempt to regulate who gets to enter their national territories – what David FitzGerald (2019) conceptualizes as 'remote control'. In the humanitarian neoliberal diagnostic through which it has become morally acceptable to classify only *some* refugees as deserving of third-country resettlement (Sözer 2020), the bureaucratic procedures through which such remote control is exercised are organized around the notion of vulnerability. That it is only those categorized as the 'most vulnerable' who are granted such humanitarian corridor is a common sense central to contemporary humanitarian governance (Fassin 2007; Sözer 2020; Ticktin 2014).

Accordingly, during my time in Jordan, I observed how, in contrast to what the UNHCR insisted on in its information video, refugees' asylum-seeker certificate was a document distinguishing not only people of concern for the UNHCR from those who were not. Rather, it was also involved in several bureaucratic processes distinguishing, along humanitarian framings of vulnerability, different categorical memberships *within* the 'asylum seeker' label itself (Cabot 2013; Sözer 2020; Zetter 2007). Engaging with Syrian asylum seekers whose (non-)vulnerability had determined their (in)eligibility for resettlement, I witnessed how people deemed ineligible sought other alternatives for leaving Jordan. Belarus was one such alternative. By offering migrants, as described in news media (Adams 2021; Walsh 2021), tourist visas, anyone in Jordan (as well as elsewhere in the Middle East and beyond) with a valid passport and sufficient economic means could go to a tourist office and apply for a visa. Once the visa was issued, they flew as tourists to Minsk, from where they began their 'irregular' journey through the Belarusian–Polish forests to reach their destination in Europe. In this chapter, Said and Ashraf serve as an example of how classifications of vulnerability among asylum seekers differentiate their paper realities, which, in turn, affect their alleged 'personal choices' to leave or to stay in displacement. In early 2016, the UNHCR had contacted Said and his family, informing them that their dossier had been identified as a resettlement case, and hence they entered a long, slow process of resettlement – a process that was still ongoing when I arrived in Jordan in 2021. The UNHCR had never called Ashraf. Since it is the UNHCR that assesses and identifies resettlement cases, he could not contact the agency himself, and trying to do so was in vain since 'they never answer the phone' as Ashraf, and many with him, had repeatedly explained to me. For Ashraf, then, an asylum seeker not vulnerable enough for resettlement in a state where there are virtually no processes of asylum (Stevens 2013) – leaving had to be through a channel other than the UNHCR. Travelling from Jordan to Belarus, crossing the borders into Europe in October 2021, he left behind not only his friend Said but also his legal status. Although it was Ashraf's alleged invulnerability according to humanitarian common sense that pushed him into what the UNHCR called 'a personal choice' of irregular mobility, such a choice made him categorically even less vulnerable – becoming 'a migrant'. Ashraf's choice to leave Jordan, as well as Said's choice to stay, begs the question of how categorical distinctions between 'refugees' and 'migrants' have become understood as *representing* human realities while they – as I argue in this chapter – rather *produce* them. It also begs the question of how notions of vulnerability have become an essential measurement in the process of making such distinctions.

Alongside recent ethnographic scholarship on the interconnections between 'categorical fetishism' (Apostolova 2015; Crawley and Skleparis 2018; Peteet 2007), documents (Andreetta 2019; Cabot 2012; Horton and Heyman 2020; Nakueira 2019; Thomson 2012; Tuckett 2018) and mobility (Achilli 2016; FitzGerald 2019; Khosravi 2010; Monsutti 2008, 2018) in humanitarian and migratory contexts, this chapter seeks to unsettle the misleading stability of these categories. Through a combination of archival data concerning the first legal refugee identity document in 1922 and ethnographic fieldwork carried out in Jordan 2021–22, it explores historical conditions that have made possible the formation of present categorical distinctions between (vulnerable) refugees and (non-vulnerable) migrants, and of regular and irregular mobility along such distinctions.

Methods and Material: Refugees in the 1920s and the 2020s

Engaging with the archive, the empirical focus of this chapter is the fond 'Refugees Mixed Archival Group', also called the Nansen Fonds, which is one of eight fonds located in the United Nations Archive in Geneva and which contains 615 boxes (United Nations Geneva 2021). Created in 1947, the Nansen Fonds is a mixture of correspondence; administrative, financial and other written records; and brochures, newspaper clippings and some photographs – all of which address the emerging 'problem' of refugees in one way or another. Archives, Ann Laura Stoler (2016: 5) suggests, have a way of drawing scholars' attention 'to their own scripted temporal and spatial designations', generating an understanding of historical events and makings as distant pasts: things that are no longer, things that are separated from contemporary life. As a result, historical continuities in the present can easily be left unnoticed. In this sense, as institutions 'founded on a claim to be a neutral body of preservation' (Azoulay 2019), archives set the conditions for what we are able to see in and through them (Azoulay 2013). One such condition is 'the omnipresence of categories shaped by the political regime' (Ibid.: 549), serving as a prism through which we as scholars tend to study the past as distinct from the present. It is through such conditions that categorical distinctions between refugees and migrants have become conceptual conventions on which we as scholars rely when we look for them in archives, and elsewhere. Looking beyond such 'conditioned sight' demands attention to the archive itself, not only the artefacts it preserves. Accordingly, alongside the notion of 'archiving-as-process rather than archives-as-things' (Stoler 2010: 20), I attend simultaneously to the written lines in archival documents, the processes through which they have come to exist in archives and how such processes condition what we as scholars look for when we approach them. Doing so allows for approaching these archival documents as sites of situated knowledge production rather than as sources of ready-made knowledge.

Further, it is crucial in looking beyond such conditioned sight to pay close attention to the connectivities between past and present makings, an exercise for which ethnography serves us well – allowing us to disrupt the often hard surface of bureaucratic officialdom (Heyman 1995: 264–65) visible not only in records of policy and law but also in archival records. During my research in Jordan between 2021 and 2022, I engaged daily in different bureaucratic processes that allowed me to follow the various procedures of eligibility assessments of humanitarian services, and how refugees and humanitarians alike navigated them. In this chapter, I situate some of these engagements with an ethnographic reading of the archive. Addressing, in tandem, the archive and the everyday documentary strategies of asylum seekers in the present day constitutes an attempt to explore how processes of categorical makings from about 100 years ago bear on categorical distinctions today. When conceptualizing bureaucratic 'thought-work', anthropologist Josiah Heyman (1995) talks about worldviews as the general guidelines on which bureaucrats rely in their everyday thinking and decision-making. He suggests that, while expert knowledge suffices for routine tasks, it is the worldview of the workers that influences their actions and informs their common sense. Addressing contemporary categorical distinctions between refugees and migrants as conceptual conventions, I think along Heyman's conceptualizations. How did the worldviews of the deputies and delegates of the League of Nations in the 1920s guide their ways of knowing – that is, their 'thought-work'? What bearings do such worldviews have on humanitarian governance in the present? Attending both to the archive and the contemporary documentary strategies of Ashraf and Said is an ethnographic endeavour to examine the worldviews of the deputies and delegates' 'thought-work' as both a condition through which certain bureaucratic categories came into being *and* a condition through which humanitarian workers and bureaucrats, but also we as scholars, have come approach them today. As such, this chapter is also a methodological endeavour to disrupt our own 'thought-work', which conditions our outlook as anthropologists of migration and humanitarianism. Accordingly, conducting ethnographic research in Jordan, I followed the everyday bureaucratic work of humanitarian nongovernmental organizations (NGOs) in urban spaces, irregular tented settlements throughout Jordan and in Azraq refugee camp.[5] I participated in both 'street-level' documentary practices (Andreetta 2019; Cabot 2012, 2013; Gatter 2023; Heyman 1995; Tuckett 2018), such as processes of eligibility assessments of various humanitarian services, and in more institutionalized processes such as staff meetings and community-representative meetings. These engagements allowed me to trace procedures of data registration and the production of reports, proposals, minute sheets and project evaluations – as well as refugees' and humanitarians' navigations in and with them. In this chapter, I engage in particular with the story of Ashraf and Said and their own bureaucratic navigations alongside categorizations of refugees' (non-)vulnerability. Central to contemporary humanitarianism (Fassin 2007; Sözer 2020; Ticktin 2014), vulnerability assessments have become key when differentiating between refugees – people in 'real' need of protection – and migrants, as described in the UNHCR information video on irregular mobility – people who, rather than being exposed, expose themselves to danger. Yet, vulnerability has also become a means to differentiate *among* refugees, separating the 'really vulnerable' refugees from those 'not-so-vulnerable' (Sözer 2020). It is along such lines that Ashraf and Said's experiences have become divided. In this respect, after years of living in Jordan under the precarious legal status of 'asylum seeker', Ashraf's search for a solution beyond third-country resettlement and Said's wait for the same serve here as an incitement to examine, in their lives, the durabilities of the historical conditions shaping the first legal refugee identity document. That is, to explore how and to what extent categorical makings in the past have become categorical conventions in the present (Stoler 2016).

The Nansen Passport

Created in 1922, the first legal identity document for refugees, known as the Nansen Passport, emerged in a political context in which the world transformed from empires and colonial mandates into nation-states, producing '"extra" populations' that exceeded the people of the emerging nations (Azoulay 2019; Soguk 1999; Watenpaugh 2015, Rodogno 2021) – a transformation that Dawn Chatty (2013: 38) has called 'the "unmixing" of peoples'. The question of what to do with emerging denationalized subjects laid the ground for the Nansen Passport, following the legal refugee status, and for what has come to lie at the heart of modern humanitarianism (Fassin 2007, 2012; Malkki 1995; Ticktin 2014; Watenpaugh 2015). Devised by the Norwegian explorer and politician Fridtjof Nansen, the High Commissioner for Russian Refugees at the League of Nations, the Nansen Passport was first envisioned for displaced and dispossessed Russian refugees in the early twentieth century (Robson 2017; Soguk 1999: 129). As the refugee problem 'grew', the word 'Russian' would disappear from the title a few years later. Nansen served as High Commissioner for Refugees between 1921 and 1930, which is a time period of concern for this chapter. In particular, I engage with (1) the correspondence and reports concerning the proposal and implementation of the Nansen Passport for Russian refugees in 1922, (2) the labour exchanges of refugees along the same process, (3) the attempts to extend the Passport's provisions to Armenian refugees in the French mandates of Syria and Lebanon between 1924 and 1929. Exploring how deputies and delegates of the League of Nations dealt with questions of responsibility towards refugees, alongside imperial projects of population exchange and refugee labour highlight ambiguities around how refugees were to be categorized and governed. The attempts a few years later to extend the Nansen Passport to contexts beyond Europe further raised questions about *what* a refugee was and how to define and distinguish refugees from non-refugees.

Keith Watenpaugh (2015) suggests that while there are distinctions between the structure and scope of humanitarian responsibility for refugees in the post-Ottoman Middle East in the early twentieth century and the postwar Europe following 1951, the Nansen Passport played an important role as a 'humanitarian-bureaucratic tool' (Ibid.: 174) in what constituted 'an early example of what today's relief or development workers would call the substitution of humanitarianism for politics' (Ibid.: 161). Vulnerability, although more closely linked to national citizenship than a measurement of deservingness for humanitarian assistance, was nevertheless central to the idea that there was an international obligation to '"do something" about refugees' (Ibid.: 169). While the creation of the Nansen Passport has been afforded some attention by historians (Housden 2010; Long 2011, 2013), archival materials are commonly treated as 'items of a complete past rather than an active element of a present' (Azoulay 2012: 4), which situates the Nansen Passport as a historical trace rather than a durable mark (Stoler 2016: 6) in the paper-realities that refugees and migrants experience today. Consequently, the distinction between 'refugees' and 'migrants' has become a conceptual convention (Ibid.: 8), hampering our capability to 'look beyond the use (and abuse) of categories' (Crawley and Skleparis 2018: 61) and the features that distinguish the individuals assigned to them (Stoler 2016: 17). Hence, while Watenpaugh cautions against conflating the limited nature of governing and the defining of refugees in the 1920s with refugee policies that took shape after the 1951 Refugee Convention, I believe that there is potentiality in examining early examples alongside contemporary ones. For, as Stoler (2016) convincingly argues, in imperial histories of the present categories do not abruptly disappear while others accidentally emerge. Rather, categories are constantly reanimated, remodelled, sequential and consequential of each other. Intertwining everyday conditions generated by the contemporary legal asylum-seeker category in Jordan with bureaucratic negotiations at a moment in history when such categories were still in the making, I look for historical continuances rather than ruptures. In what follows I begin by examining the official report of the first conference regarding the Nansen Passport held in 1922. Attending to the thought-work of government representatives in this conference concerning refugees' right to mobility and legal status allows for exploring such historical continuances in today's humanitarian governance.

Proposing an Identity Certificate: Mobility as a Refugee Right?

Created 'through the unfolding of one conference from the materials produced at another', reports are part of an institutional trajectory (Riles 2006: 83). A 'document's career' (Ibid.) – the procedure through which it becomes a concrete printed object – is thus at once sequential and consequential. That is, while the procedure of well-defined steps through which a finished report comes into being is part of the document, it is also the context of its making (Ibid.: 85). Once a successful printed product, the report itself becomes part of the wider trajectory, shaping the context of the chain. Accordingly, the first conference 'On Passports for Russian Refugees', held in 1922, was an early step in a long chain of conferences, documents and reports that 'both conceptually and organizationally' (Soguk 1999: 120) would come to mediate refugees' right to mobility as well as governments' rights to control it (FitzGerald 2019). Organized to deal with the creation of a distinct legal identity document for Russian refugees, this conference was part of a larger and longer resettlement plan, which, as historian Davide Rodogno (2021) shows, largely failed in the end, as most refugees were never resettled. Here, I pay close ethnographic attention to the questions that emerged among the government representatives during this conference. Despite the ultimate failure of the ambitions of the larger plan, exploring how mobility regulations took shape alongside negotiations and (dis)agreements on governments' rights and responsibilities towards refugees, this conference highlights a moment in history when irregular and regular mobility was yet to be distinguished along defined categories.

On 8 June 1922, a letter was sent from the Assistant High Commissioner for Russian Refugees to the Secretary General of the League of Nations 'concerning the activities of the High Commissariat, especially in regard of the question of legal status, papers of identity and visas for Russian refugees'. Claiming that previous meetings with different states had shown the difficulty of coming to 'any definite result in these questions on an international basis', the Assistant High Commissioner requested the summoning of a conference 'intended to find the quickest means of making practical progress in the question of identity papers and visas' (Nansen Geneva Office 1922).

> Not only will the discussions deal entirely with questions of a technical legal nature, with which the members of the High Commissariat are not conversant, but it seems also essential, in order to come to some practical conclusion, that a definite scheme be worked out which will take into consideration the criticisms and objections made hitherto by the various governments and that this scheme be circulated among the members of the two conferences before they meet . . . The question is, it must be admitted, of a highly complex nature. It may appear necessary to enter into special negotiations with the various governments and ascertain the general attitude of the legal advisers of these governments on the question of the refugees and the policy they are pursuing at present or intend to adopt in the near future. (Ibid.)

Said and done. Between 3 and 5 July 1922, the conference was held in Geneva, hosting representatives from sixteen nations, the International Labour Office (ILO) and the League of Nations. The negotiations at the conference unfolded around the idea of creating an identity certificate on which refugees could apply for visas, as Nansen had proposed in a report three months earlier.

> The two principal questions before the conference were:
>
> Would the Governments be ready to grant through their competent organisations such certificates of identity as were described in the Nansen report?
>
> Would the Governments be prepared to grant visas to certifications of identity issued by other Governments, and on the same conditions as ordinary passports? (Governmental Conference 1923)

While some states already had their own bureaucratic systems in place with specific documents for noncitizens and did not see the point of introducing the Nansen Passport, others had no objection. The French representative claimed that the French government

> could not issue Russian refugees documents of identity which would allow them to move freely about Europe under conditions which would perhaps be better than those granted to nationals of neighbouring [*sic*] and friendly countries. (Ibid.)

The Hungarian representative, however, 'felt in a position to state that [his government] would make no objection to the certificate of identity or to the reduction of the expenses of transport and of visas', a view shared by the Serb-Croat-Slovene government as long as 'all the other states were in agreement'. Yet, the Swiss representative

> feared that the certificate of identity which was asked for by Dr. Nansen required wither [*sic*] too much or too little. It was indeed difficult to regard such a document as a regular document granted by the states. If, on the other hand, it was granted subject to the laws and regulations in force for the admission and resilience of foreigners, the state concerned would be taking away with one hand what it granted with the other. To arrive at a practical result it would be necessary to abolish all police provisions regarding foreigners. (Ibid.)

Governments' own attempts at similar solutions were conditioned by the geopolitical context of the time and informed the debate. For instance, bounded by the Peace Treaty of Riga, an arrangement that had ended the Polish–Soviet war of 1920 (Stanisławski 2022; Wandycz 1969), Poland noted that '[t]he legal situation of the Russian refugees in Poland differ[ed] essentially from their legal situation in the countries which [had] signed no Treaty with the Soviet Government'. The country stressed the fact that in recognizing the Moscow government, it had been compelled to 'take into consideration certain rules laid down by the Soviet Authorities'. Consequently, Poland could 'not agree to the delivery of certifications of identity on which it was specified that the bearer belonged to the Russian State'. For 'humanitarian reasons and in consideration of the precarious situation of the refugees', the Polish government had therefore, about a year earlier, issued 'a special passport' that enabled 'the bearer freely to cross the frontier of the republic'. Regrettably, the Polish delegate complained that almost all diplomatic or consular representatives in Warsaw had refused to issue visas based on such a passport (Governmental Conference 1923). Accordingly, stating that the proposed identity certificates for refugees 'would in no way encroach [upon] the rights of States with regard to their control of foreigners', the president of the conference gave room for further arguments to be raised regarding the transit visa. It would, he cautioned,

> perhaps be difficult for a country to accept a refugee coming from another country if it were not certain that it could send him back to that country if necessary. On the other hand, it would be difficult for the governments to undertake an obligation to take back their Russian refugees. (Ibid.)

The suggested solutions to this 'extremely delicate' question involved the possibility of states demanding the return of refugees 'to the State whence they had come'. Problems arose around whether states would accept the return of refugees who had left their territory. The French representative asked if it would not be preferable to make optional states' 'mentioning or not mentioning the permission to return' – that is, having 'full liberty to prevent the return if it did not put on the certificate "with authorization to return if necessary"' (Ibid.). The negotiations back and forth regarding this suggestion did not reach a final solution during the conference as few representatives felt that they had the authority to take such decision without referring to their governments.

The ability to produce official documents and declarations of rights, Ariella Azoulay (2019) notes, 'already marks the excess of particular rights' held by those who do the granting. She suggests that to *unlearn* human rights, we need to differentiate between disabled, textual and imperial rights – that is, to study the connectivities between rights that have been 'put out of action' and replaced with rights inscribed in universal documents and declarations to maintain the unwritten rights of some people in exercising imperial power over others. Consequently, often studied in relation to the heavy, rights-based discourses that followed the 1951 Refugee Convention (Watenpaugh 2015), documents have become understood as 'timeless and integral element[s]' (Sharma 2020: 31) in all forms of migratory and humanitarian governance. Scholars have contributed to the unmaking of such understanding. Radhika Viyas Mongia (1999) cautions against assuming the emergence of the passport in regulating mobility between states to be an intrinsic part of state sovereignty; she sees it rather as a means of ensuring its very effectivity. Through her work on Canada's emerging demand for Indian immigrants to hold passports in the early twentieth century, she shows how the pseudo-universality of the passport was enabled through the principle of pseudo-reciprocity between nation-states. Rather than simply reflecting a new world order, she notes, the emergence of the passport extended the rule of colonial difference. The creation of the passport on colonial and racial grounds – wrapped in the language of universality – is likewise observed by Nandita Sharma (2020), who links documentary controls and the 'emergence of the figure of the (Im)migrant' (Ibid.: 33) with the British slave trade in the early nineteenth century. She suggests that the implementation of immigration controls – governed through papers – was part of an effort 'to find new ways to discipline labor in the absence of slavery' (Ibid.: 31). Accordingly, the 1922 invention of the first legal document for refugees was hardly a 'mere historical coincidence' (Soguk 1999: 133). In the new world, 'everyone had to become a citizen of a state' (Ho 2006: 306), and thus national passports became instrumental for '"envisioning" the state and its counterparts, the citizen and the nation' (Soguk 1999: 128). In this context, the creation of the Nansen Passport became part of the process of distinguishing non-nationals from nationals, constituting 'an early international juridical notice of the permanence of the refugee's exile' (Watenpaugh 2015: 174).

> *Fieldnote, Amman, September 2021*
> 'How much sugar do you want?' Ashraf asks me, standing in the tiny kitchen of the humble apartment that he shares with three other young men in Western Amman. They are all out working, and we had decided to have tea and shisha here after having dinner at a neighborhood restaurant close by. 'Like you' I answer, 'a little'.
> We sit down in one of the two sofas in the small living room. As he places the teacups on the little table and puts the coal on the shisha-head he says, 'I'll tell you all the details. I have already left my passport at an office to get the visa.' Telling me about his doings these last few days in preparation for the travel to Belarus and the wait for the visa, he wants to hear what I think about it. He tells me that no one knows that he will travel, not his roommates, and not even Said.

Indeed, throughout my time in Jordan in 2021–22, the UNHCR asylum-seeker certificate seemed to generate permanent precarious conditions in displacement rather than securing the humanitarian promise of regular, secure mobility that the UNHCR continuously promoted. Ashraf was one of those who, with the passing of time, had realized that leaving Jordan would probably never happen for him through the UNHCR. Hence, Belarus became another way for him to exit his asylum-seeker status. Yet, beyond the asylum seekers themselves, third-country resettlement was also a central topic of conversation among humanitarian workers. In opposition to asylum seekers' testimonies to the extended processes and the ambiguities and injustices in and around them, humanitarian workers often insisted that third-country resettlement is *one* solution proposed for refugees, not a right for them to claim (*tawṭīn ḥall w mish ḥaqq*). During the 1922 conference, however, such rationale regarding refugees' rights and states' responsibilities in securing such rights was evidently yet to take shape. The draft report of the 1922 conference demonstrates a search for consensus between parties. Delegates were not only concerned about *whether* there should be an identity certificate specifically for refugees but also what form such certificate should take, and whether the accompanying rights and regulations should resemble (or not) those of identity documents issued for citizens. Reading the discussions that unfolded during this conference as sites where 'epistemological and political anxiety' was mediated (Stoler 2010) thus helps to unsettle chronological understandings of *first* the emerging issue of already-defined refugees, leading, *then*, to a rational response in the form of a legal status representing them. Beyond indicating a legal document in the making, it also shows the creation of a parallel categorical membership – which process forms the central focus of the following sections. Through an ethnographic reading of correspondence sent between different delegates working for the League of Nations – mainly, the Assistant High Commissioner, Thomas Frank Johnson and the League's representative in Beirut, Georges Burnier, who was also a delegate of the International Committee of the Red Cross (ICRC) – I trace how questions around labour and legal status mediated understandings of refugees' vulnerabilities, rights and responsibilities, and how these in turn informed refugees' deservingness of humanitarian assistance.

Refugee Labour: The Movement of Humans and Archival Documents

While the documents examined in this chapter are today located at the Archives of the United Nations Office in Geneva, they have travelled between different organizations and offices before ending up there. A refugee section for arranging and archiving documents about the subject was first created at the League of Nations when Nansen became the High Commissioner for Russian Refugees. The files were then moved in 1925 as the High Commissioner's Office was transferred to the ILO, which hosted the files for four years before they returned to the League again in the end of 1929. With the establishment of the autonomous Nansen Office for Refugees two years later, most of the files of the refugee section were moved there. At its closure in 1938, the files rejoined the Secretary of the League (United Nations Geneva 2021). The mobility of these archived documents tells a story not only about the administrative history of the organizations involved but also about the history and mobility of the refugee category and the features assigned to it.

In contemporary refugee policy, I suggest, the assessment of vulnerability has become a vital bureaucratic technique for exercising a form of 'remote control' (FitzGerald 2019). It is through such assessment processes that the understanding of third-country resettlement as an entitlement only for the deserving ones, rather than a political right for anyone displaced, becomes easily justifiable. The UNHCR webpage explains that it only seeks to assess highly vulnerable families against the resettlement criteria. That definitions of 'the most vulnerable' differ between resettlement countries, however, makes it difficult for asylum seekers in Jordan to navigate which criteria that must be fulfilled to be considered eligible. Humanitarian workers have in many conversations likewise stressed the lack of authority of the UNHCR to make any final resettlement selections. In the introduction of the UNHCR resettlement handbook, it is explained that resettlement is

> a process that enables refugees to relocate to another country with a legal status ensuring international protection and ultimately permanent residence. It is a unique opportunity, offering individuals and families a meaningful chance to rebuild their lives in an environment where their rights are protected from day one, and where access to naturalization and citizenship promise an end to years of displacement. Depending on the operational context, resettlement may be primarily implemented as a response to individual protection needs, or as a mechanism to achieve broader strategic protection and durable solutions goals for particular groups or populations. As well as being a tool for protection and solutions, resettlement is also a practical way for countries to demonstrate solidarity with host communities who assume the greatest share of responsibility for protecting refugees. (UNHCR 2024)

What are the historical conditions through which third-country resettlement has come to be considered 'a practical way to demonstrate solidarity' with host communities, rather than governments' political obligation towards those who have been forcedly displaced? In this section, I turn to correspondence concerning the coordination of the labour exchange of refugees in the early twentieth century. Attending to the terms and conditions that took shape at the intersection between questions of labour and refuge highlights a blurry boundary between governments and the League's responsibility, accountability and, moral obligations towards the Russian refugees whose mobility they sought to govern. Following Ashraf's story along such questions allows for addressing how today's vulnerability criteria for third-country resettlement ultimately force people deemed 'not-so-vulnerable' to find ways to mobility beyond it.

In June 1922, a letter was sent to Nansen raising the problem that refugees being moved to Austria as agricultural labour had instead 'began to look for work in other industries'. Stressing 'the necessity of their keeping to agricultural work', the letter suggested that Russian refugees should formally confirm their understanding that 'they look for no other than agricultural work' in Austria:

> It would be very desirable if a written undertaking could be obtained from individual refugees in which they agree not to seek any other employment in Austria than that to which they are sent, on the understanding that the Austrian government would be at

> liberty to expel them in the event of the undertaking being broken. (Nansen Geneva Office 1922)

The letter further stressed that a transfer of 200 agriculturalists from Egypt and Cyprus had been delayed as some Russian refugees had declined the relocation to Austria, pleading 'that they were not strictly speaking agriculturalists, although they had registered as such'. Arguing that the work 'by reason of [the refugees'] unwillingness to proceed' would be 'unsatisfactory and thus prejudice the reception of further Russian refugees by the Austrian Government', it was suggested that a full transport of refugees from other sources, proceeding via Bulgaria, would be arranged instead. About a week beforehand, the Assistant High Commissioner for Russian Refugees had raised concerns about the refugees' own negotiations regarding the labour exchanges. Writing to Burnier, he stated that

> [w]ith reference to the difficulties which the refugees appear to raise in regard to their evacuation to other countries, I really think that you would be fully justified in pointing out that every possible precaution is taken by the High Commissariat to ensure that suitable employment conditions are offered to refugees in the countries to which they are evacuated and that *it is not reasonable for them*, in the circumstances, to ask for details as to wages, hours of labour and the exact localities in which they will be employed . . . *It does not appear to us that it is for the refugees to say* whether they will accept employment or not, but that they should be informed that suitable employment has been found for them and that, if they do not accept it, they must bear the consequences mentioned above. (Ibid.; emphasis added)

Following this, he provided Burnier with a number of arguments for why the refugees should have no say in arrangements that the League had undertaken for them, signaling a political reality that assumed some people to be fully entitled to decide over the lives of others. Indeed, in imposing evacuation through labour exchanges, the commissioners 'acted as if they could exercise their right to decide who belongs where, why, and in which way, for the sake of whose good' (Azoulay 2019: 479). While Azoulay's critique is directed at forced displacement in the postwar period following the Second World War, this letter signals a similar political worldview among the bureaucrats.[6] While this correspondence shows the League's early attempts to govern refugees, the discussions also highlight how mobility regulations were (re)shaped and negotiated by refugees themselves – who did not easily submit to the proposals provided by the League and governments. By refusing work in different sectors and resettlement based on certain employments, or seeking employment in other sectors once resettled, the refugees' activities brought about new questions for the delegates which generated new conditions and bureaucratic procedures in the projects of the League.

Further, the political context of the early twentieth century raised the question not only of what to *do* with emerging denationalized subjects but also of whose responsibility they were. In the closing years of the Russian civil war and the fall of the Ottoman Empire, people from the Russian Empire who had directly or indirectly supported the anti-communist White Army led by Pyotr Wrangel were, in 1922, evacuated to Constantinople, the Ottoman capital, at the time occupied by the Allied powers. In June that year, a telegram was sent to the Secretary General of the League, questioning how it was that 'governments who [were] in a position to support a military and political organization comprising several tens of thousands of refugees' were not able to provide with practical help for the civilians affected by the military occupation in Constantinople. Appealing, on behalf of Dr Nansen, for more money to be 'devoted entirely to [the] evacuation and employment' of Russian refugees, the telegram stressed the moral obligations of the French government towards the refugees considering that they had recognized the 'Wrangel Government and encouraged its venture'.

> It must not be forgotten that the responsibility for the maintenance of 27,000 Russian refugees in Constantinople lies not with the League of Nations but with the Allied Powers who actually occupy the town. The Council has repeatedly announced that the League cannot assume any kind of responsibility for the material welfare of the refugees. (Nansen Geneva Office 1922)

At this time, various Russian unions were formed in Constantinople to make different claims on behalf of the refugees there. For instance, only about two weeks before the League's appeal to governments to take responsibility for the suffering they had caused, a letter from 'the Russian Committee of Constantinople' had requested the League to 'take steps for their protection'. The League refused such responsibility:

> Dr. Nansen point out, however, that in appointing him High Commissioner for Russian Refugees, the League, contrary to the suggestion of your Committee, assumed no responsibility towards the refugees and expressly confined his task to an endeavour [*sic*] to find the refugees productive employment where possible. (Ibid.)

The questions of *whose* responsibility refugees were, and *what* such responsibility should imply suggest an imperial context wherein some people were entitled to formulate rights and restrictions for others. Yet perhaps even more importantly, such questions testify to a moment in time when refugees were yet to be stripped of their personhood, histories and politics (Agamben 1995; Malkki 1995, 2015) – reduced, through vulnerability assessments, to basic human needs (Azoulay 2019) and yet to become a problem for *humanity* rather than states (Watenpaugh 2015: 169).[7] In the following section, I turn to the attempts to expand the Nansen passport to Armenian refugees in the Levant. Following how the League's representatives navigated this attempt in a context beyond Europe, I pay close attention to the initial negotiations of defining – along questions of responsibility – the refugee category itself.

The Problem of Legal Status: Contesting Visions among Refugees and Delegates

Fieldnote, Amman, March 2022

It's a few months after Ashraf arrived in Europe. I am spending the day in Azraq refugee camp when he texts me. We decide to have a videocall once I am back in Amman the same evening. During the call I ask him whether he has talked to Said lately. 'He always tells me he is busy' Ashraf says. It upsets him that Said has somewhat disappeared and that they don't talk as much anymore. But he knows why that is. It is because Ashraf travelled without him. Yet, Ashraf tells me that he waited for Said to take a decision whether he should leave or not, but that he, in the end, could not jeopardize his family's resettlement dossier at the UNHCR. Realizing that Said was not going to travel, Ashraf explains, he had to leave without him.

Between 1924 and 1929, the League of Nations sought to extend the Nansen Passport to Armenian refugees, who – as a consequence of massacre, dispossession and expulsion during the fall of the Ottoman Empire – had fled to the Levant, mainly to the French mandates of Syria and Lebanon. This process of relocation and forced displacement had been ongoing since the Armenian Genocide in 1915 (Watenpaugh 2015). Although many relief associations and organizations – together with the League – had provided shelter and other kinds of relief, with time, the question of Armenians' legal status became more pressing. Although the Nansen Passport was to some extent used as a travel document in Europe until the end of the Second World War, extension attempts beyond Russians and Armenians were generally opposed and failed due to a lack of governmental will. The Nansen Passport was issued by the member states of the League themselves and gave its holders the ability, not the right, to travel between nations – echoing the common sense in contemporary refugee governance that the criteria for third-country resettlement are set by the resettlement countries themselves. Although differing today between the UN member states, it is vulnerability assessments that reduce refugees' experiences to human basic needs, making possible the materialization of third-country resettlement as a *provision* that can be taken away from them, or not granted at all (Azoulay 2019). Indeed, it is almost always not given at all. The number of resettled refugees is so small (UNHCR 2022) that the chances of being considered eligible are almost as remote as 'winning the lottery' (FitzGerald 2019: 3). Attentive to states' varying and ever-changing criteria, refugees are well aware that any change in their dossiers may undo their resettlement eligibility. In many of my encounters in Jordan, people have testified to both eligibility delays and withdrawals in relation to documentary adjustments. Said, for instance, knew that if he were to travel to Belarus he would have to be 'removed' from his family's dossier, which consequently would generate a reassessment of their eligibility. Having already waited for six years since they were first selected for resettlement in 2016, he was not prepared to take that risk. Ashraf, on the other hand, coming to Jordan as a 19-year-old, was registered alone at the UNHCR, and – as a single man – not really considered vulnerable enough for resettlement anyway (Turner 2019). In this respect, in contrast to the UNHCR's ruling that leaving Jordan meant losing the protection and humanitarian assistance that Syrians' legal status secured, Belarus was a way for Ashraf to exit the life conditions it produced.

As for the Nansen Passport, Watenpaugh (2015: 167–75) shows how, about 100 years earlier, the motives behind its extension to Armenian refugees differed between the League and the French authorities in Syria and Lebanon, which, I suggest, influenced the procedure of distinguishing the refugee category from other categorical memberships. Here, I trace how delegates' 'competing interpretations of law' (Andreetta 2019: 93) and refugees' own documentary strategies (Cabot 2012; Nakueira 2019; Tuckett 2018) jointly mediated the categorization, and reduction, of refugees into 'basic human needs'. While conferences and reports provide a space for definitions and policies to be negotiated and settled between governmental and nongovernmental actors, they manifest and unfold outside of (although never disconnected from) such space. The letters examined in this subsection show how the conferences that examined 'the refugee problem' in the early twentieth century took place not only in sequence and as a consequence of each other (Riles 2006) but also through the 'street-level' practices and the everyday life that took place between them (Andreetta 2019; Cabot 2013; Horton 2020; Tuckett 2018).

In February 1928, about 2,000 Nansen Stamps were sent to Beirut based on the 'definite promise' made by Burnier to sell all of them to Armenian refugees. Disappointed by the outcome, the Deputy High Commissioner for Refugees sent a letter questioning why Burnier had, contrary to what he had advocated for in Geneva, only sold 129 Nansen Stamps (International Labour Office 1926).

In his response, Burnier repeated a point he had made on numerous previous occasions: that the conditions in Lebanon and Syria differed from Europe, making it impossible for the Armenian refugees to pay the taxes for the Nansen Stamps. He also emphasized that Armenians had the right to acquire both Syrian and Lebanese passports, which were cheaper than the Nansen Passport. Hence, it was generally not a document they desired:

> Since 1926, I have always made it known to you that the local conditions in Syria and Lebanon, and the regime under which refugees live there, make it impossible to implement the Nansen stamp tax as it can be practiced in European states. It is with great difficulty that we have managed to collect this tax from emigrants, and of course, only from those who possess a Nansen passport. This passport is generally not desired given that Lebanese and Syrian passports are cheaper and that Armenians, under the Treaty of Lausanne, have the right to obtain them. (Ibid.)[8]

This dispute had been preceded by lengthy attempts to impose a tax system through the issuing of so-called Nansen Stamps to be affixed on the already existing identity certificates of Armenians in the Syrian and Lebanese French mandates. The system was motivated by the idea that refugees should 'pay back', and thus contribute to the funding of the humanitarian services they were provided with. Such a tax system on Armenian refugees was already in place in France, and commissioners thus envisioned that it could in principle be applied in the mandates too. The challenge, however, was that most Armenians could obtain Syrian and Lebanese citizenship and were thus not in need of any specific refugee identity. This issue was further raised by Thomas Frank Johnson in a minute sheet written in May 1926:

> There is however, one administrative difficulty, and that is that the Armenian refugees in Syria are not provided either with Nansen passports or with cartes d'identité, on the basis of which the five francs tax could be levied, but it may not perhaps be impossible to devise some means for this purpose, even in case of need by making the taking of the carte d'identité by the Armenian refugees in Syria compulsory. (Ibid.)

The fact that the situations in the Near East and France differed was discussed in various conversations between Burnier and Johnson in attempts to overcome the difficulties of imposing the Nansen Stamp on Armenian refugees. In August of the same year, Burnier further explained the situation:

> During my absence, there have been no changes in the material situation of the refugees. They still live in the precarious and unstable manner that I explained to you during my visit to Geneva. . . However, their personal status is now definitively

settled. Under the Treaty of Lausanne, all Armenians residing in Mandate States for two years, which applies to all of them, automatically become citizens of the states they inhabit. (International Labour Office 1925)[9]

Additionally, he claimed that since the municipality of Beirut had already collected 160,000 francs from the Armenian refugees by taxing all its citizens, adding another tax system would be extremely difficult to implement. These matters were not without misperceptions or contestations. In a response to Burnier, Johnson expressed his confusion regarding the rather conflicting information furnished around the question:

> . . . as pointed out to you by the Red Cross committee with reference to your letter of August 7th . . . you state that all Armenian refugees who have resided in the mandated territory for two years, or practically the whole of the Armenian refugees in Syria, have acquired or have the rights to acquire Syrian nationality. On the other hand, you reiterate that measures are being contemplated for applying the Nansen stamp system through all Armenian refugees in Syria. If, however, the Armenian refugees become Syrian citizens, it would not appear to be possible to require them to purchase the Nansen stamps. In that event our original proposals would require considerable modification . . . As you may imagine, we are most anxious to have your observations on this somewhat difficult point and particularly as to the interpretation placed by the competent authorities on the relevant article of the Lausanne Treaty (Art 30. Section II). (Ibid.)

In quoting an article of the Lausanne Treaty, Johnson further argued that there was 'no reference' to the right of Armenian refugees to obtain Syrian nationality after two years of residence, in contrast to what Burnier had claimed. Rather, he suggested that the fact that Armenians had been able to acquire Syrian nationality was a result of a 'generous interpretation' of the article. Further, he raised the problem that the High Commissioner at Beyrouth, who 'had been instructed to impose the Nansen tax on the Armenian refugees in Syria', appeared to regard the refugees in line with 'the meaning of the definition adopted by the inter-Governmental Conference' held in May that same year, which defined only Armenians *without* nationality as refugees. Stressing the difficulties of appealing for any funding if having to do so in favour for Armenians 'with Syrian nationality' rather than Armenians defined as refugees, he warned Burnier,

> You will not fail to appreciate the importance [of] attaching to a clear definition of the status of the Armenian refugees in Syria, not only insofar as it concerns measures for the reimbursement of any funds advanced for the settlement of those refugees, but also for the development of that activity. (Ibid.)

'Social etymologies', Stoler (2010: 35) suggests, 'trace the career of words and the political practices that new categories mark or that new membership in old categories signals'. Accordingly, visible in these letters, while the word 'refugee' was repeatedly used by commissionaires, delegates and deputies to denote emerging non-national subjects (in this case the Russians, following the Armenians), it was never really explained in the documents they produced. *Who* the refugees were seemed self-evident. *What* a 'refugee' was, or what kind of membership the category should encompass, was, however, less obvious. The competing understandings regarding whom among the Armenians to define as refugees were linked to the opposing visions of the League and the French authorities. Citizenship, while instrumental in the French mandates for making room for non-Muslim and non-Arab refugees to alter the demography (Watenpaugh 2015: 174), was a *problem* for the League, which needed refugees to remain noncitizens in order to proceed with their activities. More importantly, the parties' different visions demonstrate how notions of vulnerability unfolded mainly around questions of citizenship. If refugees were to gain citizenship, they would not be considered vulnerable enough for the League to justify the need to implement the Nansen Passport – which would function as a source of continued funds. Other than looking for a measurement to distinguish between refugees and non-refugees, or between deserving and less deserving refugees, as is common sense in the 'neoliberal face' (Sözer 2020) of contemporary governance of humanitarian assistance (Feldman 2018; Gatter 2021), in the 1920s the question unfolded, rather, around how to make refugees *maintain*, rather than being maintained by, humanitarian projects. More importantly, the correspondence suggests that Armenian refugees in Syria and Lebanon were not *without* identity documents and in need of a solution, or at least not a solution of this sort. Rather, coming from a political world that was evidently not theirs, the Nansen Stamp appeared irrational for most of them (Stoler 2010: 26). Accordingly, ethnographic engagement with these archival documents allows for examining not what the delegates, commissionaires and deputies knew or not, what they did or not, but the procedures and activities on which their 'thought-work' (Heyman 1995) – that is, their different ways of knowing – relied (Stoler 2010: 42). What these letters make visible, then, is that the political world of the League was a rationale in the making. For some parties, the Nansen Passport was the only solution for dealing with people affected by state violence and the dissolution of some nations in the making of others. For other parties, the issue was more complicated. The contesting prospects of how many Nansen stamps could be sold in relation to how they were received by the Armenians in Syria and Lebanon highlight an arena of different perspectives within and between different parties: the League, the French authorities and the refugees alike.

Hence, as participants in an emotional economy where the relationship between different parties, epistemologies and social worlds were still in the making, these letters illustrate the connection between the career of official documents (Riles 2006) and the career of categories (Stoler 2010) – that is, how the refugee category took form at the intersection between policy production and implementation, between conference halls and everyday 'street-level' governance.

Conclusion: Durable Marks in Contemporary Paper Realities

> The ethnographic space of the archive resides in the disjuncture between prescription and practice, between state mandates and the maneuvers people made in response to them, between normative rules and how people actually lived their lives. (Stoler 2010: 32)

Examining how asylum seekers' documentary practices affect and (re)shape their spatiotemporal (im)mobility in Jordan, I have followed the life trajectories of many Syrians since our first encounters in 2016. Throughout the years, some of them, like Ashraf, have left Jordan, returned to Syria or gone elsewhere in the world. Most of them, however, like Said, have stayed. When I met Said one afternoon about two weeks after Ashraf had left for Belarus, he told me, 'When Ashraf travelled, I got sick of this . . . There is no one here, I am alone here.' For years, Ashraf and Said shared the same legal status and, although many of their experiences differed, they shared a similar experience of being *there*, together, in Jordan – and of aspiring to a life elsewhere. That Ashraf had left reminded Said that he had not, forcing a sense that their shared experience was now different – a 'difference' I have sought to unsettle in this chapter.

Attending to the ethnographic space of the archive, I have examined the processes through which the first legal refugee identity certificate took form, and the regulations of mobility that unfolded alongside them. In an attempt to unsettle 'our habits of studying the shared world through political concepts and categories' (Azoulay 2019: 15), I have in parallel combined ethnographic engagement with those who live with the durable marks of these processes today. While refugees' right to mobility in the present is closely linked to *how* vulnerable one is, the correspondence examined in this chapter testifies to a time when present notions of refugee vulnerability were yet to take shape. Yet, demonstrating such difference is less about distinguishing the past from the present than it is about unsettling the categorical conventions on which we rely when we study processes of humanitarian governance today. Examining the archive and the contemporary documentary strategies of Ashraf and Said in tandem, I have attended to the worldviews that guided the deputies' and delegates' bureaucratic 'thought-work' in the 1920s (Heyman 1995) as both the condition through which certain bureaucratic categories came into being *and* the condition through which we as scholars (and bureaucrats in humanitarian and migratory contexts) approach such categories in the present. Questioning the distinction made in the UNHCR information video between third-country resettlement and irregular mobility – and hence also between Said's remaining in, and Ashraf's travel from, Jordan – I have sought to demonstrate not only that migrants' and refugees' experiences are products of the same system but that such a system is a *reanimation* of, rather than a replacement for, earlier systems – systems through which the Nansen Passport has, sequentially and consequentially, become a durable mark in humanitarian governance, and thus also in refugees' and migrants' paper-realities today.

Hanna Berg is a PhD candidate at the department of Anthropology and Sociology at the Geneva Graduate Institute. Her research explores the role of bureaucracy in (re)shaping and sustaining the aftermath of humanitarian emergency interventions in Jordan. Following an ethnographic approach, she works across theoretical conversations on humanitarian interventions, practice and governance in the Middle East region, and anthropology of documents and bureaucracy.

Notes

1. To protect the identity of my interlocutors, I have used pseudonyms for all names of the persons whose stories I engage with in this chapter.
2. The intended audience for this video comprised Syrian asylum seekers in Jordan. Hence, like all ethnographic material in this chapter, the video was recorded in Arabic. All translations are my own.
3. Although Jordan is not a signatory of the 1951 Refugee Convention and Syrian refugees are regarded as asylum seekers (*ṭālibīn lujū'*) – which in Arabic literally means 'seekers of refuge' – this status confirms them as people of concern, and under the protection of, the UNHCR in the same manner as in countries that are signatories of the convention.
4. In conceptualizing 'humanitarian aftermaths', I attend to the bureaucratic procedures through which the slow transformation of humanitarian interventions into development projects is navigated, negotiated and justified – and its effects on the lives of local humanitarians and Syrian refugees.
5. Opening in 2014, Azraq camp is the second largest Syrian refugee camp in Jordan, after Zaatari camp that was built in 2012. Officially, Azraq hosts around 40 000 Syrian refugees.

6. Historian Davide Rodogno (2021) provides a comprehensive examination of the imperialist and colonialist ideologies that informed the League and other humanitarian actors' operations in the Near East during this time period.
7. A direction of politics which Fassin (2007, 2012), Malkki (2015) and Ticktin (2014), among others, have explored extensively.
8. 'Depuis 1926 je vous ai toujours fait savoir que les conditions locales de la Syrie et du Liban et du régime où y vivent les réfugiés rendaient impossible l'application de l'impôt du timbre Nansen comme il peut se pratiquer dans des Etats Européens. C'est à grand peine que nous sommes parvenus à faire payer cette taxe aux émigrants et, bien entendu, à ceux seuls qui sont munis d'un passeport Nansen. Ce passeport n'est généralement pas recherché étant donné que les passeports Libanais et Syriens coûtent meilleur marché et que les arméniens, en vertu du traité de Lausanne, ont le droit de s'en munir.'
9. 'Il n'y a pas eu, pendant mon absence de changements dans la situation matèrielle des réfugiés. Ils vivent toujours de la façon précaire et instable que je vous ai exposée lors de mon passage à Genève . . . Leur statut personnel par contre est maintenant règlé (sic) de façon définitive. En vertu du traité de Lausanne, tous les Armeniens établis dans les Etats sous Mandat depuis deux ans, c'est le cas pour la totalité, deviennent automatiquement citoyens des Etats qu'ils habitant.'

References

Achilli, L. (2016), 'Back to Syria?: Conflicting Patterns of Mobility among Syrian Refugees in Jordan', *Orient* 57(1): 7–13, http://cadmus.eui.eu//handle/1814/38826.

Adams, P. (2021), 'How Belarus is Helping "Tourists" Break into the EU', BBC News, 21 October, https://www.bbc.com/news/world-58952867.

Agamben, G. (1995), 'We Refugees', *Symposium: A Quarterly Journal in Modern Literatures*, 49(2): 114–119. https://doi.org/10.1080/00397709.1995.10733798.

Andreetta, S. (2019b), 'Writing for Difference Audiences', *Journal of Legal Anthropology* 3(2): 91–110, https://www.berghahnjournals.com/view/journals/jla/3/2/jla030206.xml.

Apostolova, R. (2015), 'Of Refugees and Migrants: Stigma, Politics, and Boundary Work at the Borders of Europe', *American Sociological Newsletter*, 14 September, https://asaculturesection.org/2015/09/14/of-refugees-and-migrants-stigma-politics-and-boundary-work-at-the-borders-of-europe/.

Azoulay, A. (2012), *Archive*, Political Concepts: A Critical Lexicon, http://www.politicalconcepts.org/archive-ariella-azoulay/.

——— (2013), 'Potential History: Thinking through Violence', *Critical Inquiry* 39(3): 548–74, https://doi.org/10.1086/670045.

——— (2019), *Potential History: Unlearning Imperialism*. London: Verso.

Cabot, H. (2012), 'The Governance of Things: Documenting Limbo in the Greek Asylum Procedure', *PoLAR: Political and Legal Anthropology Review* 35(1): 11–29, https://doi.org/10.1111/j.1555-2934.2012.01177.x.

——— (2013), 'The Social Aesthetics of Eligibility: NGO Aid and Indeterminacy in the Greek Asylum Process', *American Ethnologist* 40(3): 452–66, https://doi.org/10.1111/amet.12032.

Chatty, D. (2013), 'Refugees, Exiles, and Other Forced Migrants in the Late Ottoman Empire', *Refugee Survey Quarterly* 32(2): 35–52, https://doi.org/10.1093/rsq/hdt001.

Crawley, H. and D. Skleparis (2018), 'Refugees, Migrants, Neither, Both: Categorical Fetishism and the Politics of Bounding in Europe's "Migration Crisis"', *Journal of Ethnic and Migration Studies* 44(1): 48–64, https://doi.org/10.1080/1369183X.2017.1348224.

Dunn, E.C. (2012), 'The Chaos of Humanitarian Aid: Adhocracy in the Republic of Georgia', *Humanity: An International Journal of Human Rights, Humanitarianism, and Development* 3(1): 1–23, https://doi.org/10.1353/hum.2012.0005.

Fassin, D. (2007), 'Humanitarianism as a Politics of Life', *Public Culture* 19(3): 499–520, https://doi.org/10.1215/08992363-2007-007.

——— (2012), *Humanitarian Reason: A Moral History of the Present*. Berkeley and Los Angeles: University of California Press.

Feldman, I. (2018), *Life Lived in Relief: Humanitarian Predicaments and Palestinian Refugee Politics*. Oakland: University of California Press.

FitzGerald, D. (2019), *Refuge beyond Reach: How Rich Democracies Repel Asylum Seekers*. New York: Oxford University Press.

Gatter, M. (2021), 'Preserving Order: Narrating Resilience as Threat in Jordan's Azraq Refugee Camp', *Territory, Politics, Governance* 11(4): 695–711. https://doi.org/10.1080/21622671.2020.1860812.

——— (2023), *Time and Power in Azraq Refugee Camp: A Nine-to-Five Emergency*. Cairo and New York: American University in Cairo Press.

Governmental Conference (1923), *Minutes of the Governmental Conference on Passports for Russian Refugees (Geneva, 3-5 July 1922)* (R1728/45/21597/15833), United Nations Library & Archives Geneva, https://archives.ungeneva.org/proces-verbaux-de-la-conference-gouvernementale-pour-les-passeports-aux-refugies-russes-geneve-3-5-juillet-1922.

Heyman, J. McC. (1995), 'Putting Power in the Anthropology of Bureaucracy: The Immigration and Naturalization Service at the Mexico–United States Border', *Current Anthropology* 36(2): 261–87, https://www.jstor.org/stable/2744108.

Ho, E. (2006), *The Graves of Tarim: Genealogy and Mobility across the Indian Ocean*. Berkeley: University of California Press.

Horton, S.B. (2020), 'Introduction. Paper Trails: Migrants, Bureaucratic Inscription, and Legal Recognition', in S.B. Horton and J. McC. Heyman (eds), *Paper Trails: Migrants, Documents, and Legal Insecurity*. Global Insecurities. Durham, NC: Duke University Press, pp. 1–26, https://doi.org/10.1515/9781478012092-001.

Horton, S.B. and J. McC. Heyman (eds) (2020), *Paper Trails: Migrants, Documents, and Legal Insecurity*. Global Insecurities. Durham, NC: Duke University Press, https://doi.org/10.1215/9781478012092

Housden, M. (2010), 'White Russians Crossing the Black Sea: Fridtjof Nansen, Constantinople and the First Modern Repatriation of Refugees Displaced by Civil Conflict, 1922-23', *The Slavonic and East European Review* 88(3): 495–524, https://www.jstor.org/stable/20780433.

International Labour Office (1925, 1926), *International Labour Office Refugees Service—Proposed Settlement of Armenian Refugees in Syria* (C1429/325/Ra.413/70/1/Jacket1), United Nations Library & Archives Geneva, https://archives.ungeneva.org/international-labour-office-refugees-service-proposed-settlement-of-armenian-refugees-in-syria.

——— (1926, 1929), *Russian Refugees—Distribution of Nansen Stamps—Syria [and Lebanon]*. (C1435/331/Rr.401/001/9/70), United Nations Library & Archives Geneva, https://archives.ungeneva.org/russian-refugees-distribution-of-nansen-stamps-syria-and-lebanon.

Khosravi, S. (2010), *'Illegal' Traveller: An Auto-Ethnography of Borders*. Basingstoke: Palgrave Macmillan.

Lenner, K. and L. Turner (2019), 'Making Refugees Work? The Politics of Integrating Syrian Refugees into the Labor Market in Jordan', *Middle East Critique* 28(1): 65–95, https://doi.org/10.1080/19436149.2018.1462601

Long, K. (2011), 'Refugees, Repatriation and Liberal Citizenship', *History of European Ideas* 37(2): 232–41, https://doi.org/10.1016/j.histeuroideas.2010.10.016.

——— (2013), 'When Refugees Stopped Being Migrants: Movement, Labour and Humanitarian Protection', *Migration Studies* 1(1): 4–26, https://doi.org/10.1093/migration/mns001.

Malkki, L.H. (1995), 'Refugees and Exile: From "Refugee Studies" to the National Order of Things', *Annual Review of Anthropology* 24(1): 495–523.

——— (2015). *need to help: The domestic arts of international humanitarianism*. Duke University Press.

Mongia, R.V. (1999), 'Race, Nationality, Mobility: A History of the Passport', *Public Culture* 11(3): 527–55. https://doi.org/10.1215/08992363-11-3-527.

Monsutti, A. (2008), 'Afghan Migratory Strategies and the Three Solutions to the Refugee Problem', *Refugee Survey Quarterly* 27(1): 58–73, https://doi.org/10.1093/rsq/hdn007

——— (2018), 'Mobility as a Political Act', *Ethnic and Racial Studies* 41(3): 448–55, https://doi.org/10.1080/01419870.2018.1388421.

Nakueira, S. (2019), 'Governing through Paperwork: Examining the Regulatory Effects of Documentary Practices in a Refugee Settlement', *Journal of Legal Anthropology* 3(2): 10–28, https://doi.org/10.3167/jla.2019.030202.

Nansen Geneva Office (1922), *Nansen Geneva Office—Correspondence sent, General, June 1922.* (C1318/214/03), United Nations Library & Archives Geneva, https://archives.ungeneva.org/nansen-geneva-office-correspondence-sent-general-june-1922.

Peteet, J. (2007), 'Unsettling the Categories of Displacement', *Middle East Report* 37(244): 2.

Riles, A. (ed.) (2006), *Documents: Artifacts of Modern Knowledge.* Ann Arbor: University of Michigan Press.

Robson, L. (2017), 'REFUGEES AND THE CASE FOR INTERNATIONAL AUTHORITY IN THE MIDDLE EAST: THE LEAGUE OF NATIONS AND THE UNITED NATIONS RELIEF AND WORKS AGENCY FOR PALESTINIAN REFUGEES IN THE NEAR EAST COMPARED', *International Journal of Middle East Studies* 49(4): 625–44, https://doi.org/10.1017/S0020743817000629.

Rodogno, D. (2021), *Night on Earth: A History of International Humanitarianism in the Near East, 1918–1930* (1st ed.). Cambridge: Cambridge University Press.

Sharma, N. (2020), 'The "People Out of Place": State Limits on Free Mobility and the Making of Im(migrants)', in S.B. Horton and J. McC. Heyman (eds), *Paper Trails: Migrants, Documents, and Legal Insecurity.* Global Insecurities. Durham, NC: Duke University Press, pp. 27–52.

Soguk, N. (1999), *States and Strangers: Refugees and Displacements of Statecraft.* Minneapolis and London: University of Minnesota Press.

Sözer, H. (2020), 'Humanitarianism with a Neo-Liberal Face: Vulnerability Intervention as Vulnerability Redistribution', *Journal of Ethnic and Migration Studies* 46(11): 2163–80, https://doi.org/10.1080/1369183X.2019.1573661.

Stanisławski, W. (2022), 'The Peace Treaty of Riga: A Stop-gap for Russian Expansion', trans. M. Sekrecki, Polish History, 18 March, https://polishhistory.pl/the-peace-treaty-of-riga-a-stop-gap-for-russian-expansion/.

Stevens, D. (2013), 'Legal Status, Labelling, and Protection: The Case of Iraqi "Refugees" in Jordan', *International Journal of Refugee Law* 25(1): 1–38, https://doi.org/10.1093/ijrl/eet001.

Stoler, A.L. (2010), *Along the Archival Grain: Epistemic Anxieties and Colonial Common Sense.* Princeton, NJ: Princeton University Press.

——— (2016). *Duress: Imperial Durabilities in Our Times.* Durham, NC: Duke University Press.

Thomson, M.J. (2012), 'Black Boxes of Bureaucracy: Transparency and Opacity in the Resettlement Process of Congolese Refugees', *PoLAR: Political and Legal Anthropology Review* 35(2): 186–205, https://doi.org/10.1111/j.1555-2934.2012.01198.x.

Ticktin, M. (2014), 'Transnational Humanitarianism', *Annual Review of Anthropology* 43(1): 273–89, https://doi.org/10.1146/annurev-anthro-102313-030403.

Tuckett. A. (2018), *Rules, Paper, Status: Migrants and Precarious Bureaucracy in Contemporary Italy*. Stanford, CA: Stanford University Press.

Turner, L. (2019), 'Syrian Refugee Men as Objects of Humanitarian Care', *International Feminist Journal of Politics* 21(4): 595–616, https://doi.org/10.1080/14616742.2019.1641127.

UNHCR (2024), *Introduction, UNHCR Resettlement Handbook*. Retrieved 7 March 2024 from https://www.unhcr.org/resettlement-handbook/introduction/.

UNHCR (2022), 'Resettlement', UNHCR Jordan, https://help.unhcr.org/jordan/en/helpful-services-unhcr/resettlement-unhcr/.

UNHCR Jordan (2021), 'UNHCR Jordan'—المفوضية في الاردن. Facebook, https://www.facebook.com/search/top?q=unhcr%20jordan.

United Nations Geneva (2021), *League of Nations Refugees Mixed Archival Group (Nansen Fonds)*, UN Archives Geneva. Retrieved 7 March 2024 from https://archives.ungeneva.org/refugees-mixed-archival-group-nansen-fonds.

Walsh, N.P.W. (2021), 'Belarus Floods the European Union with Migrants, Taking a Page Out of Putin's Playbook', CNN, https://www.cnn.com/2021/08/13/europe/belarus-lithuania-border-migrants-eu-cmd-intl/index.html.

Wandycz, P.S. (1969), 'THE TREATY OF RIGA: ITS SIGNIFICANCE FOR INTERWAR POLISH FOREIGN POLICY', *The Polish Review* 14(4): 31–36, https://www.jstor.org/stable/25776871.

Watenpaugh, K.D. (2015), *Bread from Stones: The Middle East and the Making of Modern Humanitarianism*. Oakland: University of California Press.

Zetter, R. (2007), 'More Labels, Fewer Refugees: Remaking the Refugee Label in an Era of Globalization', *Journal of Refugee Studies* 20(2): 172–92, https://doi.org/10.1093/jrs/fem011.

Postscript

Anthropology, Bureaucracy and Paperwork

Thomas Bierschenk

For a long time, anthropologists shied away from the study of bureaucracy. In fact, the ethnographic study of bureaucracy was largely initiated outside anthropology – that is, in political science – with Michael Lipsky's (1980) seminal study on street-level bureaucrats, as well as in sociology (Crozier 1963), while in anthropology early authors like Don Handelman and Elliot Leyton (1978), Gerald Britan and Ronald Cohen (1980) and Josiah Heyman (1995) for a long time remained on their own. After 2000, there were two major drivers intensifying anthropologists' interest towards bureaucracies. The somewhat older one was development anthropology, which, in line with the evolution of development policies themselves, shifted its focus from projects to global public policies, development agencies and public bureaucracies (Olivier de Sardan 2005; Bierschenk 2014). Arguably of more impact, however, was the so-called migration crisis of the past ten years – which was, rather, a crisis of state bureaucracies in dealing with different forms of migration. While the migration crisis, for the anthropological profession, must be considered a windfall, as it has been providing its practitioners with new, unexpectedly large and often well-funded fields of scholarly and practical engagement (see the critical review by Cabot 2019), anthropologists also slowly expanded their vision from the originally exclusive focus on the figure of the migrant to that of the bureaucrat. In this process, linked to the by now established field of the anthropology of the state, 'the study of bureaucracy has become a standard prerogative of English-language [and French, and German!] anthropology in recent years' (El Khachab 2018). 'Recent' is the correct word: the large majority of topical texts cited in the contributions to this book are no older than ten years.

On the other hand, the study of organizations – of which bureaucracy is an ordering principle – had actually already been initiated by anthropologists back in the 1920s (Schwartzman 1993: 1–26). Some of the early findings can be taken for granted now: there is always a gap between organizational norms and practices; large-scale organizations are heterogeneous phenomena (theorized by sociological institutionalism with the concept of 'loose coupling' [Weick 1976]; Lindberg and Borrelli, this volume); implementation is a fragmented process, always also going in unplanned directions (Pressman and Wildavsky [1973] 1984). All contributors to this book subscribe to such views. There is also early work by sociologists on the ethics of bureaucracy and bureaucrats, starting with Max Weber and including for example Richard Hilbert (1987) and Thomas Osborne (1994); anthropologists have added interesting findings to this study of bureaucrats' ethical and affective labour, even when they are crafting depersonalized documents (Andreetta, this volume). One area where interactionist sociology has been in advance over anthropology, with the latter slowly catching up, was in the ethnographic study of (semi-)professionals whose work has a strong bureaucratic aspect, like police officers or medical personnel (Becker et al. 1961; Bittner 1967).

The long-time aversion of many anthropologists to positioning themselves, epistemologically speaking, with the bureaucrat – which means taking bureaucrats, in Malinowskian fashion, as the 'natives' and trying to see the world with their eyes, being interested in what they think and say about themselves – might have been an effect of the genetic imprint on the discipline. This genetic imprint seems to linger on in the recent enthusiasm of many anthropologists for the topical writings of David Graeber (2015), a political manifesto based on anecdotal evidence framed by anarchist convictions which might be considered a typical first-world luxury – certainly by my African colleagues (Bierschenk 2021). For it could very well be argued, also contra the much-cited James Scott (1998), that the (Global) South needs more, and not less, bureaucracy and stateness, provided it is well functioning (see Metzker 2017). Anthropology, up to the present day, is fascinated by the margins, the peripheral, the exotic and subaltern. The anthropology of the state tellingly started in the margins (Asad 2004) before recently moving more closely to its centres.

Bureaucrats as the Evil Twins of Anthropologists

I propose that in addition to this genetic imprint, there might be another, subcutaneous reason for this aversion: bureaucrats are the unrecognized 'evil twins' of anthropologists. After all, as writers, do we not essentially do a similar type of 'thought-work' (Heyman 1995): enquire, summarize, translate, select information, categorize, draft – that is, establish – paperwork? Inspired by a particular worldview, and with a particular audience in mind? Do we not, as writers, obey aesthetic rules analogous to those which Mirco Göpfert (2013) has beautifully described for the case of African gendarmes? Do we not also try to formulate authoritative statements on the world and attempt to impose them on others? And do we not, as fieldworkers, find those people most despicable who are the closest to us – that is, in our case, tourists? This aversion to the ones who are most similar to us would not surprise a psychologist, who might call it transference – that is, seeing (parts of) yourself in the other.

Furthermore, migration bureaucrats resemble anthropologists in another, more immediate way. Insofar as asylum bureaucrats, nongovernmental organization (NGO) officials and police officers produce cultural knowledge about their clients, they might be called para-ethnologists (Lindberg and Borrelli; Andreetta – both this volume; see also Islam 2015; Beek and Bierschenk 2020). In fact, they might even have been trained as anthropologists, as many people active in the management of migration nowadays are. But in any case, as scientist-practitioners they must professionally deal with cultural diversity and do their own theorizing, produce cultural analysis of what they see and experience, much of it in written form, and some of it directly influenced by academic anthropology.

At first glance, the difference between this kind of para-ethnology and academic anthropology seems to lie, first, in the fact that para-ethnology does not serve pure knowledge production but is oriented to action and problem-solving. It produces applied, or applicable, knowledge in the organization and is supposed to assist in decision-making. However, on further inspection, this distinction is not as clear as it first seems to be, as academic ethnographic research in modern organizations is also always faced with the expectation that it would be of benefit to the organization, or some of its members (Bierschenk and Olivier de Sardan 2019).

Complicit Positionings

This points to a particular positioning of the anthropologist of bureaucracies, a topic which is taken up only in passing in this book. I want to underline three characteristics of bureaucracies as objects of study with strong epistemological implications. One of the defining characteristics of any organization is its strong boundary management. This strict gatekeeping means research always needs to be done in explicit cooperation with the organization, or at least part of it, more specifically with its leadership. The researcher is thus in a particular reciprocity relationship with the informants, and they are increasingly expected to give something back. Furthermore, the anthropologist of bureaucracy must assume that the people under study will actually read what they write – a situation which mainstream anthropology encountered only much later in the context of postcolonial anthropology, when the 'native started to write back'. In this sense, anthropologists of organizations might be called 'embedded anthropologists' (as Andreetta and Nakueira hint at in their chapters in this volume). This obviously raises the question of the analytical independence of the researcher.

Second, the ethnography of bureaucracy is confronted with a particular nexus between basic research and its impact on reality. In organizational research, rendering research results – at least, to the 'bosses' – is almost obligatory. Thus, the anthropology of organizations and of public bureaucracies, in many cases, has an applied dimension, at least in the eyes of the organization's heads. This applied aspect must often be inserted, right from the beginning, into the research approach itself, even if the main objective of the research is academic, and may lead to a 'complicit positioning' of the researcher coming from the outside (Sedgwick 2017).

Third, working at the interface of basic and applied research, from very early on, anthropologists of organizations have been confronted with ethical problems ('who do we work for?') well ahead of the crisis of representation in mainstream anthropology. This is a particularly pressing problem when the object of study is emotionally and politically heavily charged, as is the case in the field of migration and migration bureaucracies. Consequently, it becomes difficult to disentangle a positioning of the researcher, interested in the emic views of actors, from those of the citizen with moral and political concerns. It is almost impossible to undertake organizational anthropology without being constantly challenged as to one's political and ethical convictions. In fact, for many anthropologists, doing research on power-wielding bureaucracies is legitimate only if there is a disclaimer that the research is done from the position of *a priori* political critique (Karpiak and Garriott 2018; the term 'power-wielding bureaucracies' is borrowed from Heyman 2004). This obviously needs to be reflected on, including possible compensation strategies like becoming a moral and political prosecutor. This might stand in the way of the required analytical distance as much as the opposite position, which would be becoming a spokesperson for the organization under study.

The upside of these challenges is that the anthropology of bureaucracy has the potential to unsettle traditional distinctions between natives and researchers, emic and etic, inside and outside. Ethnographically studying bureaucrats is a particular form of 'studying sideways' (Hannerz 2006), partly also of studying up (Nader 1972). Thus, research on bureaucrats opens the way for a more symmetric anthropology wherein researcher and researched meet on a more equal footing, and it is not necessarily the anthropologist who is in command of a knowledge/power complex.

Paperwork and Documents

This book points to an emerging subfield in the anthropology of bureaucracy: an increasing interest in paperwork. This focus on materiality is, in fact, the result of interdisciplinary cross-fertilization, in this case with science and technology studies. Files are the essential infrastructure of any bureaucracy (Vismann 2008). They order the institution where they are produced; they link it to other institutions (including fragments of the state to other fragments; Andreetta, this volume); they control, or try to control, clients as well as, often forgotten, bureaucrats themselves (Lindberg and Borrelli; Vetters – both this volume). Anthropologists can be interested in their content, their form (Göpfert 2013) and what may be called their social life (Hull 2012). Most of all, however, anthropologists, like the contributors to this volume, are interested in documentary practices: how paperwork turns into documents; how these documents are produced; the work they do, e.g. creating legal categories (Berg, this volume); how they are being used (not always in the sense originally given to them by the producers; Cabot 2012); how they might be 'brokered'; and how they are being contested – mostly by the production of other documents (Nakueira, this volume). Paperwork can be contested only with paperwork, documents with other documents: this is the inevitability of bureaucracy which Weber had in mind, both in the public and the private sector (Hibou [2012] 2015). In the case of migration governance, this is done in 'complex multi-regulatory landscapes' with a multiplicity of sources of norms, layered systems of law and other regulations, often only loosely defined legal terms, rapidly changing legal contexts and weak representation of those who are governed (Gargiulo; Vetters – both this volume). However, while Weber ([1921] 1972: 562) insisted that bureaucracy was all the more efficient as it was 'dehumanised', anthropologists turn this perspective on its head and bring to the fore the social practices behind the production of 'dehumanised' documents, which often appear authorless or where the author is hidden in a collective (Berg, this volume).

When producing paperwork, bureaucrats collect, select and densify information. They select information according to their relevance criteria – for example, criteria of suffering or deservedness – and in reference to specific purposes. Files and documents are drafted to create coherence between observations and their bureaucratic processing. In other words, it would be naive to assume such paperwork simply reflected reality; rather, it produces an (official) reality, in the process turning into documents and turning migrants and refugees into legal subjects (Berg, this volume). These documents serve as much to foster transparency as to avoid blame or responsibility for something or prevent oneself from experiencing negative, for example legal consequences (Lindberg and Borrelli, this volume). Furthermore, as our contributions show, paperwork is in most cases assembled, in case files, with particular audiences in mind – some of them direct, some indirect. In this sense, these audiences are co-authors. The same is true for the counter case files which migrants assemble to support their claims. This functionality of its production does not prevent paperwork, once established, from following trajectories of its own, being reframed, landing on the desks of people for whom it was not originally intended, sometimes being used against its original objective (Andreetta, this volume), or by way of contrast serving as 'hostile witnesses' (Nakueira, this volume) – that is, in fact weakening the claim for which it was presented.

The result of these documentary practices is not uniform. Some of the contributors to this book, inspired by Foucault if not Kafka, stress the resulting opacity and the illegibility effect of paperwork (Lindberg and Borrelli, this volume). The latter might be too strong a term, but in any case there is no doubt that the regulatory situation is particularly opaque for migrants (Gargiulo, this volume). On the other hand, documents also turn people into legal subjects, which is the base for potential contestation even if the playing field is skewed and the 'power to complain' (*Beschwerdemacht*: Feest and Blankenburg 1972) of migrants relatively low. Sophie Andreetta, in turn, shows in this volume how bureaucrats might try to exploit interstices and contradictions in the regulatory landscape for migrants and in fact against (parts of) the state, while Sophie Nakueira insists on the agency of migrants and their capacity to navigate these landscapes, if not always successfully. Larissa Vetters, finally, shows that attempts at legal ordering by bureaucrats can also be the entry gate to at least indirectly increasing stakeholder participation, with migrant organizations and NGOs lobbying for greater transparency; or, inversely, lower bureaucratic levels might resist such ordering from above (Gargiulo, this volume). Therefore, taking this book as a whole, it seems to make sense to acknowledge the double face of bureaucracy as a form of domination and oppression as well as of protection and liberation, and all the ambivalences this dialectic entails.

Thomas Bierschenk is Emeritus Professor of Anthropology and African Studies at the Johannes Gutenberg University of Mainz, where he is currently conducting a research project, with Jan Beek and Bernd Meyer, on the management of cultural difference by German police (see Beek et al. 2023). He is the co-editor of *States at Work: Dynamics of African Bureaucracies* (2014) and, more recently, co-author of 'How to Study Bureaucracies Ethnographically' in *Critique of Anthropology* (2019) as well as of 'The Anthropology of Bureaucracy and Public Administration', in the *Oxford Research Encyclopedia of Politics*, 2 vols, edited by B. Guy Peters and Ian Thynne (Oxford University Press, 2022) – all three with Jean-Pierre Olivier de Sardan. ORCID ID: https://orcid.org/0000-0002-2423-7358. Email: biersche@uni-mainz.de

References

Asad, Talal (2004), 'Where Are the Margins of the State?' in Deborah Poole and Veena Das (eds), *Anthropology in the Margins of the State*. Santa Fe, NM: School of American Research, pp. 279–88.

Becker, Howard S., Blanche Geer, Everett C. Hughes and Anselm L. Strauss (1961), *Boys in White: Students Culture in Medical Schools*. Chicago: Chicago University Press.

Beek, Jan and Thomas Bierschenk (2020), 'Bureaucrats as Para-Ethnologists: The Use of Culture in State Practices', *Sociologus. Journal for Social Anthropology* 70(1): 1–17. https://doi.org/10.3790/soc.70.1.1.

Beek, Jan, Thomas Bierschenk, Annalena Kolloch and Bernd Meyer (eds) (2023), *Policing Race, Ethnicity and Culture. Ethnographic Perspectives across Europe*. Manchester: Manchester University Press, https://manchesteruniversitypress.co.uk/9781526165589/.

Bierschenk, Thomas (2014), 'From the Anthropology of Development to the Anthropology of Global Social Engineering', *Zeitschrift für Ethnologie* 139(1): 73–98.

——— (2021), 'On Graeber on Bureaucracy', Focaal Blog, 19 October 2021, https://www.focaalblog.com/2021/10/19/thomas-bierschenk-on-graeber-on-bureaucracy/.

Bierschenk, Thomas and Jean-Pierre Olivier de Sardan (2019), 'How to Study Bureaucracies Ethnographically?', *Critique of Anthropology* 39(2): 43–257. https://doi.org/10.1177/0308275X198429.

Bittner, Egon (1967), 'The Police on Skid-Row: a Study of Peace Keeping', *American Sociological Review* 32(5): 699–715.

Britan, Gerald M. and Ronald Cohen (1980), *Hierarchy and Society: Anthropological Perspectives on Bureaucracy*. Philadelphia, PA: Institute for the Study of Human Issues.

Cabot, Heath (2012), 'The Governance of Things: Documenting Limbo in the Greek Asylum Procedure', *PoLAR: Political and Legal Anthropology* 35(1): 11–29.

——— (2019), 'The Business of Anthropology and the European Refugee Crisis', *American Ethnologist* 46(3): 261–75.

Crozier, Michel (1963), *Le phénomène bureaucratique*. Paris: Seuil.

El Khachab, Chihab (2018), 'Current Trends in the Anthropology of Bureaucracy – A Report', Allegra Lab, 25 April, https://allegralaboratory.net/current-trends-in-the-anthropology-of-bureaucracy-a-report.

Feest, Johannes and Erhard Blankenburg (1972), *Die Definitionsmacht der Polizei: Strategien der Strafverfolgung und soziale Selektion*. Düsseldorf: Bertelsmann Universitätsverlag.

Göpfert, Mirco (2013), 'Bureaucratic Aesthetics: Report Writing in the Nigérien Gendarmerie', *American Ethnologist* 40(2): 324–34.

Graeber, David (2015), *The Utopia of Rules: On Technology, Stupidity and the Secret Joys of Bureaucracy*. London: Melvin House.

Handelman, Don and Elliot Leyton (1978), *Bureaucracy and World View: Studies in the Logic of Official Interpretation*. St John's: Institute of Social and Economic Research, Memorial University of Newfoundland.

Hannerz, Ulf (2006), 'Studying Down, Up, Sideways, Through, Backwards, Forwards, Away and At Home: Reflections on the Field Worries of an Expansive Discipline', in S.M. Coleman and P. Collins (eds), *Locating the Field. Space, Place and Context in Anthropology*. Oxford: Berg, pp. 23–41.

Heyman, Josiah McC. (1995), 'Putting Power in the Anthropology of Bureaucracy: The Immigration and Naturalization Service at the Mexico–United States Border', *Current Anthropology* 36(2): 261–87.

——— (2004), 'The Anthropology of Power-Wielding Bureaucracies', *Human Organization* 63(4): 487–500.

Hibou, Béatrice [2012] (2015), *The Bureaucratization of the World in the Neoliberal Era: An International and Comparative Perspective*. London: Palgrave Macmillan.

Hilbert, Richard A. (1987), 'Bureaucracy as Belief, Rationalization as Repair: Max Weber in a Post-Functionalist Age', *Sociological Theory* 5(1): 70–86.

Hull, Matthew (2012), *Government of Paper: The Materiality of Bureaucracy in Urban Pakistan*. Berkeley: University of California Press.

Islam, Gazi (2015), 'Practitioners as Theorists: Para-Ethnography and the Collaborative Study of Contemporary Organizations', *Organizational Research Methods* 18(2): 231–51.

Karpiak, Kevin G. and William Garriott (2018), 'Introduction: Disciplines, Fields and Problems', in Kevin G. Karpiak and William Garriott (eds), *The Anthropology of Police*. New York: Routledge, pp. 1–20.

Lipsky, Michael (1980), *Street-Level Bureaucracy: Dilemmas of the Individual in Public Services*. New York: Russell Sage Foundation.

Metzker, Julian (2017), '"Was ist (immer noch) todlangweilig und kann die Welt retten?" [What is (still) deadly boring and can save the world?]' *Perspective Daily*, 9 October, https://perspective-daily.de/article/363/probiere.

Nader, Laura (1972), 'Up the Anthropologist: Perspectives Gained from Studying Up', in Dell Hymes (ed.), *Reinventing Anthropology*. New York: Random House, pp. 284–311.

Olivier de Sardan, Jean-Pierre (2005), 'Classic Ethnology and the Socio-Anthropology of Public Spaces in Africa', *Africa Spectrum* 40(3): 485–97.

Osborne, Thomas (1994), 'Bureaucracy as a Vocation: Governmentality and Administration in Nineteenth Century Britain', *Journal of Historical Sociology* 7(3): 289–313.

Pressman, Jeffrey L. and Aaron Wildavsky [1973] (1984), *Implementation: How Great Expectations in Washington are Dashed in Oakland; Or Why It Is Amazing That Federal Programs Work at All*, 3rd edn. Berkeley: University of California Press.

Schwartzman, Helen B. (1993), *Ethnography in Organizations*. London: Sage.

Scott, James C. (1998), *Seeing Like a State: How Certain Schemes to Improve the Human Condition Have Failed*. New Haven, CT: Yale University Press.

Sedgwick, Mitchell W. (2017), 'Complicit Positioning: Anthropological Knowledge and Problems of "Studying up" for Ethnographer-Employees of Corporations', *Journal of Business Anthropology* 6(1): 58–88.

Vismann, Cornelia (2008, German orig. 2000), *Files: Law and Media Technology*. Stanford, CA: Stanford University Press.

Weber, M. (1972 [orig. 1921]), *Wirtschaft und Gesellschaft. Grundriß der verstehenden Soziologie*. Tübingen: Mohr Siebeck.

Weick, Karl E. (1976), 'Educational Organizations as Loosely Coupled Systems', *Administrative Science Quarterly* 21(1): 1–19.

Index

www.ingramcontent.com/pod-product-compliance
Ingram Content Group UK Ltd.
Pitfield, Milton Keynes, MK11 3LW, UK
UKHW021836150926
8656IPUK00004B/16

9 781805 396116